In Defence of Politics

Some titles are not available in North America.

In Defence of Politics

Bernard Crick

B L O O M S B U R Y

LONDON • NEW DELHI • NEW YORK • SYDNEY

Bloomsbury Academic
An imprint of Bloomsbury Publishing Plc

50 Bedford Square
London
WC1B 3DP
UK

175 Fifth Avenue
New York
NY 10010
USA

www.bloomsbury.com

First edition published 1962 by Weidenfeld and Nicolson
Fifth edition published 2000 by Continuum
This edition published 2013 by Bloomsbury

British Library Cataloguing-in-Publication Data
A catalogue record for this book is available from the British Library.

ISBN: PB: 978-1-7809-3692-5

Typeset by Newgen Imaging Systems Pvt Ltd, Chennai, India
Printed and bound in India

Contents

Preface to the Fifth Edition

Almost forty years ago my Preface to the first edition began by saying that here was simply an essay 'occasioned' – in the words of Thomas Hobbes – 'by the disorders of the present time'. It was an attempt 'to justify politics in plain words by saying what it is . . . I believe the essential matter to be very simple. The reader may welcome an unfashionable attempt to avoid covering him with all the author's chaff on everything before ever the grain is reached. . . . I am constantly depressed by the capacity of academics to over-complicate things. . . . [So this is not] a systematic treatise . . . simply an attempt, inspired by seeing a fairly obvious impatience with politics in the new nations of the world, and provoked by a personal dislike of exhortation and mere cant about "the ideals of freedom", to describe what in fact are the minimum benefits of politics as an activity . . .'

The essay arose mainly from conversations with a German friend to share grounds for hope that her people could exorcize the past and establish a political or republican tradition of active citizenship (as they have done so remarkably). But because this was an essay written with some intensity, in one deep breath and at one particular time, I have not in subsequent editions risked spoiling it by making substantial changes to the text, only some minor corrections (as now). References to past events once topical are merely illustrative of general points, not important in themselves, so I have left them unchanged with an occasional explanatory footnote; I have observed that for most people knowledge of what happened in the generation before they became adult is less than it is for earlier periods (such has been the decline of contemporary history in schools – or was it ever so? The broad shape of the distant hills can be seen but not the dead ground in between).

Since this book had been in print so long (and is now revived by a new publisher), I have felt the need in each new edition to add something timely or more fully explanatory rather than to rewrite. So the brevity of which I once boasted, always enjoying the speculative essay more than the monograph, has suffered. The tail is now almost as big as the dog. But each of these added 'Footnotes' can be read separately, and where only the original text is still in print in translation (with publishers too poor or mean to add the 'Footnotes'), the essential point comes across, not too much is lost. Indeed, I was delighted when I learned that pirated and illicit translations of Chapter 1, sometimes also of Chapter 7, had been circulating in the USSR and in Pinochet's Chile.

Some excuse for the Footnotes may, none the less, be needed. 'A Footnote to Rally the Academic Professors of Politics' was added because, although this was a book intended for the general reader, it has become much read by students. And at that time an absurd either/or debate raged among teachers of politics: that the study must be either science and neutrality, or else commitment and action! The 'fallacy of the excluded middle' was long ago diagnosed but there is still no easy cure. So I wanted to argue that the study of politics is necessarily part of politics, is committed to the preservation of free-politics, but not to any particular form of politics, still less to party doctrine. The professors deceive themselves (and others) in thinking that the study can be a science (except at the cost of intense triviality) or that it can, in some refined, pure philosophical way, avoid relevance to actual politics. But commitment to freedom and political rule becomes discredited if the authority of the teacher or the curiosity of the student is tied tightly to a particular cause or orthodoxy, becoming, in Michael Oakeshott's scathing words, 'a hedge-priest for some doubtful orthodoxy'.

Having said that, however, I came to see that my position was often misunderstood. I did not mean to argue for less commitment to political life (indeed I find little that is new, though much that is very welcome, in the current rediscovery of positive citizenship), only that academic authority should not be invoked for comprehensive commitments; and, above all else, that all commitments should and could take a political form. A whole chapter had dealt with the dangers of three typical positions: the non-political conservative, the a-political liberal and the antipolitical socialist. Perhaps the polemic against the latter sounded so strong (as family quarrels could be in the far-off days of

Marxist intellectual hegemony – or so they thought) that some readers took me for an eccentric Burkean conservative. They did not seem to notice that I had said in that very section, deliberately polishing an epigram, that 'indifference to human suffering discredits free regimes' (thinking of unemployment and poverty quite as much as of famine and concentration camps). And I also said, with only a little irony, that 'to think of the growth of the British Labour movement is to be impressed not with the efficacy of a single doctrine, but with the wonder of politics' (meaning that when judged by behaviour and deeds, not by rhetoric, the British Labour Party has always practised and sustained parliamentary politics in a pluralistic manner, as much as the other main parties in Great Britain).

So I added the 'Footnote to Rally Fellow Socialists' (which grew into a Fabian pamphlet and then a small book) to defend a democratic socialist tradition that is thoroughly political. Perhaps this was a self-indulgence which risked that some readers would then see this as a committed book, and switch off. But I thought it important to tell some fellow socialists bluntly to stop pretending that they had an all-embracing, self-sufficient and exclusive system, superior to normal (what they called bourgeois) political restraints and values; and also to tell some Conservatives that they discredit and devalue political debate if they portray all socialism as either a spendthrift half-way house to old Communism or a frustrated form of it. I was stung into this Footnote by a chance incident. A thoughtful Derbyshire miner (in the days when there were miners) said to me, after reading the book in an extra-mural class: 'Ay, I gets all that; but does thee not believe in anything, Professor lad?' He deserved a temperate answer. Of course, some of the pragmatic mystics of 'The Third Way' may now think that my temperate reply is way-out, certainly a little 'off-message'. We must wait and see. I am a democratic socialist.

Lastly, this book was written during the depths of the Cold War. Like most people I did not believe that the Soviet Communist system and its empire could collapse or wither away. But unlike some of my friends and students, I neither expected nor feared a Third World War. The atomic arsenals were unusable, the deterrents did deter, but the great tragedy was that they made the Iron Curtain seem indestructible and permanent. We might enjoy a kind of peace but only at the price of a war mentality, inhuman misuse of scarce resources and an acceptance of the permanent unfreedom of others – as when the tanks moved into Budapest in 1956 and into Prague in 1968. Influenced by Hannah Arendt's *Origins of Totalitarianism* I believed that once people got into that condition, there was little hope of change – at best, a dilution of totalitarianism into autocracy. The answer then became not to risk going that way at all, when and where choice was still possible. So I offered a defence of politics, not a pseudo-proof of its inevitability. But now, whatever happens to the countries of the former Soviet Union, and to China indeed, totalitarianism seems a faded relic of the mid-twentieth century, a perversion of modernism that ultimately failed, however much damage it did and left behind. The events of November 1989 in Eastern Europe showed a civic courage greater than anything seen since the Second World War, perhaps since the French Revolution or the uprisings against Britain and then Spain in the Americas. But, as in all revolutions, nothing went according to plan: there were unexpected consequences; expectations were aroused that could not be fulfilled; and the rest of the world was slow to grasp the full significance and opportunity of such events, and has failed to help with the skills and resources needed.

The price to be paid in terms of human suffering in times of transition can be greater than under some periods at least of the old oppression. The market determines prices but it does not solve, indeed can exacerbate, moral problems of distribution and the environment, ultimately of human survival. It must always be responded to and mediated by a democratic politics. So in 1992, after the fall of the Wall, I added 'A Final Footnote to Rally Those Who Grudge the Price', which contains some modifications of the more optimistic tone of the last chapter proper, 'In Praise of Politics', and I have now had to add an even darker Epilogue.

Alas, in one respect at least I have been too clever. Few noticed that, in the title of those footnotes, 'to rally' was an antique pun to convey a deliberate ambivalence. Stand fast, indeed; but when we lose self-irony, then dogmatism or even fanaticism takes over.

Acknowledgements

In the first edition I spoke enigmatically of having 'bitten two of the hands that had fed me' at the LSE. I meant Harold Laski, socialist, and Michael Oakeshott, conservative. I did learn much from both. By the second edition I was aware how much in debt I had been to the late Carl Joachim Friedrich at Harvard and to the writings of Hannah Arendt. Ernest Gellner gave me stern and helpful criticism of my first draft, and my friends Dante Germino, Melvin Richter and the late Harold Swayze reacted to the first edition to help the second. Irene Coltman Brown's *Private Men and Public Causes: Philosophy and Politics in the English Civil War* (Faber, 1962) appeared at about the same time, and our letters crossed in the post saying how good we thought the other's book, how similar our basic argument, and that we didn't normally write to strangers. That is a good way to make a life-long friend and most helpful critic, such as has also been Dr Sally Jenkinson. Each of the Footnotes contains some reaction to criticism by good students at LSE, Sheffield and finally Birkbeck.

Some paragraphs in the 'Footnote to Rally Those Who Grudge the Price' have been adapted from my essay 'The High Price of Peace' in Hermann Giliomee and Jannie Gagiano (eds), *The Elusive Search for Peace: South Africa, Israel and Northern Ireland* (Oxford University Press, Cape Town: 1990), and many friends and others in each of those countries have contributed to my change of tone from a qualified optimism to the qualified pessimism of the Epilogue. My tone is much the same as that of J. M. Ross in his *Forward to Basics – Back from the Brink* (Pentland Press, 1999). Some paragraphs in the Epilogue draw on the last chapters in my *Essays on Citizenship* (Continuum, 2000). I thank

Penguin Books for permission to quote passages from Thucydides, *The Peloponnesian War,* in Rex Warner's fine translation (first published 1954). Lastly I thank Dr Francis Celoria for interrupting his labours on 'Folly' to help me with the proofs of the fourth edition.

Bernard Crick
Edinburgh
4 July 2000

There are limits to everything. In all this time something definite should have been achieved. But it all turns out that those who inspired the revolution . . . aren't happy with anything that's on less than a world scale. For them transitional periods, worlds in the making, are an end in themselves. They aren't trained for anything else, they don't know anything except that. And do you know why these never-ending preparations are so futile? It's because these men haven't any real capacities, they are incompetent. Man is born to live not to prepare for life.

PASTERNAK, *Doctor Zhivago*

I immediately discerned within the Russian Revolution the seeds of such serious evils as intolerance and the drive towards the persecution of dissent. These evils originated in an absolute sense of the possession of truth grafted upon doctrinal rigidity. What followed was contempt for the man who was different, For his arguments and his way of life. Undoubtedly, one of the greatest problems each of us has to solve in the realm of practice is that of accepting the necessity to maintain, in the midst of the intransigence that comes from steadfast beliefs, a critical spirit towards these same beliefs and a respect for the belief that differs. In the struggle, it is the problem of combining the greatest practical efficiency with respect for the man in the enemy; in a word, of war without hate.

VICTOR SERGE, *Memoirs of a Revolutionary*

Chapter 1
The Nature of Political Rule

*Who has not often felt the distaste with democratic politics
which Salazar expressed when he said that he 'detested
politics from the bottom of his heart; all those noisy and
incoherent promises, the impossible demands, the hotchpotch
of unfounded ideas and impractical plans . . . opportunism
that cares neither for truth nor justice, the inglorious chase
after unmerited fame, the unleashing of uncontrollable
passions, the exploitation of the lowest instincts, the distortion
of facts . . . all that feverish and sterile fuss?'*

J. H HUIZINGA in *The Times*, 16 November 1961

Boredom with established truths is a great enemy of free men. So
there is some excuse in troubled times not to be clever and inventive
in redefining things, or to pretend to academic unconcern or scientific
detachment, but simply to try to make some old platitudes pregnant.
This essay simply seeks to help in the task of restoring confidence in
the virtues of politics as a great and civilizing human activity. Politics, like
Antaeus in the Greek myth, can remain perpetually young, strong, and
lively so long as it can keep its feet firmly on the ground of Mother Earth.
We live in a human condition, so we cannot through politics grasp for
an absolute ideal, as Plato taught with bewitching single-mindedness.
But the surface of the earth varies greatly, and being human we are

restless and have many different ideals and are forced to plan for the future as well as to enjoy the fruits of the past, so equally politics cannot be a 'purely practical and immediate' activity, as those who cannot see beyond the end of their own noses praise themselves by claiming.

Politics is too often regarded as a poor relation, inherently dependent and subsidiary; it is rarely praised as something with a life and character of its own. Politics is not religion, ethics, law, science, history, or economics; it neither solves everything, nor is it present everywhere; and it is not any one political doctrine, such as conservatism, liberalism, socialism, communism, or nationalism, though it can contain elements of most of these things. Politics is politics, to be valued as itself, not because it is 'like' or 'really is' something else more respectable or peculiar. Politics is politics. The person who wishes not to be troubled by politics and to be left alone finds himself the unwitting ally of those to whom politics is a troublesome obstacle to their well-meant intentions to leave nothing alone.

To some this may seem very obvious. But then there will be no harm in reminding them how few they are. All over the world there are men aspiring to power and there are actual rulers who, however many different names they go by, have in common a rejection of politics. Many Frenchmen in 1958, warm defenders of the Republic, argued that General de Gaulle was saving the French nation from the politicians; in 1961 an army rebellion broke out in Algeria in which the same General was then accused of seeking a 'purely political solution' to the Algerian problem, and the rebel Generals went on to deny that they themselves had any 'political ambitions'. Fidel Castro told a reporter in 1961: 'We are not politicians. We made our revolution to get the politicians out. We are social people. This is a social revolution.' In so many places the cry has gone up that *the* party or *the* leader is defending *the* people against the politicians. 'Politics, ill understood, have been defined,' wrote Isaac D'Israeli, 'as "the art of governing mankind by deceiving them".' Many people, of course, even in régimes which are clearly political, think that they are not interested in politics, and even act as if they are not; but they are probably few compared to the many who think that politics is muddled, contradictory, self-defeatingly recurrent, unprogressive, unpatriotic, inefficient, mere compromise, or even a sham or conspiracy by which political parties seek to preserve some particular and peculiar social systems against the challenge of the inevitable future, etc. The anti-political are very right to think that politics is an achievement far more limited in time and place than politically-minded men, or men who practise this odd thing politics, normally presume.

Many politicians, publicists, and scholars in Western cultures are apt to leap to the defence, or the propagandizing, of words like 'liberty', 'democracy', 'free-government', and then to be puzzled and distraught when, even if their voices are heard at all elsewhere, they are only answered by proud and sincere assurances that indeed all these good things exist and are honoured in styles of government as different as my Soviet Union, my China, my Spain, my Egypt, my Cuba, my Ghana, my Northern Ireland, or my South Africa. Even if precise meanings can be attached to these words, they are too important as symbols of prestige to be readily conceded. Publicists would perhaps do better simply to defend the activity of politics itself. For it is a very much more precise thing than is commonly supposed; it is essential to genuine freedom; it is unknown in any but advanced and complex societies; and it has specific origins only found in European experience. It is something to be valued almost as a pearl beyond price in the history of the human condition, though, in fact, to overvalue it can be to destroy it utterly.

Perhaps there is something to be said for writing in praise of an activity which seems so general that few people can feel any great passion to appropriate it, or to nationalize it, as the exclusive property of any one group of men or of any particular programme of government.

It is Aristotle who first states what should be recognized as the fundamental, elementary proposition of any possible political science. He is, as it were, the anthropologist who first characterizes and distinguishes what still appears to be a unique invention or discovery of the Greek world. At one point in the second book of his *Politics,* where he examines and criticizes schemes for ideal states, he says that Plato in his *Republic* makes the mistake of trying to reduce everything in the *polis* (or the political type of state) to a unity; rather it is the case that: 'there is a point at which a *polis,* by advancing in unity, will cease to be a *polis*: there is another point, short of that, at which it may still remain a *polis,* but will none the less come near to losing its essence, and will thus be a worse *polis.* It is as if you were to turn harmony into mere unison, or to reduce a theme to a single beat. The truth is that the *polis* is an aggregate of many members.'[1] Politics arises then, according to great Aristotle, in organized states which recognize themselves to be an aggregate of many members, not a single tribe, religion, interest, or tradition. Politics arises from accepting the fact of the simultaneous existence of different groups, hence different interests and different traditions, within a territorial unit under a common rule. It does not matter much how that unit came to be – by custom, conquest, or geographical circumstance. What does matter is that its social structure, unlike some primitive societies, is sufficiently complex and divided to make politics a plausible response to the problem of governing it, the problem of maintaining order at all. But the establishing of political order is not just any order at all; it marks the birth, or the recognition, of freedom. For politics represents at least some tolerance of differing truths, some recognition that government is possible, indeed best conducted, amid the open canvassing of rival interests. Politics are the public actions of free men. Freedom is the privacy of men from public actions.

Common usage of the word might encourage one to think that politics is a real force in every organized state. But a moment's reflection should reveal that this common usage can be highly misleading. For politics, as Aristotle points out, is only one possible solution to the problem of order. It is by no means the most usual. Tyranny is the most obvious alternative – the rule of one strong man in his own interest; and oligarchy is the next most obvious alternative – the rule of one group in their own interest. The method of rule of the tyrant and the oligarch is quite simply to clobber, coerce, or overawe all or most of these other groups in the interest of their own. The political method of rule is to listen to these other groups so as to conciliate them as far as possible, and to give them a legal position, a sense of security, some clear and reasonably safe means of articulation, by which these other groups can and will speak freely. Ideally politics draws all these groups into each other so that they each and together can make a positive contribution towards the general business of government, the maintaining of order. The different ways in which this can be done are obviously many, even in any one particular circumstance of competing social interests; and in view of the many different states and changes of circumstance there have been, are, and will be, possible variations on the theme of political

---

[1] *Politics of Aristotle,* edited by Sir Ernest Barker, p. 51.

rule appear to be infinite. But, however imperfectly this process of deliberate conciliation works, it is nevertheless radically different from tyranny, oligarchy, kingship, dictatorship, despotism, and – what is probably the only distinctively modern type of rule – totalitarianism.

Certainly it may sometimes seem odd, in the light of contemporary usage, to say that there is no politics in totalitarian or tyrannical régimes. To some it would be clearer to assert that while there is plainly some politics in all systems of government, yet some systems of government are themselves political systems: they function by or for politics. But usage does not destroy real distinctions. And this distinction has a great tradition behind it.[2] When Chief Justice Fortescue in the mid fifteenth century said that England was both *dominium politicum et regale,* he meant that the King could declare law only by the consultation and consent of Parliament, although he was absolute in power to enforce the law and to defend the realm. But a régime purely *regale* or royal would not be *politicum* at all. In the early modern period 'polity' or 'mixed government', that is the Aristotelean blending of the aristocratic with the democratic principle, were terms commonly used in contrast both to tyranny or despotism and to 'democracy' – even when democracy was just a speculative fear, or a theoretical extension of what might happen if all men acted like the Anabaptists or the Levellers. In the eighteenth century in England 'politics' was commonly contrasted to the principle of 'establishment'. Politicians were people who challenged the established order of Crown, Court, and Church; and they challenged it in a peculiar way, not by the Palace intrigues of despotism, but by trying to create clear issues of policy *and* by making them public. Politicians were people, whether highminded like Pitt the Elder, or low-minded like Jack Wilkes, who tried to assert the power of 'the public' and 'the people' (in reality, of course, always publics and peoples) against what Dr Johnson called 'the powers by law established'. The term was pejorative. The Tory squires called the Whig magnates 'politicians' because they enlisted the help of people like Wilkes; and the 'big Whigs' themselves regarded people like Wilkes as politicians because he made use of 'the mob', or rather the skilled urban workers. So being political in fact usually meant recognizing a wider 'constituency', than did the powers-that-be of the moment, whom it was felt to be necessary to consult if government was

---

[2]See further 'Semantic Digression' in the first Appendix.

to be effectively conducted, not in the past, but in the present which was the emerging future.

So in trying to understand the many forms of government that there are, of which political rule is only one, it is particularly easy to mistake rhetoric for theory. To say that all governing involves politics is either rhetoric or muddle. Why call, for instance, a struggle for power 'politics' when it is simply a struggle for power? Two or more factions within a single party, or the clients of two great men, struggle for a monopoly of power: there may be no political or constitutional procedures whatever to contain this struggle, or powerful enough to do so, and the contestants will regard any compromise as a pure tactic or breathing-space on the way to the complete victory of one faction and the suppression of the other. Certainly there is a sense in which, even in a tyranny or totalitarian régime, politics exists up to the moment when the ruler finds himself free to act alone. While he is not free to act alone, while he is forced to consult other people whom he regards as his enemies, either through necessity or through a temporary ignorance of their real power, he is in some kind of a political relationship. But it is essentially fragile and unwanted. The ruler will not, nor may anyone else, regard it as normal, even if it could be shown that it is perennial. Politics is then regarded simply as an obstacle – and, in a sense, it is an obstacle, but it may not be an at all secure or effective one. Some politics may exist in unfree régimes, but it is unwanted – a measure to their rulers of inadequate progress towards unity; and every effort will be made to keep such disputes secret from the ruled, to prevent the formation of a 'public'. For Palace politics is private politics, almost a contradiction in terms. The unique character of political activity lies, quite literally, in its publicity.

There is no need, then, to deny that elements of politics can exist in tyrannical and other régimes – rather the contrary. Sophocles makes this point in the *Antigone*:

CREON: Then she is not breaking the law?

HAEMON: Your fellow-citizens would deny it, to a man.

CREON: And the *polis* proposes to teach me how to rule?

HAEMON: Ah. Who is it that's talking like a boy now?

CREON: Can any voice but mine give orders in this *polis*?

HAEMON: It is no *polis* if it takes orders from one voice.

CREON: But custom gives possession to the ruler.

HAEMON: You'd rule a desert beautifully alone.

Suppose I had made my point less strongly by rendering *polis* as simply 'city'; we would still see a word being contested for by two different theories of government – call it 'civil society' or 'political society'. Both claim that their theory is inherent in the concept – the primacy of autocracy or citizenship respectively. And which is the more realistic? The great hope for the political way of Haemon is that it is, in the long run, a more workable way of maintaining order than the one Creon chose or stuck to. Politics thus arises from a recognition of restraints. The character of this recognition may be moral, but more often it is simply prudential, a recognition of the power of social groups and interests, a product of being unable, without more violence and risk than one can stomach, to rule alone. (An anti-political moral heroine like Antigone may arouse the city, but it is the power of the city that counts. Creon is a bad man to refuse to let her bury her rebel brother, but he is a bad ruler because he does not allow for the power of the city on this issue.) It is, of course, often possible to rule alone. But it is always highly difficult and highly dangerous. 'To make a desert and to call it peace' is not impossible, nor is it uncommon. But fortunately most ordinary politicians realize the incalculability of violence, and do not always need to wreck the State in learning this lesson.

Politics, then, can be simply defined as the activity by which differing interests within a given unit of rule are conciliated by giving them a share in power in proportion to their importance to the welfare and the survival of the whole community. And, to complete the formal definition, a political system is that type of government where politics proves successful in ensuring reasonable stability and order. Aristotle attempted to argue that these compromises of politics must in some sense be creative of future benefits – that each exists for a further purpose. But it is probably wiser to keep what we want to defend as simple as possible and simply to point out that no finality is implied in any act of conciliation or compromise. Each compromise has at least served some purpose, teleological or not, if at the time it is made it enables orderly government to be carried on at all. Orderly government is, after all, a civilized value compared to anarchy or arbitrary rule; and political government, other things being equal, clearly remains more acceptable to more people if they are ever given any chance or choice in the matter. Advocates of particular political doctrines – as will be seen – should beware of denying the context in which their doctrines can operate politically: their claims can never be exclusive. The political process is not tied to any particular doctrine. Genuine political doctrines, rather, are the attempt to find particular and workable solutions to this perpetual and shifty problem of conciliation.

Why cannot a good ruler do this, without all the muddle and uncertainty of politics? – it will always be asked. When the academic is asked this question by an ordinary person in urgency or innocence, he coughs and blushes, feels that he is meant to utter a platitude and tries to remember correctly Lord Acton's words about all power corrupting. Aristotle, however, took this as a perfectly serious issue of principle. If there was a 'perfectly just man' he should, by right and reason, be made king (just as we *should* obey any party which could prove that it knows which way the iron laws of history are unfolding for our future benefit). This for some is at least a theoretical possibility – and an interesting one. There is no similar hope for an absolute justification of political rule. The answer is a practical one; Aristotle thinks, not surprisingly, that such a man is not very likely to be found. We have no particular need to take his word for that when faced with our own modern gallery of moralistic autocrats, dictators promising the moon and various 'fathers of their people'. Many of these men are not, in any ordinary sense, bad men; but few, to put it mildly, could be described as 'perfectly good'. And to Aristotle the slightest flaw will disqualify one, will put one in need of some restraint. It was only the *perfectly* good man who would not need to listen to his fellows, who would not need to have rival powers so firmly entrenched that he has to listen. Indeed, he remarks that the man who can live outside the *polis* is either a beast or a god. God is the only possible being who does not need to consult, having no fellows; God is the only possible being whose command is identical with law and justice. Aristotle's sometime pupil, Alexander, had to try to become a god in order to solve the problem of finding the authority – and hence the power – to rule, not merely conquer, diverse types of *polis,* indeed whole empires which had never known politics at all. Plato's philosopher king, in the parable of the *Republic,* after all his intense scientific training, has to undergo a mystical experience of illumination or conversion, an utter change of quality, before he is fit to rule the ideal state. The Caesars were to find deification a practical response to the problem of authority in consolidating an empire gained by conquest. And the notion of descent from God has been typical of Oriental and of pre-Hispanic American empires (an 'imperium' or empire being kingship which aspires to govern men of different histories and cultures, and thus has need of a greater authority than can stem from custom alone). The utility of such a notion for rulers is less surprising than the willingness of many followers, even in our own times, to treat their leaders as if they were God: the declarer of the law, the one above criticism, above the need to consult, the only truly self-sufficient man.

Politics, then, to Aristotle, was something natural, not of divine origin, simply the 'master science' among men. Politics was the master-science not in the sense that it includes or explains all other 'sciences' (all skills, social activities, and group interests), but in that it gives them some priority, some order in their rival claims on the always scarce resources of any given community. The way of establishing these priorities is by allowing the right institutions to develop by which the various 'sciences' can demonstrate their actual importance in the common task of survival. Politics are, as it were, the market place and the price mechanism of all social demands – though there is no guarantee that a just price will be struck; and there is nothing spontaneous about politics – it depends on deliberate and continuous individual activity.

Now it is often thought that for this 'master science' to function, there must be already in existence some shared idea of a 'common good', some 'consensus' or *consensus juris.* But this common good is itself the process of practical reconciliation of the interests of the various 'sciences', aggregates, or groups which compose a state; it is not some external and intangible spiritual adhesive, or some allegedly objective 'general will' or 'public interest'. These are misleading and pretentious explanations of how a community holds together; worse, they can even be justifications for the sudden destruction of some elements in the community in favour of others – there is no right to obstruct the general will, it is said. But diverse groups hold together, firstly, because they have a common interest in sheer survival and, secondly, because they practise politics – not because they agree about 'fundamentals', or some such concept too vague, too personal, or too divine ever to do the job of politics for it. The moral consensus of a free state is not something mysteriously prior to or above politics: it is the activity (the civilizing activity) of politics itself.

Now, of course, our aspirations and actions will be sadly disembodied spirits if they cannot go beyond a mere appreciation of what politics is all about. We shall all want to do something with it. Those who sit tight and drift, murmuring incantations which did not wreck us yesterday, are apt to be cast away on hostile shores. Those who urge us to remember that our only clearly demonstrable task is simply to keep the ship afloat have a rather curious view of the purpose of ships. Even if there is no single predetermined port of destination, clearly all directions are still not equally preferable. 'What politics is' does not destroy or exhaust the question 'What do we want to get out of it?' But we may not go about trying to get what we want in a political manner at all.

For politics is to be seen neither as a set of fixed principles to be realized in the near future, nor yet as a set of traditional habits to be preserved, but as an activity, a sociological activity which has the anthropological function of preserving a community grown too complicated for either tradition alone or pure arbitrary rule to preserve it without the undue use of coercion. Burke's aphorism about the need to reform in order to preserve is a characterization of the political method of rule far more profound than that of those conservatives who hold that politics is simply a communication received from tradition.

Politics is, then, an *activity* – and this platitude must be brought to life: it is not a thing, like a natural object or a work of art, which could exist if individuals did not continue to act upon it. And it is a *complex activity*; it is not simply the grasping for an ideal, for then the ideals of others may be threatened; but it is not pure self-interest either, simply because the more realistically one construes self-interest the more one is involved in relationships with others, and because, after all, some men in most part, most men in some part, have certain standards of conduct which do not always fit circumstances too exactly. The more one is involved in relationships with others, the more conflicts of interest, or of character and circumstance, will arise. These conflicts, when personal, create the activity we call 'ethics' (or else that type of action, as arbitrary as it is irresponsible, called 'selfish'); and such conflicts, when public, create political activity (or else some type of rule in the selfish interest of a single group).

Consider another human *activity,* almost as famous as politics – something which is again neither an implementation of principles nor a matter of pure expediency: sexuality. They are both activities in which the tacit understanding of presuppositions often makes more formal propositions unnecessary; the sympathies that are a product of experience are better than the doctrines that are learnt from books. Sexuality, granted, is a more widespread activity than politics, but again the suspicion remains that the man who can live without either is either acting the beast or aping the god. Both have much the same character of necessity in essence and unpredictability in form. Both are activities which must be carried on if the community is to perpetuate itself at all, both serve this wider purpose, and yet both can become enjoyable ends in themselves for any one individual. Both activities can be repeated in an almost infinite variety of forms and different circumstances; and yet in both, the activity often becomes attached to a quite arbitrary or fortuitous individual instance, which we then proceed to treat as if that he or she, or Fatherland or Motherland, were the most perfect example ever found of the whole great enterprise. And both are activities in which the range of possible conduct is far greater than any conceivably desirable range of actual conduct. Both are activities in which the human group maintains itself amid the utmost variations in, for the actors involved, success and failure, tragedy and joy, passion and prudence, and in those dialectic syntheses more often domestic and familiar. Politics, then, like sexuality is an activity which must be carried on; one does not create it or decide to join in – one simply becomes more and more aware that one is involved in it as part of the human condition. One can only forsake, renounce, or do without it by doing oneself (which can easily be done – and on the highest principles) unnatural injury. To renounce or destroy politics is to destroy the very thing which gives order to the pluralism and variety of civilized society, the thing which enables us to enjoy variety without suffering either anarchy or the tyranny of single truths, which become the desperate salvation from anarchy – just as misogamy and celibacy are forms of salvation for the overly passionate mind.

For political rule must be preceded by public order just as love must be preceded by social acquaintance and contained by social conventions. Politics and love are the only forms of constraint possible between free people. Rule or government preserve and often even create communities. 'Electoral representation', 'liberty', 'rights' and even, or especially – as we will see, 'democracy' are specific and subsequent achievements of a civilization which has already established order and constraint in a known territory. Those who glibly say that all government is based on consent, as if that settles anything, are being as passionately vague as those who say, for instance, that all love must be based on the absolute freedom of the partners in love. If there were absolute freedom, there could be no love; if there is absolute consent, there could be no government. But people have every right to say that all government is based on consent, and there may be no harm in their saying so, so long as the small word 'all' is taken seriously. For this shows us that the assertion can have little to do with any possible distinction between freedom and oppression – the most absolute tyrant must have his faithful dogs around him.

And equally the word 'government' must be taken seriously and recognized for what it is: the organization of a group of men in a given community for survival. Thomas Hobbes, after all, spent a great deal of time arguing the massively simple point that if one does not survive, there is no knowing whether one has made the right choice. But there are good grounds for thinking that politics is often a more effective way of ensuring survival than the absolute rule of Leviathan. Whether Leviathan is a monarch, a dictator, a party, or a 'nation in arms', he is apt to be a pretty clumsy fellow who has few reliable ways of knowing what is really going on (representative electoral institutions, for instance, seem a fairly good way by which a government can find out what people will do and what they will stand for). But this ignorance on the part of autocracy only arises because one part of survival is a continuous process of adaptation to complicated social changes, economic and technological; this need to consult cannot eliminate the other type of survival which is military, or at least militant, the capacity to act without compromise or normal consultation in a state of emergency, whether flood, famine, pestilence, or war itself. Leviathan must be there already – he cannot be created in a hurry, but he is the guarantor of politics, neither the single leader nor the negation. His authority, like that of the two Dictators of Republican Rome, ceases with the end of the emergency. *Quis custodiet custodes?* Who, indeed, shall guard the guardians? There is, perhaps it should be simply said, no possible general answer to this question. History is rich with experiment and examples, some relatively successful, some complete failures. Only the problem is clear enough. As Lincoln put it amid the agony of Civil War: 'It has long been a grave question whether any government not too strong for the liberties of its people, can be strong enough to maintain its liberties in great emergencies.'

The guardians may, indeed, try to carry on ruling the country after the end of the emergency or, more often, by prolonging the emergency – if they can get away with it. There is no possible 'right' of revolution to check this, as John Locke tried to argue: revolution is the destruction of a particular order of rights. But, thinking in sociological rather than legal terms, Locke had an obvious point; there may come a time when people are driven to rebel by the failure of a government to govern politically at all. The state of emergency is the time of sovereignty – when all power has to go to and to come from one source, if the community is to survive at all. 'Those republics,' wrote Machiavelli, 'which in time of danger cannot resort to a dictatorship will generally be ruined when grave occasions occur.' But in normal times in some fortunate states the 'sovereignty' of governments is a very formal abstract thing compared to the reality of politics. Hobbes's *Leviathan* saw government as a perpetual state of emergency. Hobbes may have been frightened in the womb by the guns of the Spanish Armada, and he may have thought sixty years later that there was nothing more terrible than Englishmen killing Englishmen in civil war, but that is no excuse for not studying, as Machiavelli did, the problem of how to maintain a state through time (which is a problem of spreading power), as well as how to preserve it in crisis (which is a problem of concentrating power). Surely we have less excuse. Some modern states in times of infinitely greater threat have been able to preserve politics, even to recreate it, as even in part of Germany where for a generation it was wiped out with a unique and deliberate fury. 'The secret of liberty is courage,' as Pericles declaimed. It is not a very safe world anyhow. Free men stick their necks out.

Even with luck and courage, we must not hope for too much from politics, or believe that we see it everywhere. It can exist only where it has been preceded by sovereignty or where sovereignty can be quickly called into being. So if politics, to be a stable and possible method of rule, requires some settled order, as well as tolerance and diversity, then the relationships between states themselves can be seen at their best only as a kind of quasipolitics. The will to conciliate and compromise may actually be stronger at times in international relations, simply because it is more difficult to calculate whether one is powerful enough to ignore diplomacy, than it is to know whether one can govern unpolitically in a single, settled country. But the possibility of politicizing an established order is largely absent simply because there is no established order – only a speculative and doubtful common interest in peace, or some more certain, but more abstract, moral fact of human brotherhood. The agony of international relations is the need to try to practise politics without the basic conditions for political order. The 'cold war' would not have surprised Hobbes, for he defined 'War' simply as 'time men live without common power to keep them all in awe'. International society was no society at all, but simply the state of nature – war. For 'the nature of War consisteth not in actual fighting, but in the known disposition thereto, during all the time there is no assurance to the contrary'. And there are no assurances to the contrary, outside the realm of a particular sovereign or 'common power'. This I take to be the case of 'international politics'. One wishes it were otherwise, but it is not. Certainly diplomacy and politics have much in common: the urge to conciliate and act prudently are much alike, indeed can be, as we have said, actually stronger in diplomacy. But in diplomacy the basic fact of order is lacking. Even in times of emergency, of threat to what international order there is, there may not be a clearly superior and effective power. In a territorial society, government makes politics possible; but in an international 'society', politics (or rather diplomacy) has to try to make any even minimal government or order possible. Political maxims and experience (even though as aspirations and not an established activity) will be some help in international problems. Clearly, for instance, a country powerful enough to threaten world peace cannot be permanently excluded from any institution which even purports to be concerned with world order. But genuine politics remains an ideal in international relations. Distinctions can in fact be drawn. The United Nations Organization is not, for instance, a political assembly because it is not a sovereign assembly. There are, strictly speaking, no politicians at the United Nations; there are only 'statesmen' and 'ambassadors' who are mere delegates of bodies regarded as sovereign. Unlike politicians, they cannot settle issues of government among themselves; they depend upon instructions. For the politician is not a delegate; the politician has power to act in conjunction with other politicians; his power is limited by acceptance of periodic elections, but is not bound by daily instructions. Where government is impossible, politics is impossible. Once again, distinctions can in fact be drawn. Everything is not politics. Struggles for power are struggles for power. And the task of diplomacy is a somewhat different task from that of politics. Certainly it can be a universal activity among states – whereas politics is not a universal activity even within states. Let us defend politics, then, as an actual activity without thinking that so-called international politics is more than, at the best, a kind of aspirant, quasi-politics.

Similarly, common usage may encourage us to talk about politics in the small group – in the trade union, in the office, and even in the family; and anthropologists find that many tribal societies are more 'political' and less 'autocratic' than once supposed. Some social scientists, perhaps being a little too clever, make quite a song and dance about 'the politics of small groups'. They hope by studying the microcosm to understand the macrocosm. But the difference is not just one of scale: a valuable qualitative distinction is lost. If all discussion, conflict, rivalry, struggle, and even conciliation is called politics, then it is forgotten, once more, that politics depends on some settled order. Small groups are subordinate parts of that order. They may help to create politics, but their internal behaviour is not political simply because their individual function is quite different from that of the state itself. And, unlike the state, they have no acknowledged legal right to use force if all else fails.

If the argument is, then, that politics is simply the activity by which government is made possible when differing interests in an area to be governed grow powerful enough to need to be conciliated, the obvious objection will be: 'why do certain interests have to be conciliated?' And the answer is, of course, that they do not have to be. Other paths are always open. Politics is simply when they are conciliated – that solution to the problem of order which chooses conciliation rather than violence and coercion, and chooses it as an effective way by which varying interests can discover that level of compromise best suited to their common interest in survival. Politics allows various types of power within a community to find some reasonable level of mutual tolerance and support. Coercion (or secession or migration) need arise only when one group or interest feels that it has no common interest in survival with the rest. Put at its most obvious, most men would simply agree that coercion needs justification: conciliation justifies itself if it works. There may not be any absolute justification of politics. Let us be brazen and simply say, 'We prefer politics'. But such modesty had better be somewhat truculent. For it is, after all, too hard (indeed perverse) to respect the morality and wisdom of any who, when politics is possible, refuse to act politically.

Political rule, then, because it arises from the problem of diversity, and does not try to reduce all things to a single unity, necessarily creates or allows some freedom. Political freedom is a response to a need of government – it is not, as so many sentimentally think, an external impetus that somehow forces, or persuades, governments to act tolerantly. The freedom of a group will be established at the moment when its power or its existence cannot be denied and must be reckoned with in governing a country as it actually is. The American Revolution took place, for instance, not because people suddenly became supersensitive to their rights, or – an even more unlikely theory – because they suddenly became nationalistic, but because the existing government broke down. The British Government had failed to recognize the peculiar interests and the peculiar character of the colonies which it suddenly tried to govern, with the Stamp Act of 1765, after a long century of what Burke had called 'wise and salutary neglect'. And it failed to recognize their interests because they were not represented. If they were 'virtually represented' in Parliament, this was in numbers so few compared to their real power and commercial importance that they were not taken seriously until too late, until they had been driven into revolutionary violence. Political representation is, then, a device of government before ever it can be sensibly viewed as a 'right' of the governed. If it is not made use of, a government may not be able to govern at all – unless it is willing to practise coercion and to suffer fear to the degree that it is ignorant of the interests of the governed. Almost any system of representation, however ramshackle, incomplete, and at times even corrupt, is better than none; and is better than one that will represent only an alleged single interest of the governed. The English Reform Bills of 1832 and 1867 did not take place because old Whig gentlemen in Westminster suddenly became convinced, out of some movement in abstract ideas, that those Radical fellows were morally right, but because it became increasingly clear that government could not be carried on in an industrialized society unless the power and existence first of the entrepreneur and then of the skilled manual worker were recognized and represented.

'Politics', then, simply summarizes an activity whose history is a mixture of accident and deliberate achievement, and whose social basis is to be found only in quite complicated societies. It is not as such motivated by principle, except in a dislike of coercion which can, in turn, be simply thought to be a matter of prudence. (To debate too hotly the rival integrity of different motives which lead to the same action is academic – either political folly or the luxury of an already established political order.) Political principles are, whatever they are, principles held within politics. Now the holding of political principles or doctrines, at some level, with some degree of consistency, seems quite inevitable for any but the beast or the god – and why not? There is a touch of doctrinaire absurdity in those conservatives who would argue that all political doctrines become doctrinaire. A political doctrine is only doctrinaire, firstly, if it refuses to recognize the power and existence of other forces and ideas within an established political order; or, secondly – and more obviously – when it seeks to argue that some of these groups must be eliminated urgently, illegally, and unpolitically if other great benefits are to follow. Political doctrines must, in fact, be genuinely political (Marxism, for instance, as we shall see, is clearly and explicitly an anti-political doctrine).

A political doctrine I take to be simply a coherently related set of proposals for the conciliation of actual social demands in relation to a scarcity of resources. As such, a political doctrine should make short shrift with the old and barren academic controversy over 'fact' and 'value' – for it is necessarily both evaluative and predictive. For a political doctrine always offers some generalizations about the nature of actual, or possible, political societies, but it always also offers some grounds, however disputable, for thinking some such possibilities desirable. By prediction I do not mean something that is necessarily measurable as in natural science, but merely something that guides our present actions according to our expectations of what will happen in the future (or, of course, of what we shall find in the past). And it is evaluative not merely because all thought is an act of selection from a potentially infinite range of relevant factors, but because we do in fact seek to justify some act of selection as in some way significant. A political doctrine will state some purpose, but it will claim to be a realizable purpose; or it may state some sociological generalization. But argument, if not analysis, will always reveal some ethical significance in wanting this relationship to be true, or to remain true. A political doctrine is thus just an attempt to strike a particular harmony in an actual political situation, one harmony out of many possible different (temporary) resolutions of the basic problem of unity and diversity in a society with complex and entrenched rival social interests. This problem is the germ of politics and freedom.

Some freedom, at least, must exist wherever there is political rule. For politics is a process of discussion, and discussion demands, in the original Greek sense, dialectic. For discussion to be genuine and fruitful when something is maintained, the opposite or some contrary case must be considered or – better – maintained by someone who believes it. The hallmark of free government everywhere, it is an old but clear enough test, is whether public criticism is allowed in a manner conceivably effective – in other words, whether opposition is tolerated. Politics needs men who will act freely, but men cannot act freely without politics. Politics is a way of ruling divided societies without undue violence – and most societies are divided, though some think that that is the very trouble. We can do much worse than honour 'mere politics' so we must examine very carefully the claims of those who would do better.

Chapter 2
A Defence of Politics against Ideology

That not all forms of government are political, and that politics is a more precise concept than is often thought, are truths which become very clear by contrast to totalitarian rule and its reliance on the theory of ideology. Totalitarian rule marks the sharpest contrast imaginable with political rule, and ideological thinking is an explicit and direct challenge to political thinking. The totalitarian believes that everything is relevant to government and that the task of government is to reconstruct society utterly according to the goals of an ideology. This ideology will offer a criticism of existing society and a prophecy – on the basis of a single 'key to history' – of a final, perfectly just, and perfectly stable stage of society. So to appreciate the unique character of totalitarian rule and the unique aspirations of totalitarian ideology should help us to understand more fully the peculiar importance of some aspects of politics. We shall find there a direct attack on the idea of a diversity of semi-independent groups in society and on the idea of the affirmative individual, so strong as to convince us that the totalitarian at least knows that these two things are at the heart of what makes politics possible. And we will find ourselves disabused about the importance of some other things.

Such a comparison will, at least, destroy any easy identification of political freedom with 'democracy'. The contrast of democratic and undemocratic régimes, so that free régimes become simply those based on willing and active consent, breaks down completely in the light of totalitarian régimes. As Hannah Arendt has written in her great

Origins of Totalitarianism: 'it is painful to realize that they are always preceded by mass movements and that they "command and rest upon mass support" up to the end.' To deny this basis of mass support to the Soviet Union and to Communist China – as once some denied it to Nazi Germany – may be a comfortable belief, but it is a false and dangerous one, a symptom of how thoroughly many of us good liberals are in the grip of a false theory of government: that the consent of the people necessarily creates freedom. Mill's essay *On Liberty* was premised on the need to defend liberty against even democracy, to give democrats a respect for liberty. Representative government, he saw, was no guarantee of liberty – if all posts were filled by men of the same mind. But somehow the point rarely sinks in. People continue to try to characterize 'free politics' in terms of democracy and can never see why, in the history of the rise of democratic institutions (which is not the same as the history of toleration), the Communist claim to be democratic is equally plausible. Totalitarian régimes, indeed, are a product of a democratic age. They depend upon mass support, and they have found a way of treating society as if it were, or were about to be, a single mass. Even opposition with more bark than bite will be destroyed, not because it offends the pride of an autocrat, but because its very existence challenges the theories of a totalitarian ideologist. No more may even sleeping dogs lie, as under autocracy. They must be whipped into action until they begin to enjoy it.

For totalitarianism is not merely an intensive word of abuse applied to old authoritarian practices 'new writ large' by modern technological opportunities. Modern technology has not just expanded opportunities for the exploitation of office, but has helped to create a new style of ideological thought of such sweeping ambition that the mere passive obedience with which most former autocrats were content has now given way to the need for an active and perpetual enthusiasm. The autocrat wanted to govern in pleasure and peace – he might have military ambitions, but even they were limited to the pleasure he could conceivably get out of them in his own life span; but the totalitarian leader aspires to 'remake this sorry scheme of things entire' and tries to think in terms of whole epochs, not just of human generations. Himmler claimed that his S.S. men were not interested in 'everyday problems' but only 'in ideological questions of importance for decades and centuries. . . .' The enjoyment of office and the perpetuation of a régime or dynasty have become secondary to the achievement by a single party of the goals of an ideology. Thus we have broken, with little warning, from the bounds of those Greek classifications of types of government which for so long seemed adequate, since they all presumed that government served limited purposes, that the State, while being the predominant social institution, yet was not omnipotent.

For the aim of totalitarian rule is not simply intense autocracy. Autocrats, once a state grew too large and complex for every group interest to be dominated by a Palace Guard, could solve the problem of power only by sharing power. Limited government (however limited), government by consultation (however one-sided), became an administrative necessity to some degree (however shallow). Mass consent, when the masses became important as towns grew and industry spread, could be gained only by mass participation in politics. For as Rousseau said in one of those flashes of empirical clarity that make up for so much else: 'the strongest is never strong enough to be always master, unless he transforms strength into right and obedience into duty.' But totalitarian ideology has provided this basis of right and duty in a plausible, intelligible, and revolutionary form. It has provided what Napoleon once said would be the politics of the future: 'the organization of willing masses for sacrifice for an ideal.' To the totalitarian régime, then, nothing is irrelevant to the government, everything is possible. The masses must be changed, or orchestrated, towards a single future harmony. It is at least clear that such a style of thought can be called, with agreement from both ideologist and politician, anti-political.

The chiliastic claims of both Nazism and Communism have been generally remarked – whatever have been their temporary compromises in practice: what was once a religious heresy, to achieve the holy reign of the saints on earth, has become in our times a secular orthodoxy held with religious intensity. There was a fanatic rejection of the compromises of mere 'politics' by the Nazis, something which challenged the conventional belief of the bureaucracy and the officer corps that they could live beside and yet avoid 'politics', could dwell in some aloof but dutiful *Überparteilichkeit*. The belief that race and race alone was the sole determinant of social action gave rise to the belief of the Nazi élite in a 'Final Solution'. Few denied that the 'Final Solution of the Jewish problem' would not become a gross political liability, even in Germany, when it became widely known; but the system had swept beyond mere politics. Racial purity was offered to the masses as being infallibly able to ensure the subjection or transformation of the two great demons of the old liberal systems, those two things of great dread which, after 1914, had seemingly proved uncontrollable in the rational liberal world: war and mass-unemployment. War was transformed from something to be excused politically into something to be glorified racially; and unemployment was banished by attempting to put the whole economy on a permanent war-footing. Politics became anti-politics, as when Hitler wrote: 'Politics is the art of carrying out the life struggle of a nation for its earthly existence. Foreign politics is the art of ensuring for a nation its living space in size and wealth whenever and however necessary. Domestic politics is the art of maintaining for a nation the power necessary for this aim in the form of its racial equality and size of population.'[1]

If the idea that class struggle is the sole determinant of social action appears at least more plausible than that of racial struggle, it also gave rise to killings and cruelties so great that comparisons of more or less become themselves inhuman. One trembles with horror at the person who thinks either that one should count heads, or that any distinction between a Nazi 'irrational' terror and a Communist 'rational' terror would help one to set oneself up as a judge who must – strangely and terribly – pardon one or the other. For the Communist too, terror and 'mass-resettlement' is done in the name of an advance to a final stage of history. Time and time again the real interests of Communist Parties which were involved in political situations, in China during the 1920s, in Weimar Germany, in France and Britain during the 1930s, were sacrificed for the needs of the whole ideology (and even if these needs of the whole ideology became at times suspiciously close to a traditional Russian self-interest, the fact remains that Communists abroad were willing to take this on trust and to sacrifice their own obvious immediate interests). The activity of politics itself, both in Nazi and Communist doctrine, was only a transitional stage in history. The element of diplomacy in international relations was itself irksome; it fortified the universalism and world-shaping aspirations of the ideology. Both the Communists and the Nazis took part in politics only as a temporary means to a higher – permanent – end.

---

[1] Hitler's *Zweites Buch* (Stuttgart 1961, p. 62).

To say that doctrine is of unique importance in totalitarian régimes is to misunderstand how precisely and uniquely doctrine is viewed as ideology. Ideology has now become one of the most loosely used words in the vocabulary of power. Publicists and journalists have debased it into a mere term of abuse, a synonym for fervid impracticality – or, more occasionally, a useful moral armament which the *other side* has got and which we lack. We are in danger of forgetting its precise significance as a theory of human action. The word was first coined by a philosopher, Destutt de Tracy, in 1795 as the name for a 'science' which would explain the relationship between sensations and ideas and would remove all ambiguity from language. This was to be an official project of the revolutionary government's *Institut National des Sciences et Arts.* Shortly afterwards Napoleon gave the word greater currency, using it to mock all abstract and literary schemes concocted by philosophers or publicists. The word became well established, with this invidious meaning, in the writings of French and English conservatives. But Marx, in his polemic *The German Ideology,* though he began by using the term in this way, ended by generalizing from it to create a new and precise theoretical meaning. It expressed a new and vastly influential concept – which marked the birth from the same womb of both the intellectual justification for totalitarianism and the modern study of sociology. To Marx the claim of the theory of ideology is that all doctrine is a derivative of social circumstance. All thought whatever is ideological. Contrary to the belief of many who have not read the book, Marx did not waste much space on chapter and verse of how precisely the German philosophers were serving as tame lackeys of the State, of how the Hegelian 'idealists' were in fact instruments of material class interests. The argument set down was completely general: *any* philosophy can only serve the interests of the class who control the means of production. 'The class which has the means of material production at its disposal, has control at the same time over the means of mental production.' The theory of ideology sees even 'knowledge' and 'reason', let alone ethics and custom, as mere expressions of the total structure of society, as things relative and functional to a particular social system.

Now, to examine the function of ideas as social products (rather than for their truth or falsity) is obviously a proper, interesting, and enlightening subject of inquiry; it is one way, at least, of understanding human society. Marx was indeed the virtual inventor of sociology – itself, obviously, sociology with a purpose, a theory developed to achieve an end. The old oppressive and 'self-contradictory' political order was to be replaced by a new and highly unified social order (politics and philosophy were to be exposed and surpassed by sociology). He was the precursor of the modern study of the 'sociology of knowledge'. This study has not always assumed that all ideas are ideology; and when it has done so, it has often been in the mood of abstract supposition, or of scientific hypothesis: to see what can be explained on the assumption that such a view is true. But it has had a characteristic danger (though danger is no excuse for abandoning learning – as some genteel critics of sociology would have us do). The danger is that man is dissolved away into his social circumstances; the tough-spiritedness of human will and the inventiveness of human intellect become lost in a swamp of circumstantial detail. (It is sadly interesting that Max Weber's writings contain both some of the profoundest modern scholarship and some of the deepest pessimism about the stability and survival of free politics.) But in Marx himself, right from the beginning, the theory of ideology furnished a plan of action aimed at a total change of society, not simply an academic means of understanding society as it was. For if all thought was ideology, then the only final and stable ideology would be that of the ultimate class to come to control the means of production.

So Nazi and Communist ideology became not just a uniquely effective and widecast body of doctrine, only differing in degree from previous political doctrines; for each made an explicit claim to be the necessary and exclusive outcome of the total relationships of every aspect of society – and therefore, in theory at least, claimed to be able to predict and explain everything. An ideology, thus, can be stable, final, and free of any and all internal contradictions only when society as a whole frees itself, or is freed, from those divisive elements of property ownership or racial impurity which impede its fullest possible coherence, generality, and unity. To the totalitarian mind, the limited function of 'mere' politics is both a fallacy and a deceit, a trick of the State to prevent the reign of Society. The *Communist Manifesto* itself spoke of depriving 'the public power' of 'its political character'.[2] The distinction drawn in different ways by every political doctrine between a realm of public affairs and some areas – always some – of privacy (whether that assertive privacy

---

[2]See pp. 136–37 below, for examples of Marx's explicit attack on politics.

called 'personality' or the negative privacy that there are simply some things irrelevant to politics), was deliberately obliterated by the theorists of ideology. Some recognition of privacy or of spheres of irrelevance is one of the reasons why even those who once pushed the power of the state to the utmost then imaginable, say Hobbes, say Hegel, say Papal theorists at different times, cannot sensibly be regarded as totalitarian. Totalitarianism surpasses autocracy. To the totalitarian not merely the machinery of government and the economic institutions of society, but also all education, industry, art, even domesticity and private affections, all these, both in work and leisure, are part of a completely interrelated social system, all are forces which must be accountable to the ideology. To leave any of these uncontrolled would be, in a practical sense, to leave dangerous lacunae of liberty and means of personal escape from complete dedication to public purposes; would be, in a scientific sense, to refute the claim of the theory of ideology that all aspects of society, including thought itself, are dependent on each other and are moving, or can be released, in a known and given direction. Even things which to the conventional tyrant and politician would be quite irrelevant to the needs of *government* – how men paint and make music, or the shape of the roof of a house – become, on this theory, relevant and are therefore either progressive or decadent, never subjects of indifference to the ruler or ruling party.

'The whole framework of our social life is very closely knit together, comrades', so the Soviet critic, Olesha, once cleverly put this point in publicly recanting his misguided admiration for the 'formalist' music of Shostakovich: 'In the life and activity of our State nothing moves or develops independently. . . . If I do not agree with the Party in a single point, the whole picture of life must be dimmed for me, because all parts, all details of the picture are bound together and arise out of each other, therefore there can be no single false line anywhere. . . .'[3] Thus a plausible sense of the complete involvement of all men and all things, which has anthropological significance in defining the distinctively human condition and which may have spiritual meaning – 'do thyself no harm; for we are all here' – attempts translation into political terms, but immediately becomes totalitarian. True politics cannot treat *everything* in political terms. The Marxist attempt to politicize all social relations is,

[3]From 'The Discussion of Formalism', *International Literature* No. 6 (Moscow 1936), p. 88.

in fact, the attempt to eliminate politics. For politics is concerned with limited purposes. Art, for example, cannot be politicized while remaining art. Love cannot be politicized while remaining love. If we are asked to love our country or our party more than our family or our friends (so that if necessary we would lay down our life not for another, but for the cause), we should know that we are being called to sacrifice life for ideology. And a situation will seem to demand such desperate actions only through the failure or neglect of political remedies.

The uniqueness of totalitarianism (which so vividly demonstrates, in the limitlessness of its aspirations, the uniqueness of politics) is further demonstrated in the attack on the concept of the State which was made in the name of Society. Both Nazi and Communist theorists and publicists composed to this theme. Consider the attack in Marx's *Critique of the Gotha Programme* on the idea of the 'Free State'. He tried to show the erring Social Democrats that 'Freedom consists in converting the State from an organ standing above society into one completely subordinated to it.' Hitler wrote in *Mein Kampf*: 'The State is a means to an end. Its end is the preservation and promotion of a community of physically and psychically equal living beings . . . we must sharply distinguish between the State as a vessel and the race as the content.' If society were one pure element, or even a stable solution and not just a compound of differing elements, then the State-as-coercive-power would not, indeed, be needed.

The conventional bourgeois state, precisely because its political, conciliatory function had recognized widely differing ideologies within the same territory, came to be regarded by the modern totalitarians as a mere transitory historical device which it was the purpose of *the* Party finally to resolve and remove. The bourgeois state, Marx said, contains 'inner contradictions' (indeed it does, that is what it is all about); but these contradictions are, for many high-sounding reasons, ultimately not to be tolerated; they were not, to the Nazis, a sign of civilization but of decadence, a failure to think clearly, to put first things first, a failure of nerve and a weakness of will. In order to achieve final justice, Society as a whole, treated as a unity, had to supplant the State. When the divisive elements in decadent society were removed, there would be only a single, all-embracing ideology, state and society would be at one, and an end be made to all the travail of the body politic. When the lowest class of all conquered, then class war would no longer be fundamental, and ideology would be clear and unambiguous. When the nation would be able to remove all biologically inferior and contaminatory strains, the path of triumph of the *Volksgemeinschaft* would be unimpeded, society would be one family, one brothers' band under an inspired father and leader. In both cases the triumph of Society over the State would restore a shattered sense of belonging: the masses would have become a community (just as, in the transitional stage, the mob had been given a uniform).[4]

The similarity of Nazi and Communist styles of thought can also be seen in their common stress on violence. Violence is to totalitarianism as conciliation is to political systems – something creative. Precisely because thought and action are so determined by the superstructure of traditional society, and because the elements of this structure are so inter-dependent and interlocked, society can only, with very few exceptions – entirely tactical – be smashed, broken, overturned, shattered, seldom if ever converted or persuaded peacefully. The habits of the bourgeois State are so deeply rooted that it takes class war or national war to uproot them. Revolution, not just the taking over of power, is necessary, to break up the old strata of society, to prevent 'contradictions' or 'bourgeois deviations' from lingering on into the new era. Machiavelli saw the logic of this, or rather the sociology, when he argued that a Prince who comes to power, whether by conquest or inheritance, in a new territory which has known its own laws, has two choices open to him: either he must rule according to these laws; or he must break and smash them up *utterly* with great violence and destroy all potential opposition even, in one night of long knives. This is not a mere matter of intimidation of individuals; Machiavelli was trying to get at the social structure itself, the differing laws or customs which make opposition possible. But in Machiavelli this is really a purely theoretical discovery. The Prince cannot then solve the problem of perpetuating his rule except by spreading and sharing power: Princes to save or create states, Republics to maintain them. His Prince lacked an ideology which gives a public purpose for power and at least appears to solve, in the

---

[4] Normally the substance of the two ideologies is recognized as being very different; but it does not exhaust human ingenuity to try to synthesize them, to gain – in rhetoric, at least – the best of both impossible worlds together. Dr Cheddi Jagan, the former Prime Minister of British Guiana, is reported as having said: 'We believe in race – the working class race of the world.'

presence of the modern Party, the problem of succession which has been the bane of autocracies. The regenerating Prince is no longer a lonely hero, but has the massive capability behind him of a modern militant party. If the Prince must be a demi-god, yet his son may be depressingly mortal. But nowadays, the Party goes on for ever as the priesthood of the ideology. So long as people can recognize one man or a group of men (like Hobbes we need not always be fussy as to whether Leviathan is one or several men) as the authoritative expounder of the ideology, they will continue to bind themselves in willing subjection.

Totalitarian ideology not merely purports to explain everything, but it offers a belief in necessary progress. This belief is akin to the enervating liberal belief in progress, but it far surpasses it in the precision and passion of its claim to know with certainty the iron laws of historical development, the path to the final solution of the unwanted problem of politics. Obviously this combination of ideology and prophecy raises a formidable problem: if all thought is ideology, a product of circumstance, how can a clear vision be gained of that one ideology which will be the final ideology of the ultimate condition of society (which 'vision' is supposed to be the operative ideology of totalitarian government)? The practical answer that emerged, in the persons of Hitler and Stalin, was, of course, the peculiar position of the leader: the Machiavellian demi-god Prince who alone could transcend immediate necessity. The leader himself is, it cannot be denied, inspired: if not a god, he is at least a different sort of man from you or me. The new type of leader is, indeed, no mere politician of conciliation, nor yet a tyrant with immediate sensuous enjoyments, but a dedicated master-builder: the *fauve* artist and the social scientist dialectically fused for the creation of the best and the most efficient final society. His authority derives largely from passionate popular superstition that he understands best the laws of progressive history. What right has any man to resist the ideology of society as a whole and the tactical necessities of the unfolding laws of history?

Precise knowledge about how these historical laws are discovered has, of course, never been made as public as the broad goals of the ideology. So much of so much importance is taken on trust. Our times have seen a practical revival of the Renaissance concept of the *arcana imperii,* the craft, the skill, the 'art', the 'mystery', the hidden techniques of domination known only to the leader. But mere survival of the State was a fairly clear standard of judgement in public policy compared with vast schemes to remake mankind: *raison d'état* is of crystal clarity compared to *raison de parti*. The actions of the party leader are accepted as consistent with the real goals of the unfolding ideology, even when there are substantial contradictions in the world of mere appearances. It is thus no accident that the two great totalitarian régimes of our time have both enshrined one man as head. Once the State tries to reduce the *in fact* diverse elements of society to a single composition, once society is viewed as a completely integrated work of art, whether Wagner's *Gesamtkunstwerk* or the 'artificial animal' of Hobbes's *Leviathan,* then there is need for an artist. Once statecraft is seen as *arcana,* then there is need for a charlatan-magician, as superbly shown in Thomas Mann's parable of Fascism in the story *Mario and the Magician.* There must be at least one man who can see clearly the way ahead through the inhibitions and limitations of the conventional, which otherwise determines all thought and action; one man who can substitute some trickery, cunning, or magic for what otherwise might seem unbroken vistas of the violence needed to fuse together social forces so naturally apart. And this type of 'the leader' seems to be emerging as a typical institution of ultra-nationalism – wherever nationalism has fallen into a pseudo-racial theory of history, one of the two thresholds of totalitarian ideology. The irrationalities and contradictions in such theories are hardly conducive to their being expounded and operated by the free discussion of even a small élite; there is a practical need for such theories to include some final irrational source of authority. If the *Führer* says that a (necessary) Jew is not a (Jewish) Jew, then he is not a Jew. If Khrushchev says that Marxism shows that Communist victory is inevitable *and* that co-existence is possible, then the faithful will applaud and the gullible be reassured. And the monopoly of truth which President Nasser held on the intricate question of 'what is an Arab?' seems too much of a kind with Prime Minister Verwoerd's assurance that God had given him the means to distinguish the progeny of Ham from those of Shem and Japhet.

   The academic sociologists of knowledge, notably Max Weber and Karl Mannheim, became involved in a similar difficulty. Even when using the theory of ideology purely explanatorily, not as a weapon of social change, how can even the scholar, let alone the highly moralistic Marx, achieve 'objectivity'? Am I just bound to be a product of my own ideology, interpreting all other ideologies simply as my own would condition me to do? The answer became, of course, that certain scholars could do it because they were very peculiar types of person, the 'unattached intellectuals' who had succeeded in cultivating a 'detached perspective' – obviously a quite attractive view to intellectuals. Thus thought was at least allowed an element of transcendence over circumstance, but only to furnish the grounds for the first postulate of a 'value-free' and total social theory. Let us, indeed, assume that any social theory which aims to be fully comprehensive must be allowed one initial jump, one free move to begin the game. But perhaps if the sociologists of knowledge had been writing in the first full generation of totalitarian rule, and not a decade before, they would have adopted some ethical first assumption to prevent a theory of understanding from being 'perverted' as a plan of action. For the viewpoint of 'ethical relativism' implied in this science, while a buttress for tolerance when applied to ideologies *within* a political régime, yet appears quite inadequate to explain the novelty – and to condemn the cruelty – of totalitarianism as a positive theory of ideology. There are some things, as Leo Strauss has said of the concentration camps, of which a purely objective description would seem like a satire on mankind.

Mannheim does point out that his 'concept "ideology" is being used . . . not as a negative value-judgement, in the sense of insinuating a conscious political lie, but is intended to designate the outlook inevitably associated with a given historical and social situation. . . . This meaning of the term . . . must be sharply differentiated from the other meaning.'[5] But Mannheim failed to see that once it is believed that the logic and imperative of ideas is seen as purely ideological, as simply the mirroring and maintenance of that *status quo* which is the existing social order, then his 'Utopians' (perversely unaware that they are purely culture bound – which they are probably not) will have to see any progress as dependent upon a complete shattering and a total transformation of the entire social system: ideologies as 'political lies', or plans for a complete new future, will then become necessary. The philosophical foundation of totalitarian ideology rests upon the sociology of knowledge. Both underestimate the complexity of advanced industrial societies, the coexistence, clash, and overlap between several, even many, different ideologies within a given state, the number of 'cross-cultural pressures' to which any individual is subject – a state of affairs which can be

[5]See Mannheim, *Ideology and Utopia* (London 1936), p. 111.

sensibly regarded as fairly normal and, in the variety of experience it allows, reasonably delightful. Politics is a response to this very type of situation, and politics does not set itself the impossible tasks of creating a unified social theory before it thinks any government can justify itself, or of finding a single equation or a final reduction. But politics is not simply a restatement of the *status quo,* for things never are fixed: the conservative perpetually underestimates the amount of deliberate political innovation and invention, and of reasonably well understood social change and adaptation, which is going on at any time. Just as Mannheim, and even Weber, tends to underestimate the creativity of politics, so he underestimates greatly the plausibility and coherency of that use of 'ideology' which he calls a 'political lie'. Totalitarianism is obviously far more rooted in social thought and structure than a mere 'political lie'. And politics itself is a concept which stands outside the admitted relativity of particular political aspirations and doctrines: to that degree it is autonomous and creative.

Totalitarian ideology presents a clear contrast to politics; and even the academic theory of ideology represents a false, and even dangerous, attempt to reduce all political to sociological theory. Choices are made and have to be made, and one can never describe them in such a way that they are necessarily determined. Indeed the contrast points to two characteristics of political activity: one, the importance of a diversity of group interests, explicit in the argument so far; the other, some concern with personal identity, implicit.

I have argued that we are much beholden to the great Aristotle for recognizing the political relationship as one that harmonizes and tries to elevate those differences of opinion and interest which naturally exist within any known State. This is the basic proposition of political theory. And in almost nothing is totalitarian doctrine more remarkable than in its hatred of diversifying groups and institutions. The first theoretical basis for totalitarianism was the unintended creation of the first 'armed bohemian', Jean-Jacques Rousseau, when he replaced reason with will and argued: 'If then the general will is to be truly expressed, it is essential that there should be no subsidiary groups within the State. . . . It was the magnificent achievement of Lycurgus to have established the only State of this kind ever known.' But what just made sense in Rousseau's romantic misunderstanding of the nature of the *polis,* and in the parlourrealism of his preferring Sparta to Athens, makes a very different kind of sense when applied to the great scale of the modern State, and even to the France of 1789. That his stress on the infallibility of the general will makes nonsense of his equally passionate individualism, is an old criticism, but a good one; although a better one might be that the danger, to both individualism and politics, stems from believing in such an entity at all. The 'malignant imagination' (in Sir Lewis Namier's words) of Edmund Burke was, alas, right, and the all too human Jean-Jacques wrong, when Burke saw that rights to have any meaning must adhere to particular institutions: the rights of Englishmen are, indeed, necessarily more secure than the Rights of Man. The theory of democratic-centralism robbed men more and more of any intimacy with institutions small enough to be known, worked, and loved. Industrialism threatened to complete the rout of Burke's 'small platoon', and only for an ineffective moment did the rising socialist movement pause to look at the small group as the natural unit, before plunging after a liberalized conservatism into mild or strong forms of Étatism.

The totalitarian destruction of intermediary groups only points to the relative naturalness of some of these groups. The totalitarian manufacture of a multiplicity of party or party-front organizations only points to the importance to them of providing controlled substitutes for the natural wealth of corporate life. But these controlled groups are *ersatz,* are just not-so-good substitutes, for they are made to have as little organic relevance to any non-political function as possible. No possible refuge for publicly opting out into purely private preoccupations is allowed; even the groups that there are will be periodically reshuffled, examined, or purged to prevent not just actual, but even possible, opposition forming. The sovereignty of the totalitarian general will, if it is to be made real, can allow of no competition or even flight to alternative activities. Contrary to the habits of traditional autocracies, sleeping dogs must be kicked into life, but not out of principle – out of theory. For everything in society, according to the operative theory, is either progressive or corrosive; *there are no* areas of privacy or federal divisions of authority. Hobbes unwittingly showed how the ground could be prepared for totalitarianism when he denounced all 'Corporations' as 'worms within the entrails of the body politic', although his whole theory was in fact meant to be a defence of the absolute self-identity of each and every individual against any possible group or even general interest.

The picture of the 'need' for totalitarian rule has had, alas, many helpful touches added to it in utter innocence by good liberals *too* consumed with dislike for 'peculiar institutions' which separate individuals from the State, which seem to create or leave pockets of irrational inequity in society. Any theory of political obligation must react to totalitarian ideology by a far greater stress on the pluralistic and federalistic nature of authority than has been the fashion of late. There is something, after all, to be said for continuing to venerate the great platitude of politics, perhaps as formulated by the young Harold Laski: 'We shall make the basis of our state consent to disagreement. Therein we shall ensure its deepest harmony.'

The second more specific characteristic of political activity which emerges in contrast to totalitarian rule is, I have claimed, some concern with personal identity – its assertion and its preservation. This seems, in an at first sight curious manner, to be not just a contrast but the antithesis to the totalitarian stress on violence. Here is not just the all too obvious matter that totalitarian régimes have put a very low value on human life, both of opponents and of their own people; they both take and waste life easily compared to any known political régime. The contrast is deeper than that. Violence, as we have argued, plays a creative role for the totalitarian régime in smashing up the old structure of society. But it is also constantly demanded, in the form of self-violence, of sacrifice, from the individual.

Totalitarian régimes, to say something very obvious, try hard to gain willing sacrifice from their inhabitants, even to the death, even in quite normal tasks. Few Communists have shared the humanism of Brecht's Mother Courage who remarks that only bad generals need brave soldiers. Rather, the ideal man is the man who will sacrifice himself for his cause, whether on the military or the industrial front (and even, as some of the great State trials of the 1930s in Russia showed, on the political front). Now this kind of pleasant appeal is not unknown even in political régimes; but there it is usually clap-trap more than effective policy, except in time of war. No one would be so silly as to applaud one for working oneself to death building a road for the Ross and Cromarty County Council – however badly they need roads; or even if one took a huge and fatal risk in trying to exceed production norms in the great mission of the State itself to electrify the Highlands of Scotland. Totalitarian régimes, however, encourage just such an absurd ethic of sacrifice at all times – for again, all times are emergency times. But this is absurd only to the free man. The true believer thinks himself happy to sacrifice himself for the future of the cause – or at least to run the risk. He does not think that he sacrifices freedom; he comes to think that sacrifice is freedom. 'Oh God, . . . whose service is perfect freedom' – the emotion is familiar but the confusion between heaven and earth is vastly novel. If there are spiritual truths, they are clearly only perverted by being treated as political truths; if there are states of mind in which we feel not just free, perhaps not free at all, but 'liberated', then we could imagine them extended to the whole of society – if society were indeed one mind. The Christian 'service' is, of course, far too other-worldly and humble for the totalitarian true believer. If Christianity to Nietzsche was a 'slave morality', by the same token it could not command true sacrifice on a vast scale. Sacrifice is not a characteristic of slaves, slaves are sacrificed; only the free man can sacrifice himself. So, if one has no capacity for enjoying real freedom, one sacrifices oneself to prove that one is free, or one tries to command the sacrifices of others to the end of the great and final cause – the last fight (which is perennial). Violence in the service of the cause is thus self-liberating: it liberates one from oneself and fuses one with the great collectivity:

> They but thrust their buried men
> Back in the human mind again.
> You that Mitchel's prayer have heard,
> 'Send war in our time, O Lord!'
> Know that when all words are said
> And a man is fighting mad,
> Something drops from eyes long blind,
> He completes his partial mind,
> For an instant stands at ease,
> Laughs aloud his heart at peace.

Yeats obviously reaches more deeply into the psychology of Fascism and Nazism than of Communism, but some such terrible perversion of human instinct marches alongside every attempt to sacrifice the present generation so that the future can lay down all burdens. The destination of such fanaticisms may be vague, but this may actually strengthen the joy in the march itself. 'A man never goes so far,' said Oliver Cromwell, 'as when he does not know whither he is going.' Politics 'in contrast' is obviously both prudential and prudent. A political state does not call on its citizens to risk their lives except in the defence of the realm in time of emergency. But there is more to the antithesis than this. There is a seeming irrational violence in totalitarian régimes which is in fact rationally aimed at destroying a belief essential to politics.

Let us consider one of the strangest and most characteristic institutions of totalitarian régimes, probably one of the most horrible inventions in human history: the Concentration Camp. 'The remembrance of them is grievous unto us; the burden of them is intolerable.' For mass extermination or incarceration can be, after all, very obvious practical solutions to the administrative problems represented by political diversity – this need not be denied. One searches for heightened language because it is clear that the actual practices of the camps went beyond all such criteria of the utility of power. Witness after witness has paid tribute to the lengths to which the Nazi camps especially would go, not merely to work their inmates to death rather than work them efficiently, but to smash their spirit utterly before they died. They had not merely to be killed, but to be degraded utterly. If it was said that the Jews were *Untermenschen,* then they had to be made *Untermenschen.* David Rousset wrote in *Les Jours de Notre Mort*: 'The triumph of the S.S. demands that the tortured victim allow himself to be led to the noose without protesting, that he renounce and abandon himself to the point of ceasing to affirm his identity.'[6] It seemed as if the guards were probing, blindly but surely, to expose an essence of personality that many would not expect to find even, or particularly, in themselves, so as to degrade it and render it passive before death. It is as if they were trying to prove hollow even the comfort offered in: 'Do not fear those who kill the body, but cannot kill the soul.'

These deep-thrusting cruelties have been part of the regular administration of totalitarian régimes, something far beyond the occasional ecstasies of sadists. These practices seem of profound importance to the totalitarian pattern of controls. Rousset has seen in this degradation of the prisoners not just the attempt by the S.S. to exalt their own belief in their spiritual superiority, but also a proof that to

---

[6]Quoted by Hannah Arendt, *The Origins of Totalitarianism,* 2nd ed. (London 1958), p. 455. See also Gerald Reitlinger, *The Final Solution* (New York 1953), especially pp. 414–28, and Eugon Kogon, *The Theory and Practice of Hell* (London 1950) *passim* – in German *Der S.S. Staat.*

the totalitarian 'everything is possible', an assertion that ordinary men, who do not or will not know of these things, cannot believe – for even to know of them can begin to create an intolerable burden. The same refined attack on human personality took place in the Soviet Camps. Certainly it was less immediately deliberate in Communist hands. Communist forethought in these matters was usually more selective and was more often reserved for the punishment of specific political prisoners and the 'reconstruction' of exemplary victims for the State Trials. The mass cruelty and death in the Soviet camps mainly arose from the vast inertia and indifference to human life of the bureaucracies in charge of the camps. The Nazis invented new ways to kill and degrade people, the Soviets left them to rot. But the inertia and indifference is itself directly attributable to ideological thinking. Men who do not act and believe as the ideology says they should are no longer men.

The inmate of a concentration camp has not just ceased to have any human rights whatever by losing his identity as a citizen, but he must be deprived of his spiritual strength as well, not merely his life, before the full claims of the ideology can be proved. It is 'proved' that those who oppose or are indifferent to the ideology have no ultimate defence for any scrap of pride, dignity, or sense of personal identity, once they are removed from normal social relationships. The general theory of totalitarian ideology cannot be proved true while there is the slightest spark of absolute personality alive in its actual or potential opponents. Only when the individual is stripped of all previous social identity and finds that he has nothing else to fall back upon, only then can it be seen that the general theory of ideology is true: *that there is nothing in the world but social identity – the individual is independent in nothing.* But it should also be proved to us, through the horror of such observations, that there is such an aspect of man which must be independent of social circumstance, that personal identity does not depend entirely on social consciousness; and as the totalitarians seek to destroy this human autonomy, so political régimes hold it to their very hearts. Any normal man who dares to read the perfectly well-known books and documents on the totalitarian use of genocide and terror as regular methods of government (which we – as normal people – find so many excuses not to face), cannot but be filled with compassion and understanding for those isolated individuals who challenge such systems and who are either forced into a life of 'double-think' and constant verbal treachery to freedom, or who are broken by them and 'reconstructed'. The man who is reborn is seldom reborn free. But, equally, this compassion should create a hatred, for the sake of human values, for those in free régimes who seek to find excuses for such things.

There is really little mystery about the importance of group diversity and of the affirmative individual for politics. Aristotle, once again, saw this more clearly than many moderns when he said that a tyrant to rule successfully must forbid above all: '. . . common meals, clubs, education, and anything of a like character – or, in other words, a defensive attitude against everything likely to produce the two qualities of *mutual confidence and a high spirit.* '[7] Mutual confidence arises from corporate experiences, so these must be destroyed if they do not serve the immediate purposes of the régime. And if the Greek 'high spirit' or *arete* is a moral quality with a specific content not wholly applicable to our times, yet it points to exactly the same dimension of individual experience, the liveliness of men, that the totalitarian must destroy and the modern political man must nurture. A political régime cannot insist upon its citizens in fact asserting themselves in the public realm, even though it will be weaker if they do not; but it will not be a political régime at all if it tries to deny their spirited right to live inside their own privacy or outside in the public realm, as they choose.

If we act so unnaturally as to try for ourselves to merge *all* our individuality and *all* our corporate differences in one common enterprise, then that enterprise is inevitably crazy and destructive – like the chase of the white whale Moby Dick, heroic, but inhuman and fatal: 'They were one man, not thirty. For as the one ship that held them all; though it was put together of all contrasting things oak and maple and pinewood; iron and pitch and hemp – yet all these ran into one another in the one concrete hull, which shot on its way, both balanced and directed by the long central keel; even so, all the individualities of the crew, this man's valour, that man's fear; guilt and guiltlessness, all varieties were welded into one mass, and were all directed to that fatal goal which Ahab their one lord and keel did point to.'

Politics may be a messy, mundane, inconclusive, tangled business, far removed from the passion for certainty and the fascination for world-shaking quests which afflict the totalitarian intellectual; but it

[7]Barker's *Politics,* p. 244, my italics.

does, at least, even in the worst of political circumstances, give a man some choice in what role to play, some variety of corporate experience and some ability to call his soul his own. The most we can believe with certainty about politics is that it is unavoidable – unless a régime goes to great lengths of coercion; and that it is also limited – unless a régime thinks in great terms of ideology; and that within a political community agreement about 'fundamentals' is never likely except by force or fraud; the only basic agreement in a political régime is to use political means. Politics is an activity and so cannot be reduced to a system of precise beliefs or to a set of fixed goals. Political thinking is to be contrasted to ideological thinking. Politics cannot furnish us with an ideology; an ideology means an end to politics, though ideologies may combat each other within a political system – if they are weak and the system is strong. 'Isn't it high time,' someone wrote to the London *Times,* 'that we in the west (*a*) realized that it takes an ideology to cope with an ideology; (*b*) found and lived our own ideology, the ideology of freedom?' Probably such Buchmanite writers think that ideology means no more than a kind of passionate certainty. Even so, the idea of an ideology of freedom is a contradiction in terms: when everything is knowable, determined, or certain, freedom is impossible. Free actions are always, strictly speaking, unnecessary actions. Ideology cannot be taken up and set down by politicians as a weapon; it devours its manipulators. At least the ideologist knows that political habits are indeed his great enemy. *He* may make use of politics for a while, but then only to destroy it. The inscription on the base of a statue of President Nkrumah in Accra, 'Seek ye first the political kingdom and all other things shall be added unto it', is in fact a threat to, and a perversion of, true politics.

Politics is not, then, a grasping for the ideal; but neither is it a freezing of tradition. It is an activity – lively, adaptive, flexible, and conciliatory. Politics is the way in which free societies are governed. Politics is politics and other forms of rule are something else.

Chapter 3

A Defence of Politics against Democracy

There are those who would tell us that democracy is *the* true form of politics. Some would even say that it is politics, or that it is clearly and always a form of government, value, or activity superior to mere politics. But politics needs to be defended even against democracy, certainly in the sense that any clear and practical idea needs defending against something vague and imprecise. We will argue that while democracy as a social movement must exist in nearly all modern forms of political rule, yet, if taken alone and as a matter of principle, it is the destruction of politics.

Democracy is perhaps the most promiscuous word in the world of public affairs. She is everybody's mistress and yet somehow retains her magic even when a lover sees that her favours are being, in his light, illicitly shared by many another. Indeed, even amid our pain at being denied her exclusive fidelity, we are proud of her adaptability to all sorts of circumstances, to all sorts of company. How often has one heard: 'Well, at least the Communists claim to be democratic'? But the real trouble is, of course, that they do not pretend to be democratic. They are democratic. They are democratic in the sound historical sense of a majority actively willing to be ruled in some other way.

So while democracy has most often been used to mean simply 'majority rule' (which in a sizeable state can only mean majority consent), all kinds of special meanings have arisen (many to refute rather than to refine this common view). Perhaps its primary meaning to most people at the moment is no more than 'all things bright and beautiful', or some such rather general sentiment. Then others hold that, surprisingly enough, democracy 'really means' liberty, even liberalism, or even individualism, even to defend the (democratic) individual against the (democratic) majority – this is certainly an amiable view. The late Ernest Bevin once told a Trade Union Conference that it was not democratic for a minority to continue to question the decisions of a majority – and he received the equally sincere and astonishing reply that democracy meant that he – an offending Brother – could say what he liked, when he liked, how he liked, against whom he liked, even against a majority of the T.G.W.U. The word can be used, as Tocqueville used it, as a synonym for equality, or, as Herbert Spencer used it, to mean a highly mobile free-enterprise society with great (Darwinian) differences in station and wealth. Or it may be seen as a political system which places constitutional limitations even upon a freely elected (democratic) government (the most sought-after use, but the most historically implausible and rhetorical); or, on the contrary, as the 'will of the people', or the 'General Will', triumphing over these 'artificial' restraints of constitutional institutions. To many democracy means little more than 'one man, one vote' – to which others would hopefully add: 'plus real choices'. And in broad terms embracing all of these usages, democracy can be seen as a particular recipe of institutions, or as a 'way of life', some style of politics or rule, as when it is said that the 'spirit of democracy' is more important than any institutional arrangements, or that a democracy is where people behave democratically in their speech, dress, amusements, etc.

There was a time when 'the meaning' of democracy was thought more certain, but was also thought by many, even in the most politically advanced country of the time, to be simply and only an affair of small units of rule. 'It is ascertained by history,' George Mason told the Virginia Convention of 1788 which met to ratify the proposed Federal Constitution, 'that there never was a government over a very extensive country without destroying the liberties of the people. History also, supported by the opinions of the best writers, shows us that monarchy may suit a large territory, and despotic governments over so extensive a country, but that popular governments can only exist in small territories.' Only in small territories could the people themselves see what was going on, and take part in what was going on. The democrats of the day, for this reason, argued vigorously that power should reside in the separate States of the Union. Some of the national government men launched an equally fierce polemic against popular government, against democratic tendencies, on precisely this same logic. There was a danger that the alternatives would be seen as either a strong oligarchical national union or a mere alliance of popular governments. But the solution had already been seen. Few indeed really argued for *a* democratic government: the question was how strong should the democratic *element* be? Mason himself was reported saying at Philadelphia: 'he admitted that we had been too democratic, but was afraid that we should incautiously run into the opposite extreme.' The solution, an invention or recognition fundamental to modern politics, had already been stated by James Wilson of Pennsylvania: 'He was for raising the Federal pyramid to a considerable altitude, and *for that reason* wished to give it as broad a basis as possible.' Thus to achieve strong government at all, it must rest on 'the confidence of the people'. This was true, even in this pre-industrial society, because there was already 'a people', at least a large number, who had already exercised for many years, in their provincial and local assemblies, the habits, rights, and duties of political citizenship. They could not be ignored: the administration of any possible form of government depended upon them. But neither could conscript soldiers be ignored if the problem was, as Napoleon made it, to put a nation in arms against a system of dynastic professional armies. And nor could the skilled industrial workers be ignored if the survival and welfare of a country depended upon rapid industrialization – whether in the case of Victorian England or Stalinist Russia. In this context, too, is to be seen Michels' famous dictum explaining the unique strength of the modern political party: 'that every party organization represents an oligarchical power grounded upon a democratic base.'

The difficulty is that this discovery or invention is completely general. When it occurs in the context of a society which already enjoys free institutions, such as Colonial America, the result is an extension of political liberties; when it occurs in Revolutionary France or Russia, the result is very different: it can then actually strengthen centralization and autocracy. The need for democracy as an instrument of government then creates the need to manufacture popularity, to sustain mass enthusiasm, to mechanize consent, to destroy all opposition. The people are ground down in fear by constant news (half-real or wholly invented) of conspiracies against the nation and the party, and then are raised up in hope by grandiose promises of vast future (always future) benefits. Democracy, then, not merely stabilizes free régimes, it makes stronger unfree régimes, and it has made possible totalitarianism. For the first time every stratum of society is important to the ruler and is open to exploitation, whether moral or economic. Let no one think that I am lumping together for all purposes people as different as Hitler, de Gaulle, Baldwin, and Kennedy to say that they are all figures, for good or evil, who could only have arisen in states with a democratic franchise. But let us not be too sceptical. No propaganda can manufacture opinion which does not correspond to some real need. The experience and fear of poverty and war everywhere make men willing to sacrifice some liberty (particularly if they have never known it on any regular basis) to parties and governments which promise them relief (sometime) from these two grimmest burdens of mankind. Even let us grant that some, much, or most mass support for a totalitarian régime is a 'genuine' and free surrender of freedom (as for so many in the German elections of March 1933), if only in the sense that people are led to believe that 'true freedom' *is* sacrifice for the cause; yet the point still remains that Wilson of Pennsylvania was right: the higher the pyramid of power is pushed, the broader must be the base. But he was right in a sense that embraces all important forms of modern rule: democracy is not necessarily related to political popular government based upon free citizenship. And even where democracy, in this sense, does coexist with free politics, as in modern America, with an intimacy almost inextricable, yet there is tension as well as harmony; the parties in this marriage are involved in famous quarrels – democracy is jealous of liberty and liberty, at times, fears democracy. Nowhere else in the world, both to the horror and honour of Americans, is the large question of the 'tyranny of public opinion' so debated. 'If ever the free institutions of America are destroyed,' Tocqueville wrote, 'that event may be attributed to the omnipotence of the majority.'

Majoritarian democracy appears in its most unsatisfactory and unpolitical form in the famous doctrine of the 'Sovereignty of the People' (which people?). The *Declarations of the Rights of Man* of 26 August 1789 stated: 'The source of all sovereignty is essentially in the nation; no body, no individual can exercise authority that does not proceed from it in plain terms.' It should be the test of whether a man values liberty effectively, of whether he is in earnest about free politics, to see if he is willing to recognize the meaninglessness of this rhetorical phrase, this sadly empty doctrine. A constitution may claim to be based on the 'sovereignty of the people', but this has never helped anyone, rulers, judges, or politicians to decide what disputed words may mean or which policies to adopt. 'The people' may be consulted by a referendum, as in France, when the constitutional framework is changed: but their role is limited to 'yes' or 'no' on a complicated and predigested document. And the complicated decisions of actual governments, even the management of large political parties, can never be undertaken by a body as large as, or a concept as vague as, 'the people'. 'Sovereignty of the people' can mean little more than an affirmation that government should be in the interests of everyone and that it should be representative. But the representative assembly itself will almost invariably represent particular constituencies or particular interests or parties. In other words, it will represent an actual political situation, not a theoretical 'sovereign' situation in which all power is supposed to stem from an undivided and indivisible 'people'. Such an affirmation should be made – though it might be better made in a form that seems to exclude the representation of the people by a single party: 'the right (need?) of the people to choose the government they want', or some such. But no such affirmation solves any practical difficulty of government – whether of political governments, totalitarian governments, or forms more ancient. Indeed, the doctrine, if taken too seriously, is an actual step towards totalitarianism. For, quite simply, it allows no refuge and no contradiction, no private apathy even. 'A patriot,' said Robespierre, 'supports the Republic *en masse,* he who fights about details is a traitor. Everything which is not respect for the people and you – the Convention – is a crime.' This is but another form of the cruel chimera, already observed, of supplanting political prudence and moderation by the reign of 'society as a whole', the subsuming of the political by the ideological. The violence and the terror needed to produce unanimity are no more rendered humane by the plea of democracy than they are by the pleas of racial purity or economic equality. 'The terror,' continued Robespierre, 'is nothing but justice, swift, stern, and unrelenting, it is thus an emanation of virtue; it is less a particular principle than a consequence of the general principle of democracy applied to the pressing needs of the country.'

Even 'fraternity' can be as deceitful as 'virtue' as a purifying principle for mere democracy. As the apostate Nazi Rauschning argued in his *Revolution of Nihilism,* people at first did not march in the endless parades and torch-light processions because they were full of fraternity; they marched because marching gave them the feeling of fraternity. Or as the American longshoreman Eric Hoffer has said: 'Collective unity is not the result of the brotherly love of the faithful for each other. The loyalty of the true believer is to the whole – the church, the party, the nation, not to his fellow true believer. True loyalty between individuals is possible only in a loose and relatively free society.'[1]

Here it is as well to digress and say that not merely the concept of 'sovereignty of the people' is un- or even anti-political, but also the whole doctrine of sovereignty. The concept can, of course, mean many things. I am considering the claim of Thomas Hobbes and the English positivist lawyers, that there must be absolute power of final decision in every organized society in some clearly recognized and effective institution. This doctrine of sovereignty can, indeed, historically and theoretically be given a meaning only as a contradiction to normal political conditions even if, at times, a necessary contradiction. Sovereignty is the realm of emergency, the potentiality of defence to maintain order at all in face of clear and present danger, the justification of emergency powers by which all régimes, including political régimes, including democratic régimes in any possible sense, must find a capacity for decisive, centralized, and unquestioned (and hence nonpolitical) action – if a state is, in desperate times, to survive at all. Politics, as Voltaire said of liberty, has no relevance to a city in a state of siege. The practical difficulties of deciding when a state of emergency exists are always great – but they are practical and procedural difficulties: they do not destroy the real distinction between the time of politics and the time of sovereignty. If sovereignty is the father of politics, then once we are grown up enough to look after ourselves, we should only fly to him when in very great distress. For there are those in free régimes who harp so much on these 'toughminded' or 'realistic' themes of power and sovereignty, on every possible occasion, often with a sadly transparent masochistic relish, that they are guilty of turning the subtle play of political life into a crude melodrama. Man cannot live by fear alone – or he will fear to live. But equally guilty are those wishful tender souls who would repress any and all mention of sovereign power, except to deny its existence; this is neither political courage nor principle, but a prudishness which bowdlerizes a plain human tale. Accident as well as design, as Machiavelli reminds us, can create conditions of emergency. Yet it is only in totalitarian régimes that a continuous state of emergency is maintained, a sense of permanent

---

[1]*The True Believer: Thoughts on the Nature of Mass Movements* (New York 1951) – a remarkable and neglected book.

revolution, a belief that there is a continual desperate struggle against traitors within and aggressors without, which is often maintained quite artificially, though seemingly as a device of government essential to such régimes.

The democratic doctrine of the sovereignty of the people threatens, then, the essential perception that all known advanced societies are inherently pluralistic and diverse, which is the seed and the root of politics. Few have understood more clearly than Alexis de Tocqueville the importance of group loyalties intermediate between 'society' and the State. He was the first to see clearly why 'the species of oppression by which democratic nations are menaced is unlike anything that ever before existed in the world . . . I seek in vain for an expression that will accurately convey the whole of the idea I have formed of it; the old words *despotism* and *tyranny* are inappropriate: the thing itself is new . . .'[2] Thus he wrote even in his *Democracy in America* in which he sought to show that there were diversifying institutions in American society which could mitigate the danger of a 'tyranny of the majority'. In his *L'Ancien Régime et la Revolution* he christens this new thing 'Democratic Despotism' and characterizes it thus: 'No gradations in society, no distinctions of classes, no fixed ranks – a people composed of individuals nearly alike and entirely equal – this confused mass being recognized as the only legitimate sovereign, but carefully deprived of all the faculties which could enable it either to direct or even to superintend its own government. Above this mass, a single officer, charged to do everything in its name without consulting it. To control this officer, public opinion, deprived of its organs; to arrest him, revolutions, but no laws. In principle a subordinate agent; in fact, a master.'[3]

That the word 'democratic' can now be used to describe what earlier writers would have termed 'mixed-government' (which is a clearer interpretive translation of Aristotle's *politeia* than simply 'polity'), is a dangerous loss to political understanding. The older tradition of political theory in using the term 'democracy' had exemplified Aristotle's tripartite usage: democracy as, intellectually, the doctrine of those who believe that because men are equal in some things, they should

---

[2]Phillips Bradley's edition of the *Democracy in America* (New York 1948), Vol. II, p. 318.
[3]*Society in France Before the Revolution of 1789,* translated by Henry Reeve (London 1888), p. 140.

be equal in all; constitutionally, the rule of the majority; sociologically, the rule of the poor. Democracy he saw as a necessary element in polity or mixed government, but alone it was destructive of the political community, attempting the impossible feat of the direct rule of all – which in fact meant the unrestrained power of those who were trusted by most. Democracies were particularly prone to fall by 'the insolence of demagogues' into tyrannies. Modern experience seems to bear out Aristotle's precise description of democracy rather than that of those who would have it stand for 'all things bright and beautiful'.

The Western World, for all its good fortune in having a political tradition, has had the disadvantage that what should have been the great modern consolidation of politics – the spread of the idea of liberty from an aristocracy to the common people – took place in an age when relics of Feudalism associated all intermediate political and social groups between the individual and the State with privilege unredeemed by function. The aim of the friends of liberty became too often merely to sweep away such institutions so as to leave revealed the undoubted majestic and spontaneous harmony of a sovereign people and a sovereign State. There is no incident more significant for genuine political thought than when John Stuart Mill confesses in his *Autobiography* that reviewing Tocqueville led 'my political ideal from pure democracy' into considering 'the necessary protection against its degenerating into the only despotism of which, in the modern world, there is real danger – the absolute rule of the head of the executive over a congregation of isolated individuals, all equals but all slaves'. Indeed much of Mill's great essay *On Liberty* would be more convincing, if less dramatic, if recast on narrower grounds as simply a defence of politics itself. Liberty, in Mill's sense, is a political achievement – it is, both logically and historically, a product of politics, not a prerequisite. Democracy, in modern conditions, is a necessity of strong government. Government must be prior to politics, but democracy may or may not be political. There is both totalitarian democracy and political democracy.

Now if ever there was a natural unanimity of opinion in any society on all great issues, politics would, indeed, be unnecessary. But in societies which claim to be pure democracies, and full of such pure democrats that no one wishes to speak against the government – for all agree with its policies, it is more likely that politics has been forbidden *in order* to try to reach such a unanimity rather than that it has withered away because there is unanimity already. The eighteenth-century democrats commonly called a man a 'pure and incorruptible democrat' (as, for instance, John Wilkes was toasted in many a tavern) if he was thought (incredibly enough) to have no particular interests, only the general interest at heart. Particular interests were always a corruption of the pure common interest or the general will. But it is notorious what Rousseau thought should be done to the earnest seeker who, look into his heart as he will, purify himself and strip himself of particular prejudices and loves as he must, still does not agree with the general will: he must be 'forced to be free'. There are, of course, many things a man may be as a consequence of force – he may be less dangerous, he may be made safe despite himself, less hungry despite himself, perhaps even, in some sense, be made 'better', certainly be made ready and available for a moral re-education; but whatever he is, it is nonsense to say that he is free. It is better to admit that for democratic (or any other governmental) purposes those in power may on occasion have to take away people's freedom – far better than to claim that this taking away is freedom. Otherwise, we lose the power to understand what is right even when we cannot act. And if we lose that, then the defeat is perpetual.

The identification of democracy and freedom can, of course, be attempted in the other direction. Just as liberty can get buried by democracy, democracy can get buried in liberty. Democracy, some will tell us, means a liberal constitutional régime in which the rights of the individual are preserved even against a majority. But calling such a régime democratic, even though it will almost certainly have a strong democratic element in it, is not a help to understanding anything – except how great is the prestige of the word. For it to make historical or sociological sense, to describe an actual state of affairs, it would have to be argued that liberty can exist only in a democracy.

But, as Burke reminded us, liberty in politics can mean only 'liberties'. An ounce of law is worth a ton of rhetoric if a court will recognize certain liberties and order their preservation against the State itself. And certainly all sorts of liberties, highly important to politics, can become established, preserved, and protected in societies which are by no stretch of the imagination 'democratic'. By the 1770s in England certain liberties already existed which would seem fundamental to stable political régimes: the subject was free from arbitrary arrest; he was tried by jury, not by royal judge alone, and juries frequently flew in the face of the law in their dislike of political prosecutions; he was free to criticize the government from a platform or in print; he could report Parliamentary debates, and he could travel without passports or special permission – yet the franchise was corrupt, inequitable, and inadequate. The franchise needed to be made more democratic before the government could adequately represent the changing real interests and real power of the governed; but there is absolutely no doubt – here indeed is a platitude which needs to be taken seriously – that liberty preceded democracy and lived a life of its own. It is sadly obvious that there was more liberty in the England of the 1760s than in the People's Democracies of the 1960s – though there may have been, at times, more hunger. But the point is simply that not being hungry is not liberty: it is a different value. Other values may be deemed superior. There even may be, amid all the turbulence, injustice, and insult, more liberty of the subject in the closing stages of a Colonial régime than amid the intolerant enthusiasm for unity of a new national government. Most people will have little doubt which is to be preferred, and even sceptics will have little doubt which alone is possible. G. K. Chesterton once said of the milder fanaticisms of temperance reformers: 'Better England free than England sober'. And anyone who doubts that 'self-government is better than good government' is indeed a reactionary Canute scolding the tides of history. But unless the intellectual distinction is drawn between personal liberty and national self-determination, whatever the necessities of the moment, new states may never return to or achieve a political tradition – and the alternative is ever greater violence and propaganda to maintain the artificial unanimity once the common enemy has gone. Such states may, then, justly be called democratic, but it is, at the least, confusing to call them free. But, equally, if we call all free states democratic, we may obscure the need for them to become more democratic if they are to survive in changing circumstances.

Take the case of Great Britain. 'Democracy', to the generation before 1914, had a much more precise meaning than now. People took it to mean, amid the overtones of simple majority rule, such things as: an increased working-class representation in Parliament; an increase in the power of Trade Unions; more investigation of and more publicity about all aspects of public administration; increased educational opportunity; a decrease in the power of the House of Lords and of the landed interest. And it was beginning to show overtones of a non-doctrinaire kind of socialism, as the rising Labour Party seemed to exemplify democratic institutions and to espouse democratic habits and causes, just at the moment when the Liberals became more and more split between their radicalism and their whiggery. But the word, increasingly respectable though it was, was never used to characterize English life in general or English politics in particular. There were friends and foes of democracy, but no one in their right mind in 1913 would have called Britain, as it was, a democracy. It simply was not. It was a free society, it had a system of representative government in which some popular reforms were proving increasingly possible, but it was not democratic. Only with the First World War did it learn that it was fighting – being conscripted, indeed – *to preserve* democracy. The rhetoric of Lloyd George, the genial cynicism of Churchill and Beaverbrook, and the idealism of Woodrow Wilson, all contrived to rob the term of any precise meaning whatever. The word was established for the sovereign purposes of war at the cost of stripping it of any real political meaning. Sacrifices could be demanded in the name of democracy which could not be expected for mere patriotism for the social order as it was. Tories who should have known better, and radicals who did know better but who were hoping for better, conspired to make Britain (verbally) democratic. And it has remained (verbally) democratic ever since.[4]

Or take the case of the United States. Here indeed must be an uncontested example of a political system which can be clearly, and by popular usage must be, characterized as democratic. But even here it is necessary to remind oneself that the word came to be applied very late to the system as a whole, rather than to those parts of it which were uniquely and from the beginning democratic – the franchise (with the great Negro exception) and what was, certainly by comparison with any other country, the broad equality of social conditions. Not until this century have all Americans, except political eccentrics, called American government unequivocally a democracy. The old Aristotelian distinction, well understood by the Founding Fathers, between democracy as a force on its own and democracy as one element in mixed-government,

---

[4]Yet there was always some mordant scepticism. Even in the Second World War, British soldiers sang a song which ended:

And as the kicks get harder
The poor private, you can see,
Gets kicked to bloody hell
To save de-moc-ra-cy.

long survived the attacks of democratic rhetoric. And the situation was complicated by Party names which had little to do with the case at hand. The Democratic Party was, after all, throughout most of the nineteenth century the anti-national party. The words 'Republic' and 'Republican' were more often used in those times (which is why 'Republican' was seized to name a new party). The word had not yet lost its Roman overtones of simplicity, civic virtue, and even small proprietorship as the typical estate of a true citizen. The word 'Republic', for all its growing vagueness, avoided the majoritarian overtones of 'democracy'. Perhaps only when the original democratic social condition of America became called into question did the word become adapted to stand for the whole instead of some of the vital parts. Andrew Carnegie's *Triumphant Democracy* of 1886 may well mark this polemical turning point. When democratic forces in America were beginning to protest at some of the effects of capitalism, Carnegie wrote a triumphant hymn of praise to the material success of the Republic which systematically identified capitalism and democracy. They were not different forces. They were the same thing! Democracy meant equality of opportunity, not equality of condition: democracy enabled the most able, by a process of natural selection, 'the survival of the fittest' and all that, to rise to the top direction of material affairs. And, to Carnegie, it was part of the genius of American life that the best talents were drawn into business and not, as in England, into the wasteful channels of politics. Such men saw politics as 'mere politics': the unproductive pastime of an aristocratic oligarchy. But, in contrast, James Bryce's great work on American politics, published two years later, took deliberate refuge in the almost meaningless title, *The American Commonwealth.* Bryce in the Preface explicitly criticized Tocqueville for making his *Democracy in America* the account of an 'idea' rather than of an actual system of government. But by 1949, when Harold Laski tried to surpass both Tocqueville and Bryce, it was inevitable that the title would be *The American Democracy.*

Whatever the name, however, the dispute continues between those Americans who regard their system as too democratic to provide effective government – if not in the domestic field, at least in the great jungle of foreign affairs – and those who regard it as not democratic enough – popular democracy is still frustrated by the checks and balances of the Constitution, the division of powers, particularly the Senate, on occasion the Supreme Court. American writers can still be found in abundance who are simply naive democrats. The business of government to them is simply to find out the wishes of the people. 'Democracy,' as Justice Holmes said sarcastically, 'is what the crowd wants.' 'Populist' direct democracy is one of the great animating myths of American politics for both left and right. Nearly half the States of the American Union, for instance, have provision in their constitutions for popular initiative, referendum, and recall. They forget that the first business of government is to govern – which may at times, even in America, call for the deliberate endurance of unpopularity. 'The politician,' said Churchill at his last Washington Press Conference, at a time when President Eisenhower was trying not to make up his mind what to do about the late Senator McCarthy, 'who cannot stand unpopularity is not worth his salt.' They forget that issues fit for a plebiscite, or the questions put into public opinion polls, are inherently predigested. Such issues and questions are frequently artificial in the sense that there may not be a public opinion on any question, or that the answers to such questions have to be seen in the context of all other questions, some of which may be mutually exclusive, all of which have to be weighed against each other by someone – so long as we live in a world in which life is short and resources are limited. Government alone can establish priorities of real social effort and actual policies. Democracy can only advise and consent, and then only in an indirect and spasmodic manner. Representatives must be politicians: if they all simply represent their immediate constituents and did not mediate, compromise, and occasionally think of the interests of government, they might survive, but it is unlikely that the Republic would.

More and more, however, American writers will argue just these things themselves: that 'government by the people' is misleading because impossible, or can only be one element in government and politics. But too often they then say that therefore 'democracy' must be made to mean strong and effective government, even a responsible two-party system (a very specific piece of business indeed), checks and balances, the liberty of the subject even against public opinion, etc. The lack of history for this generous usage need not worry us too much: meanings change both as levers and as mirrors of reality. But it hides the primacy of political values. It does lead to false expectations about other systems which also call themselves democratic. It may lead people to expect too much – and the disillusionment of unreal ideals is an occupational hazard of free politics. For instance, Ghana, of which we (good Pharisees) hoped so much (and new candidates for such comparisons arise almost monthly), is seen to be plainly not 'democratic'. It is rapidly becoming what former ages would have called a 'benevolent despotism'. Much of the opposition is in prison and so not very effective. Former colonial régimes and underdeveloped areas claim to be democratic and then we learn that they are not, American-wise, democracies at all. We lose heart and we wonder whether there is any hope for liberty. But the real worry is not that Ghana is not a democracy, which it plainly is not, but that with the intolerance of the government to opposition even as criticism, it may not even be political. And however popular or democratic the régime, if political opposition (however unpopular) is not allowed, the State may be free but its inhabitants will remain servile. One must hope for politics at all before one can hope for democracy in the American liberal sense. Equally, the liberal use of the concept democracy can lead people to expect too little. If some democratic institutions may seem overdeveloped in America, they can seem underdeveloped in Britain. Britain does not need democratic reforms because she is supposed to be democratic already. But one does not need to be a Jacobin or an American to think that English life could endure considerably more democracy of manners and methods without endangering political order. Indeed, the British constraint and conceit of class might seem, in American eyes, to be the very factor limiting national energy and more open to remedy by a whiff of democratic spirit than by the present tortuous economic programmes of any of the political parties. And it is indeed a platitude to say that if the American executive is too much subject to democratic control, yet in Britain there is too little Parliamentary or popular control of the executive. Strong government needs strong opposition if it is to be free and effective government.

So if democracy is best understood as one element in free government, not as a characteristic of the whole system, then it will always be possible to argue that *more* or *less* democratic institutions or democratic spirit is needed in any particular circumstance. Once again, Aristotle more clearly defined the relationship between politics and democracy than the usually over-complicated, or purely ideological, writings of modern authors. The best form of government was to him political rule – 'polity' or mixed-government. Such a government combined the aristocratic principle and the democratic; good government is a matter of experience, skill, and knowledge – not just opinion, but is subject to the consent of the governed. If there is no democratic element, a state will be oligarchic or despotic; if democracy alone prevails, the result is anarchy – the opportunity of demagogues to become despots. Democracy, then, is to be appreciated not as a principle of government on its own, but as a political principle, or an element within politics. As an intellectual principle, the belief that because men are equal in some things they are equal in all, it can be disastrous to the skill and judgement needed to preserve any order at all, let alone the special difficulties of a conciliatory political order.

Perhaps the worst danger from the democratic dogmas in free régimes can occur, as in the United States, not in the formal political institutions at all, but in the educational system. The idea is still deeply rooted in the American Public High School that it is 'undemocratic' (and therefore bad) to teach children of unequal ability unequally. This idea is now being challenged, spontaneously and fiercely, from many different quarters, not through any reactionary love of teaching a 'subject' rather than a 'child', as the cant has it, but largely on political grounds of worry that the schools are not furnishing people of sufficient talent and abilities to serve and maintain the national life. This argument has its own dangers. But at least it is combating a situation where many believe (always with complete sincerity) that the schools have the task of teaching not merely 'citizenship' (which has been debatable), but 'democracy' in a very specific form. This is an obvious, but now quite unnecessary, hangover from the days of mass immigration. 'A legitimate aim of education,' a Professor of Political Science writes, 'is to seek to promote the major values of a democratic society and to reduce the number of moral mavericks who do not share the democratic preferences.'[5] Politics will be richer in the United States when more people come to insist that it is a legitimate aim of education to educate, not indoctrinate. Within a free system there is a place both for democracy and authority. In the formal political institutions one assumes that democracy will normally outweigh but not exclude authority; but perhaps in education the converse should be the case. Political democracy does not imply intellectual democracy; intellectual democracy can make political democracy all but unworkable. Democracy, once again, cannot be the whole; it can only be a part in whatever activity it touches.

It comes to this very simply. That no government or authority can govern and survive unless it is based on consent – be it only the

---

[5]Harold Lasswell, *The World Revolution of Our Times* (Stanford 1951), p. 31.

consent of the praetorian guard or the officer corps. But grant the social circumstances of modern industrial states, or of states wishing to industrialize, then the technical skills of manual workers become necessary for economic survival, to say nothing of progress. To govern such societies any government must govern to the general welfare. This means that it either has to enforce some single idea of what that general welfare is, or it has to find out what people think it is – and reconcile the divergent results as well as possible. And how does one find out what people think except by giving them real choices to discuss and real freedom to criticize and choose their government?

Democracy, then, if we give the word the fairest meaning we may want to give it – if we value liberty, free choice, discussion, opposition, popular government, all of these things together – is still but one form of politics, not something to be hoped for at every stage of a country's development or in every circumstance. Politics is often settling for less than what we want, because we also want to live without violence or perpetual fear of violence from other people who want other things. But democracy, in its clearest historical and sociological sense, is simply a characteristic of modern governments both free and unfree. If industrial societies need governments of unparalleled strength, activity, and energy, they must be based upon active consent.

So while democracy can be compatible with politics, indeed politics can now scarcely hope to exist without it, yet politics does need defending on many occasions against the exclusive claims of many concepts of democracy which can lead to either the despotism of People's Democracies or the anarchy of the Congo. But perhaps it needs most of all that most unpopular of defences: historical analysis applied against the vagueness of popular rhetoric. Democracy is one element in politics; if it seeks to be everything, it destroys politics, turning 'harmony into mere unison', reducing 'a theme to a single beat'.

Chapter 4

A Defence of Politics against Nationalism

Nationalism is at this time perhaps the most compelling of all motives that can lead men to abandon or to scorn politics. Every feeling of human generosity is stirred by the struggle of an oppressed people to be free. And nothing can argue people who feel themselves to be a nation out of the belief that they are a nation; and that if they are to be oppressed, it is better to be oppressed by their own people than by foreigners. Even the mildest of us feels militant when he reads news of some national uprising, ambush, bomb plot, riot, or act of assassination. And it is easier, of course, to identify oneself with the smaller scale of nationalist illegality and violence than with the extreme contempt for life shown in Hitler's Germany, Stalin's Russia, and the China of Mao Tse-tung. Nowadays it does not even seem enough to challenge domestic tyranny in the name of popular liberties; it must always be, it seems, the nation struggling against – if actual foreigners are lacking – foreign-dominated puppets. Is it cynical or is it humane to say that many of us in free régimes who are wary before any brand of patriotism are gullible to any line of nationalism? The slogans of nationalism can lead to results as good or as bad for the interests of the governed as can the slogans of democracy. Nationalism may have become, in certain circumstances, a necessary condition for political order, but in others it has made a political system almost impossible.

Nationalism, however, is a much harder claim to limit than democracy. For it can speak with any one or more of four clamant voices: it can assume all the plausibility of *democratic nationalism* itself and the 'sovereignty of the people'; it can assume all the memories of imperialistic or *alien oppression and exploitation,* which then provide a builtin excuse for every excess of the liberators; it can assume the terrible plausibility of *racialism*; and, lastly, even the *nationalism of long-established states,* whose inhabitants may normally enjoy a political tradition, can assume in times of crisis a xenophobia which too often outlives the crisis, and may affect, at the least, the prudence of one state's dealings with another. Perhaps the most that can be done with the claim of nationalism is to dilute it with enough cool scepticism to bring it down from the boiling point of totalitarian democracy to the body temperatures of political tolerance.

Nationalism, as a force in public affairs, like democracy, indeed like politics itself, is something more specific than is commonly recognized. A wise contemporary has recently written: 'Nationalism is a doctrine invented in Europe at the beginning of the nineteenth century. It pretends to supply a criterion for the determination of the unit of population proper to enjoy a government exclusively its own, for the legitimate exercise of power in the state, and for the right organization of a society of states. Briefly, the doctrine holds that humanity is naturally divided into nations, that nations are known by certain characteristics which can be ascertained, and that the only legitimate type of government is natural self-government.'[1] Perhaps the French, from the time of the first Revolutionary Armies, may be allowed priority for the invention which Kedourie sees as arising in Germany to counter their advance and to purify the resisting states. But this is a small reservation to the main deadly excellence of such a definition. It is deadly for it touches at once the two greatest weaknesses in the claims of nationalism: the assumption that there are objective characteristics by which nations are known, and the assumption that there can be any single criterion of the proper unit of population to enjoy its own government.

It is notorious that no single objective criterion of the national unit has ever been found. The difficulty is not merely that different nationalisms have pursued different paths – such as common descent, language, customs and tradition, religion, or geographical proximity – each of

---

[1]Elie Kedourie, *Nationalism,* Hutchinson University Library (2nd ed., London 1961), p. 9. My admiration for the argument of this small masterpiece is great, though I think that its pessimism is overdrawn and its misanthropy strictly *obiter dictum.*

which can prove mutually contradictory to all. But there is the greater difficulty that in actual states which claim to be national units rarely have *any* one of these principles alone proved exclusive. This should be decisive to nationalism as a theory of government. It may move us, in directions in fact determined by other considerations, but it cannot help us to understand the situation we are in. But the nationalist, none the less, is not content with mere legal allegiance, nor with a proper pride in the country one lives in and the local institutions one knows. The nationalist wants to be more than the patriot. To him the *patria* or country to be loved should only be a nation. There can be no British nationalism, but only an English, Welsh, Scotch, and (Northern) Irish nationalism. There can be no Canadian nationalism, but only an English and a French. Attachments to such states are not really national; they are, indeed, merely patriotic. To the nationalist, both the United Kingdom and Canada are bastard States at the best, not famous and legitimate examples of political rule. There was a generation of radicals, even some democrats, in England and America in the 1760s and 1770s who styled themselves 'patriots'. This was in emulation of the Roman Republican sense of free citizens who loved their country and the populace that went with it. These patriots would have recognized a considerable degree of accident in what went before to make up a particular country. They wrote history as the history of free institutions, not of nations. They would judge governments by standards of utility rather than by whom they professed to govern. They loftily saw themselves as citizens of the world as well as of a particular allegiance, and the republic of learning had no national frontiers. All this to the nationalist is shallow and detestable. The French revolutionaries started by calling themselves patriots in this old Republican sense, but they soon became French nationalists, discovering and creating a force and emotion unknown to the great Republic which they thought they followed.

The true Republican patriots, those who in the eighteenth century were regarded as disciples of the constitutional thought of Locke and Montesquieu rather than of the – as it were – 'group psychology' of Rousseau, believed that any unit of population could form a state if governed by just laws. This view may have been at times profoundly unhistorical. But this error is no reason for treating all history as national history. There is no reason why there should be any single criterion at all of what makes a state. If this is seen, then the national criterion is, at the best, only something to be treated in each case on the merits of the type of rule it provides.

Nationalism has no special relationship to political justice; but neither does it have a particular relationship to injustice. The most obvious thing about it is, after all, that it exists. It may furnish no objective criterion for statehood – and there are no objective criteria of what is a nation – but its subjective power is compelling. 'A nation, therefore,' said Renan, 'is a great solidarity founded on a consciousness of sacrifice made in the past and on willingness to make further ones in the future.' A nationality is formed by the decision to form a nation. The consciousness of being a Pole, a German, a Hungarian, an Irishman, an American, a Peruvian, an Algerian, a Ghanaian, or a Malian, is not something that somebody can be argued out of – only, perhaps, argued into not carrying it too far by trying to invent objective criteria to coerce the unilluminated.

Modern nationalism clearly fulfils a need. The need may be met in some other way. But it is not enough just to say that the 'only criterion capable of public defence' is whether the new national rulers are 'less corrupt and grasping, or more just and merciful' than the old, or whether they are just as bad.[2] They may well be just as bad. But they have arisen out of the failure of previous régimes. This should never be forgotten. They can at least enforce public order – which often the previous régime could not. Some writers on nationalism need to be reminded, as Tocqueville said of democracy to the French conservatives of the 1830s, that it has come to stay, and that the problem is not how best and most elegantly to deplore it, but how to work with it so that it can be politicized.[3] There are real grounds on which to try to persuade nationalists that they prejudice nationalism by destroying political methods and values. But the tide cannot be turned back, and so it is not very sensible or political simply 'to sit down', like some modern Augustine, 'upon the banks of the rivers of Babylon and upon the rivers of Babylon weep, either for those who are being carried away by them, or for those whose deserts have placed them in Babylon'.

---

[2]Kedourie, *Nationalism,* p. 140.

[3]'The nations of our time cannot prevent the conditions of men from becoming equal, but it depends upon themselves whether the principle of equality is to lead to servitude or freedom, to knowledge or barbarism, to prosperity or wretchedness.' Tocqueville, *Democracy in America,* ed. Phillips Bradley, II, p. 334.

Modern nationalism is a product of the French Revolution. Its function has been to provide some popular substitute for the sense of belonging in a known public order which perished with the collapse of Feudalism. As the French Revolution built, so did it destroy. Masses of people were left floating on the tide, sometimes treated more honourably than before, but uprooted and at a loss to know where they belonged. Nationalism told people in a given area that they were a family. A nation-in-arms had taken on the rest of Europe, and even in defeat had proved that citizen armies could, firstly, be trusted; and secondly, be called on for exertions and sacrifices hardly possible from professionals. Nationalism arose from the breakdown of the universalism of the French Revolution. When democracy had proved itself in terms of power and belief, but had failed miserably as a system of government, Napoleonic nationalism came on the stage. This in turn was prepared to encourage or create other nationalisms, as in Italy, when the effect would be a weakening of France's enemies. Nationalism, then, at first acted within existing states to give them a degree of unity and a strength of purpose hitherto unobtainable – and this without the delays and frustrations of politics.

This nationalism was emulated not merely in war and politics. In the eighteenth century French language and culture had been the model and the bond of educated men all over Europe. But in the early nineteenth century the actual content became disregarded abroad; what was envied was the idea of an organic relationship between the language, the culture, and the State. It became the ambition of many to have a language and culture coinciding with or determining a unit of rule. If only two elements in some such triad were present, then the third had to be created. So in some cases historians invented a 'true national territory', as in Germany; in others, philologists revived dying languages, as in Ireland (and the line between invention and artificial respiration was often extremely fine; all over the Balkans philologists had to learn to use rifles to convince other educated men of the need to speak the same tongues as their backward peasantry).

European rulers in the eighteenth century had looked something like an international society – as had the Church and the educated in Medieval Europe. Ruling classes usually had more in common with each other than with their subject fellow-countrymen. But by the middle of the nineteenth century, Marx could argue that the working man had become the true internationalist and that nationalism was part of bourgeois ideology. Seldom was Marx more wrong. Nationalism has proved to be an idea of such popularity and potency at every level of society that Communists today everywhere ride its coat-tails rather than prophesy its demise – except when they have the overwhelming power, within their own borders, to smash it or restrict it to folkdancers and acrobats.

Nationalism, then, represented a system of authority which poured into the vacuum left by both the failure of the French Revolution and, as it were, the double failure of Autocratic Legitimacy that which preceded the revolution and that which followed it until the days of 1832 and 1848. The settlement of 1815 sought to return to the systems of power which had prevailed before 1789, before democratic and national passions had established themselves on the scene. In making the attempt to ignore both, an attempt not simply conservative but literally reactionary, the identification of each with the other was assured. Henceforth to many freedom came to mean the obtaining of a national government. People who were oppressed felt that the solution was not, as the eighteenth-century Whigs thought, to gain a just constitution, but to gain a national state. And even people who were not oppressed felt stirred to despise their comforts until the affront of not being a nation had been taken from them. 'We sought liberty,' wrote Mazzini, 'not as an end, but as a means by which to achieve a higher and more positive aim . . . We sought to found a nation, to create a people.'

Much has been written of the excesses to which the principle of national self-determination was carried by the victorious allies at Versailles in 1919. The dismemberment of the Austro-Hungarian Empire is often seen as a regrettable act of folly, reducing Central and South Eastern Europe to anarchy and impotence. But it is hard to see what alternative there was. Woodrow Wilson did not bring nationalism with him – all he brought to Versailles was a belligerent optimism, drawn from American and British history, that national States were free States (whereas, in fact, America had been a free State long before she experienced nationalism). By 1914 the damage had been done. Nothing that had happened during the war could make the spirit of nationalism more tolerant, indeed the contrary – and that was probably the only thing to be hoped for by 1919. The difficulty with nationalism was that it was not, in fact, a completely subjective or fictitious theory. If all the various people within a clear-cut unit of territory under a common rule suddenly begin to think of themselves as a common nation, as in the United States during and after the Civil War, no great harm is done.

But if criteria of language or religion or race are accepted, then those who fit it but who live just over the borders – the great problem of the *Auslandsdeutschen* – must be brought into the fold.

What if, for instance, there are fellows who pass a nationalist examination on race, fail on religion, are passed on geography, but fail on wanting to join in? 'Ireland shall be free from sea to sea,' said the *Shan Van Vocht.* In 1957 a liberating 'column' of fourteen young men crosses the border and attacks a Police Station in Northern Ireland, with – for them – disastrous ineptitude. A pamphlet sold on the streets of Dublin, after a great funeral procession for one of them, says: 'His tall, spare body, topped by red hair and the beard he grew when the fight opened and said he would not shave till Ireland was free, is the picture his comrades carry of him now. Men from the North, denied the opportunity of learning Irish, will remember that every order given by him was in the ancient tongue, then translated for their benefit.' The point of this parable, small beer indeed by some standards, is not simply that this crazy lad was a martyr to a theory of language, but that he was, quite simply, in any human terms, a murderer.

Why should not a man be proud of his country and think of it as a nation? –'a proud man's a lovely man', says the poet. But why should he think that an island (of a certain size?) or a plain, a valley, some area between some rivers, necessarily makes a national state, when inhabitants of a large part of it may govern themselves under a different concept of allegiance, any more than that there should be *a* national language (which may not be the colloquial language of most or many of even those who feel themselves of the nation)? If nationalism is a matter of will, of consciousness, and not of objective rational criteria, then let it be so. If there are different national feelings within an area, why should they not count as equally important? If even partition of an area – as of a language area – works, then let it work. Injustice only arises if a majority of such an area is prevented by its rulers, by force or fraud, from organizing politically for unification. But there will be injustice equally great if such a majority then attacks and destroys the national religion or linguistic institutions of the minority.

Nationalism, we said, speaks with four strident voices. *Democratic nationalism,* the myth of the sovereignty of the people, can be the most intolerant to minorities. It thrives upon the confusion of national government with popular government and uses both sticks – is possessed by both extremes – to beat a divided people into a unity.

Only three years ago the Government of Ceylon stirred up a civil disobedience campaign among the Tamil minority by attempting to repress its language. Ceylon should be one nation. On 26 April 1961, in justifying the declaration of a state of emergency, the Prime Minister said: 'At times like these we must lay aside political and religious differences. This is the hour for everybody to unite against the enemies of the nation and of the people.' Here is the worst plausible rhetoric of nationalism. Mrs Bandaranaike is saying that politics is to be thrown away in order to achieve a national unity and that those who wish for political compromise are enemies of the people. This category of man was the terrible invention of the Jacobins, and still thrives happily: an 'enemy of the people' loses all civic rights, he is literally an outlaw – cast beyond justice; it is a small step then before he loses all human rights. What sort of man is it who can willingly, wilfully, be an enemy both of the nation and of the people? The answer may, of course, be simply – a politician. *The Times,* on 3 May 1961, reported Senator S. Nadesan, a prominent Tamil leader, as saying: 'that the true solution to the problem facing Ceylon could not be found by a resort to armed force. There had to be a political solution to the language problem if Ceylon was to go forward.' Whatever the facts of the case are, it illustrates all too well what is and what is not politics – and I think one can admit to more than a mere prejudice in favour of political solutions in all such cases. The Tamils, like the Jews, are being punished for what they cannot be, or for what they are not even allowed to be.

Alien oppression and exploitation have often created, rather than repressed, nationalism. The majority of the new African States have no semblance of 'objective nationality' by any possible criteria – except the unification both of oppression and the accidental administrative areas of alien rule. The 'new nationalisms' have seldom been based on any common history prior to European domination. Nationalism, learned from Europe every bit as much as industrialism, arose to give a positive quality to the negative ambition of getting rid of the foreigner. This ambition is wholly legitimate and, in some cases, was simply a by-product of demands for political representation on some, even broadly, democratic lines. A communion of oppression can create a community of passionate intensity. The only question now is, the past being past, will this intensity tolerate diversity once the alien is gone? Too often the habits of discipline, unity, loyalty, violence, which were virtues in the liberation movement become the vices of the new government. Solidarity (for ever) becomes, indeed, an end in itself. The struggle against imperialism has to be continued, long after the imperialists have gone, because the enemy alone creates the unity by which the governing party can hope to perpetuate itself in office. The territory to be governed has to be convinced that it is a nation – if it is to be governed to the same degree of central authority as the power of the former government allowed. And this new power must be right at hand and active every moment; it has no overseas reserves to draw on to gain its awe and obedience. Where the demand for political representation precedes the absolute claims of 'national liberation', the occupying and unifying power may have been wise enough to create political institutions. If this is done in good time, as in Nigeria, free politics may be enhanced by the change of government. Where it is done late in the day, as in Ghana and Kenya, the issue will be in doubt – the habits of those who took to violence when denied political expression may prove stronger than political prudence and more endearing to the masses than the habits of those who 'compromised themselves' by working what politics there was. But if political institutions are not created at all, as in the Congo, then the result will be anarchy. The withdrawal of the occupying power may reveal a religious, ethnic, tribal, and regional disunity which can be brought into order only by an existing political machinery, or, failing that, by a central nationalist ideology – preached with the help of a national army. There may well be, then, circumstances in which politics is not immediately possible; but there are no circumstances in which a community is so much of one mind, if it is free to speak its mind, that politics is not desirable.

Racialism is not necessarily connected with nationalism. They are, indeed, formally opposed. Racialism is a myth of the body whose mode of expression is pseudo-scientific, nationalism is a myth of the mind whose mode of expression is cultural and historical. It can act to divide a nation, as in the United States, where the Black is so incorrigibly 'American' in all his habits and aspirations; or in Germany where the Jewish community had been good, even zealous, nationalists in war and peace from the middle of the nineteenth century until the Nazis made it impossible. Race-thinking and class-thinking are the two great alternative ideologies which claim to possess *the* key to history and a scheme for remedying all the defects of the human condition. Racialism, like Marxism, is really a fellow-traveller or parasite of nationalism, not at all a prerequisite for it. Racial theories will appear useful to certain types of nationalist; he will make use of them, all too easily; he may not even see the distinction. He may raise such devils from the deep, and then be unable to get rid of them. Racialism is the characteristic perversion of nationalism. The true nationalist must believe, on the contrary, in the equality of nations. Mazzini preached the right of every people to form a nation state and the duty of no nation to oppress another. Thus nationalism is not, strictly speaking, an ideology. All history is national history, but every national history is unique; there is no one final true type of national life; there is, at the worst, a pluralism of national bigotries. But it inclines towards ideological thought by undervaluing and undermining political activity, in that it abolishes the distinction between private and public: every act should be a national act; there is a national way of doing everything and everything should be done in a national way. Racialism can furnish a nation with a full ideology to make it not just one among equals, or even *primus inter pares,* but top dog, champion thoroughbred among mongrels. Racialism can give a nation a unique role to fill in world history, a pseudo-scientific claim for predominance among other races and nations. And it can be used to build up alliances among nations, as Anglo-Saxon racialism appeared in Anglo-American and also German historical writing in the late nineteenth century; as Arab nationalism today preaches blood, stock, and descent (as being less noticeably false than other appeals for unity); and as a Black racialism threatens to arise in parts of Africa in opposition to White racialism. If a nation wishes to overstep what it will think of as its natural territorial limits, or wishes to deny that a large number of its subject inhabitants can *ever* attain national status and citizenship, it needs a justification which transcends the theoretical category of nationalism. The equal right of all nations to be an independent state leaves little room for territorial expansion. So racialism, then, becomes a theory by which one nation can oppress other nations. Before the time of nationalism, Empire or *Imperium,* the rule of different peoples in one unit of government, could be justified either on religious grounds – the Emperor with sacred duties; or simply on grounds of utility – that the Empire enforced an equitable law and order. But after nationalism had destroyed both these sanctions, only racialism could demonstrate a natural superiority of one people over another. Imperialism was the nationalistic form of Empire-building. And it might be a happier world, but it is not, if the economic motives for imperialism could ever have been clearly separated from the racial justifications.

The *nationalism of long-established states* is free from some of the dangers of the new nationalisms. Great Britain, the United States, Holland, Switzerland, Sweden, all were territorial units with a firm legal and patriotic basis before the rise of nationalism, indeed before racialism and before industrialism, which form the peculiarly difficult climate for the new states. Being states already, nationalism was not needed to create unity – indeed, when it did come, domestically it was scarcely distinguishable from patriotism. British imperialism only once seriously endangered the established domestic political institutions in the way that German imperialism strangled and frustrated the growth of German liberalism. Nationalism in Great Britain was only a summary of an existing experience, it was not a revolutionary force. The nation was defined by the unit of rule, since it included Welsh, Scots, and some Irish; the state was not defined by a nation. Ireland, of course, was the great and terrible exception. It was, in fact, a conquered territory held down by force, in which political methods had first been abandoned, with the abolition of the Irish Parliament in 1800, and then made derisory by the exclusion of Catholics from public life. Ireland, in many ways, was the laboratory of modern nationalism: the inheritor of the old nationalist theories of pre-1848; the anticipator of the new nationalist practices of the era of the ending of colonies. Simply, it fell between the case of a conquered – and thus unified – colony, and the case of the suppressed national minority in the territory of another nation state. The one great threat to politics in Britain arose on the Irish question when, in 1913 and 1914, the Conservative Opposition not merely connived at sedition in Ireland, but helped suborn the army from its duty in the Curragh Mutiny when officers announced that they would refuse to enforce 'Home Rule' on Protestant Ulster. Britain at that moment was close to civil war, when the nationalism of Catholic Ireland was suddenly met by an equally intransigent, if temporary, English Conservative nationalism (a nationalism, at that moment, literally and clearly, unpatriotic).

American nationalism is, again, a late growth, far later than that great political skill which brought the thirteen revolting colonies from a mere Congress into a Federal Union. Right from the beginning of independence, the unity did not depend on a sense of a unique common language, religion, or stock. All were too plainly derivative, anarchic, or mixed. The national identification was with the Constitution itself and the political principles of the Declaration of Independence;

it was overwhelmingly a political agreement to be governed by an agreed set of political institutions. Politics itself was the foundation of American national unity. Cultural nationalism arose only in the memory of men still living. For a long time in the life of the Republic even a national history was lacking. Nationalism arose only when this political agreement broke down over the question of slavery. Even then, it was a nationalism of the Union, which is not precisely 'the State'. (Throughout the nineteenth century travellers had commented on the truculence of Yankee patriotism, but also on their 'lack' of a 'sense of the State'.) The Union was preserved, it was proved that a free state could protect itself; and this nationalism, which arose to justify the use of sovereign power in a highly pluralistic country, was actually combating racialism. If the Southern revolt had succeeded, students of racialism might be reading the discordant out-pourings of ante-bellum Southern College Professors, rather than the orchestrated lunacies of Gobineau or Houston Stewart Chamberlain.

In Canada the case is even clearer that nationalism is not a necessary prerequisite for national unity. The motives for unification in 1867 were military and economic. There was a real fear of American expansionism and there was real need to expand trade between the colonies by the joint construction of a trans-continental railway, if the separate colonies were not to become entirely dependent on their great neighbour. The success of unification was the result of already existing political institutions and habits in the separate Colonies and Provinces. It could even contain, with some rough – but never revolutionary – passages, one of the toughest and most exclusive nationalisms in the world, that of French Canada in Quebec. But French Canada had some very great politicians. Sir Wilfrid Laurier spoke simple political truth to his fellow *Canadiens* as in 1877: 'You wish to organize all Catholics into one party, without other bond, without other basis, than a common religion; but have you not reflected that by that very fact you will organize the Protestant population as a single party, and that then, instead of the peace and harmony now prevailing between the different elements of the Canadian population, you will throw open the doors to war, a religious war, the most terrible of all wars?' Those, today, who talk about the need for *a* Canadian nationalism either mean simply patriotism, the love of a country (which in fact includes two major nations), or are engaged in an unnecessary and ridiculous task – ridiculous because it is simply a form of emulation, an unnecessary defensiveness of 'mere politics' before the dangerous prestige of nationalism elsewhere, the judging of actual circumstances in terms of a theory of alien conditions.

Only in times of crisis need the old national states, who have grown by politics, abandon politics. This may be no more than the basic need of a state to preserve itself at all in face of clear and present danger. But when this is done in the name of nationalism, there is a danger that such emotions will outlive the crisis. Hatred of foreigners can exist without nationalism, but with nationalism, xenophobia becomes a respectable theory which can gravely distort normal political prudence. However soberly limited war aims are stated, the character of the struggle may become nationalistic. The struggle is then not against certain acts or policies of the enemy, but against the people itself. The outcome is that the Peace Settlement becomes no such thing; it becomes an instrument of national vengeance rather than of political pacification. The Versailles Treaty failed to pacify Europe less because, as some argue, it created too many national states too weak to stand alone, than because French and British nationalism punished the Germans by economic reparations so great that they guaranteed political instability in Germany. A politics of vengeance is not politics. Revenge is a recklessness towards the future in a vain attempt to make the present abolish a suffering which is already past. Nationalism made the Allies act against their own national self-interest. By treating Germany as a guilty people to be punished, they ensured that, at the least, all Germans would feel bereft of national pride until Versailles was repudiated. The nationalist, unlike the totalitarian, is not willing to take over a conquered state completely, smash it, and rebuild it utterly – which, as Machiavelli saw, is one solution; but he is too passionately involved to be able to draw its teeth and leave it in peace, without stepping on its toes, breaking its heart, insulting its very being, sowing the dragons' teeth for the next generation to enjoy. To condemn Versailles is not, of course, to condone the motives of everyone who sought to repudiate it – Nazis in Germany and appeasers in England. And to argue that nationalism failed in 1919 to act in its own self-interest is not to deny that Germany had pushed war beyond the traditional boundaries of nationalistic morality – with the unlimited U-boat campaign and the plans to colonize Poland and 'resettle' the Poles further east. But he who has the power has the responsibility, and political power is the restraint of power. The German army, though not the German nation, was defeated; the Allies had both the power and the right *to dictate* a peace; but they had the greater responsibility *to make* a peace that would endure. 'It is not what a lawyer tells me I *may* do,' cried Burke, 'but what humanity, reason, and justice tell me I ought to do. Is a political act the worse for being a generous one?'

Also, it is hard not to think that the demand for the unconditional surrender of Germany in 1944 and 1945 did not cruelly prolong the war, make reconstruction more difficult, and was not a product, once again, of a nationalism which had temporarily discarded normal political sense. Indeed, the demand seemed to take on the same desperate logic as that of the totalitarian enemy. It was an indulgence in retribution, not an exercise in statecraft, based on the doubtful totalitarian slogan that all real Germans were Nazis. Despite the rhetoric – which was damaging enough to the growing German opposition – had the table not been so unusually thick, had Colonel Stauffenberg's bomb killed Hitler, it is hard to believe that America and Britain, at least, would not have allowed some political conditions to dilute the unpolitical assumptions of 'unconditional surrender'. But there were many, more plausible than Lord Vansittart, willing to strengthen our unbelief. For consider a rumbustious polemic of the time, Quintin Hogg's *The Left Was Never Right* (1945). He contrasted two passages in speeches in the House of Commons in 1944, as if any honest man could see the sober common sense of the latter compared to the wild idealism of the former. He first quoted Aneurin Bevan: 'Instead of regarding the Germans as uniquely different, let us regard the mass of them as victims equally with ourselves of the Nazi régime and as likely to act roughly in the same way when the war is over.' This may have been going a little too far. But then this brilliant shallow man quoted with purring approval Sir Anthony Eden: 'The essential factor we have to remember in deciding our plans for the future is that in the German character the unquestionable authority of the State is what counts for most. . . . Unless we are seized of that we do not understand the foundation on which Nazi doctrine was so easily superimposed. It was acceptable to the average German because it expressed in aggressive forms the belief which the average German has had for two hundred years or more.' There are some tragic over-simplifications which it is impossible to paraphrase without seeming to parody. But, of course, this was an example, fortunately not of the total collapse of a political sense of diversity before wartime nationalism, but just of some partial damage done to it. Political habits reasserted themselves because – with victory – the 'problem of Germany' lost its apparent simplicity and all Germans did not seem absolutely alike. Thus nationalism may or may not be political. It offers many specific dangers, perhaps none insuperable, to free government. There was a famous criticism by Lord Acton of John Stuart Mill's views on nationalism. 'It is in general', Acton quoted Mill, 'a necessary condition of free institutions that the boundaries of governments should coincide in the main with those of nationalities.' Acton thought this an unworthy ideal and unworkable as a general rule. But Mill also wrote that 'where a sentiment of nationality exists in any force' there is a *'prima facie* case' for creating a national government, and – further – that 'Free institutions are next to impossible in a country made up of different nationalities.' Mill is dealing with something more than the old Whig notions of nationality or patriotism, but he is recognizing a phenomenon, not espousing it; his recognition of the national state is pragmatic and circumstantial, not nationalistic and of principle. So Acton's famous riposte, if it is a riposte, somewhat misses the mark. 'If we take the establishment of liberty . . . to be the end of civil society, we must conclude that those states are substantially the most perfect which, like the British and Austrian Empires, include various distinct nationalities without oppressing them. . . . A State which is incompetent to satisfy different races condemns itself; a State which labours to neutralize, to absorb, or to expel them, destroys its own vitality; a State which does not include them is destitute of the chief basis of self-government.' Critics of Mill rarely quote this passage of Acton in full. For the last sentences make clear that Acton himself saw the force of nationalism as 'the chief basis of self-government', only he wished for some kind of Austrian Federal system or British Imperial system which allowed substantial local autonomy. The two cases he cites, while they illustrate his ideal, are scarcely typical types of state formation. So the debate never was, and never can be, one of nationalism versus political freedom. The problem, rather, is of the preservation of politics in a context overwhelmingly nationalistic.[4]

The nationalist, or rather his follower, has to be shown that he can have both national freedom and political freedom. But in practice, there is

---

[4]See especially Ernest Gellner, *Nations and Nationalism* (Blackwell, 1983) and Eric Hobsbawm, *Nations and Nationalism since 1780* (Cambridge University Press, 1990).

more often the need to remind the follower that the time of revolutionary justice should not last for ever, and that the claim of nationalism was once that national states were the best ground on which personal freedom could flourish. This has yet to be proved. Throughout the world it trembles in the balance. It has often enough been disproved. Israel, for instance, conceived in the most intense nationalism, founded by violence, living in fear, oppressing Palestinians, yet seems to preserve free politics; Ghana, whose birth, though hard, was far easier, and who is threatened by no one, yet seems in danger of losing or destroying freedom. Why? Perhaps when all the vast and obvious differences between two such histories and circumstances have been conceded, the simple fact remains that in one country there is a greater will to preserve both political freedom and national identity. Perhaps men who have known the deepest and most violent oppression crave for and become addicted to personal liberty, while people who have known only insult and injustice may undervalue liberty in their desire for national revenge and national prestige. The boast of Padraig Pearse that he would rather be a prisoner in a free Ireland[5] than a free man under alien rule, has often enough come true.

Parnell came down the road, he said to a cheering man:
'Ireland shall get her freedom and you still break stone.'

---

[5]For Ireland herself, I should now add that a 'United Ireland' is not likely to take the form of a unitary national state, as is the hope of traditional Irish republicanism, nor is it likely to be impeded by the United Kingdom hanging on to the old doctrine of parliamentary sovereignty. It will probably take the form of a federal or even confederal State with Northern Ireland retaining a strong British connection, and with the Republic of Ireland and the United Kingdom establishing some institutions in common. Such a unique arrangement will reflect neither pure nationalism nor a continuance of the full 'territorial integrity' of the United Kingdom, but arises from the actual poetics of the problem: that Northern Ireland does face both ways and has a mind of its own.

Chapter 5
A Defence of Politics against Technology

There is a great danger to politics in the desire for certainty at any price. This idea may seem exceedingly abstract and general, but it is powerful and is the strong and deep root of many simple beliefs and of many elaborate doctrines. So far we have considered types of rule of which there are actual or would-be examples. These have offered, if not desirable alternatives to political rule, at least, in varying degrees, concrete proposals for action. But there is common to all of them, and is found even in free régimes, a set of highly abstract ideas, distinctively modern, seemingly inescapable, which can deeply undermine any belief in the political way of ordering society. Such ideas may be all too obviously in the interest of certain groups – it is their own certainty which they want to impose on others; but they may be pursued with the most elevated disinterestedness, simply because people hold them to be true – 'they *must* be true because our whole modern world – is it not? – is built upon science.'

This section could almost as well be called 'A Defence of Politics Against Science' or '. . . Against Administration'. 'Science', 'Technology', 'Administration', will be understood by most of those actually engaged in such activities to have no necessary antipathy to politics. But to many they appear as related symbols, forming together a style of thought which, they imagine, could rescue mankind from the lack of certainty and the glut of compromises in politics. This belief may often be held in surprising ignorance of what is actually involved in such activities as science, technology, or administration; but it is none the less influential and convincing. Technology, however, is probably the keystone of all these imaginary constructions which seek to rehouse and redevelop mere politics. Technology creates the image of applying scientific knowledge to the administration of society. Many will talk about the benefits of science, when they in fact mean technology; many will talk as if administration should exist apart from politics, because they in fact believe that it is simply a matter of technique. Technology is, of course, simply the activity of applying scientific principles to the production of tools and goods – whether or not these principles are fully understood. But it has also become perverted into a social doctrine. 'Technology' holds that all the important problems facing human civilization are technical, and that therefore they are all soluble on the basis of existing knowledge or readily attainable knowledge – if sufficient resources are made available. This doctrine is very widespread. So powerful is it that it must seem to many, in Kharkov as well as Detroit, in Birmingham as well as Hankow, to be self-evident and completely obvious – instead of being something arbitrary, peculiar, and specific.

Now there are, it should be ungraciously admitted, some positions which one hesitates to attack because of the kind of allies attracted. Here is a defence of politics against 'scientism', not science; against technology as a doctrine, not as a practical activity. I have no desire to please that parochial British intelligentsia who give the genteel groan of agreement to any attack on science however sweeping and misplaced. Perhaps they take too seriously the claim of some anti-political doctrinaires to be 'scientific' (there is, as will be seen later, an element of mutual flattery between the doctrinaire and the traditionalist). The present argument could, in another context, be quite simply a defence of the scientific spirit against the hucksters, the manipulators and the doggedly fashionable who cover other aspirations, some quite proper and ordinary, by using the names of 'science' and 'technology' as magic incantations.

The rise of industrial technology led to a strengthening of the state – in order to regulate an urban, centralized society; and it led to a strengthening of demands on the state – in order to distribute more equitably the fruits of the technology; but it has also created this wholly new style of thought: 'technology' as a doctrine. Everything in society is seen as capable of rational manipulation if the techniques of power and production are understood. Indeed power and production are the same thing. A state maintains its power, argued Marx, so long as production expands. The modern state is simply the governing committee of the bourgeoisie; all power is economics and economics is production. The class that can expand production gains power, and for a class which acts as a restraint upon production, the writing is already on the wall, the foundations of its power have already collapsed. One of the symptoms of a declining social order is that its members have to give most of their time to politics, rather than to the real tasks of economic production, in an attempt to patch up the cracks already appearing from 'the inner-contradictions' of such a system. Politics is simply a product of those inner contradictions, or at the best a transitory device on the way to their final resolution. The whole state, then, to the 'technologist' is first seen as a factory producing goods for society. It is not seen as the protector of rights or the arbiter of differing interests, but as the producer of happiness – consumer goods. But even this is mild, liberal, and political to the true 'technologist' – a kind of Welfare State idea in which the state as servant does something for society as master. The complete concept of 'technology' is that of all society itself as one factory of which the state is manager. The factory is supposed to produce for the needs and happiness of the workers, and everyone is a worker (happiness being the superfluity of consumer goods over what is needed merely to survive); but it is known that nothing can be produced without the skill, direction, or permission of the manager. Things worth doing for their own sake, art, love, philosophy, indeed *leisure* itself as distinct from mere rest (the purpose of which, to Aristotle, was the activity of doing just those things), are irrelevant to production and therefore inefficient – unless propaganda for production controlled by the manager.

All civilizations, and the doctrines of government whose company they keep, create some image of the type of citizen they most need and value. The world of the Greek *polis* had the hero, the man of *arete,* the active 'doer of deeds *and* speaker of words' in the public realm; early Christianity had the humble, suffering, other-worldly man, the saint. Medieval Christendom had the knight and the priest, ideally fused as the crusader or the member of an order of knighthood. The English in modern times have been torn between the gentleman and the businessman, just as the Americans have between the common man and the businessman. The Nazis had their Aryan superman, and the Communists have their party man (sub-category, Stakhanovite worker). To those who see all industrial civilization as on the common path of 'technology', the typical citizen is the *engineer*. The engineer is to be the true hero-citizen of our times: he will rescue us from the dilemmas of politics and the pangs of hunger (and envy?) if 'left alone to get on with his job' free from, in various circumstances, the intrusions of the politicians, the businessmen, the bureaucrats, the generals, or the priests. The engineer is what every boy will want to be. The engineer is what every father will be ashamed of not being. The engineer is what society will strain itself to produce through the schools and colleges – and he will be trained, by accident or design, in a kind of aristocratic seclusion from, and contempt for, other types of education. The engineer will try to reduce all education to technique and training, and its object will be to produce social engineers to transform society into something radically more efficient and effective. The engineer is not interested in ordinary politics; he thinks in terms of invention and construction, not of maintenance and management. But he will naturally be attracted to doctrines which attack 'mere politics' and to régimes which have shown great technological advances and which have all-intrusive ideologies claiming to be scientific.

The vision is now an old one whose history does not concern us here. But its plausibility is enhanced by the fruits of modern technology: the vision that politics can be reduced to a *science*. By this is usually meant that there are laws of social and historical development which can be discovered and then *should* be observed, implemented, enforced on society. Such enforcing will be held to be no more than acting naturally at last: 'freedom is the recognition of necessity'. Human societies have been unstable and full of conflict because, as it were, we have been trying to fly in the face of laws of social gravitation. 'The only safety for democracy . . .' wrote an American social scientist, James Shotwell, is to 'apply scientific methods to the management of society as we have been learning to apply them in the natural world. . . . We are in the political sciences where the natural sciences were two hundred years ago.' And such a common cry is itself still in the position of Saint-Simon in 1821 – exactly a hundred years before: 'In the new political order . . . the decisions must be the result of scientific demonstrations totally independent of human will. . . . Under such an order we shall see the disappearance of the three main disadvantages of the present political system, that is, arbitrariness, incapacity, and intrigue.' Now it will immediately be obvious, to be very simple, that if one fails to observe certain laws of physics, one falls flat on one's face. But some of the promised laws of society must have been fairly often 'broken' – presumably without consequences quite as drastic as a Daedalus trying to fly and falling smashed to earth. What a science of society offers us, then, is not something necessary for society to survive at all, but necessary if there is to be complete 'safety for democracy' (or anything else), or no more 'arbitrariness, incapacity, and intrigue'. Suppose the 'arbitrariness' which Saint-Simon hated to be no more than a product of diversity; 'incapacity' simply some sense of limitations; 'intrigue' no more than the conflict of differing interests in any even moderately free State; and suppose 'safety' to be only realizable – as in the world of Hobbes – by the surrender of freedom out of fear – then we have a characterization of politics itself, indeed a rather good one: the 'scientists' often at least knew what they were attacking more clearly than the politicians knew what they were defending. At heart what disturbs those hopeful for a science of politics is simply the element of conflict in ordinary politics; what excites them has been the prestige of science, its good reputation for – so it is thought – 'unity'. Professor Harold Lasswell wrote in the article on 'Conflict' in the Chicago *Encyclopaedia of the Social Sciences* of 1930: 'Social conflict results from the conscious pursuit of exclusive values . . . the philosophy of compromise seems to concede in advance that there is no truly inclusive set of social aims. . . . It may be that the manipulation of collective opinion for the sake of raising the prestige of science will contribute towards this sense of unity of man with man.' Such a scientifically manipulated unity might indeed get rid of conflict and freedom too.[1]

The claim that politics can and should be reduced to a science is not as clear as it seems. To go no further – the 'and should' is essential to the claim, although it immediately introduces a moral or a political decision. It could be argued that politics *can* be made scientific, but then that it should not be; or it could be argued, more unlikely but possible, that it *should* be made scientific, but then the fact bewailed that it cannot. But, be this as it may, the claim can mean three rather different things. Science can be

[1] See the final section, 'Inconclusions' of my *The American Science of Politics* (London 1959).

thought of as a body of *laws* which enable measurable predictions to be made; or it can be thought of as a common *method* to be pursued in the discovery of knowledge – irrespective of whether such laws exist in every sphere; or it can be thought of as simply a logic of *verification*: science is all true knowledge and truth is only what is testable by experiment or direct observation – whether or not there are laws or there is a method. These may seem to be very abstract matters – conceits of the colleges more than concerns of the caucuses. But they do correspond to some ordinary, tenaciously popular viewpoints. The first fulfils a very common desire for certainty about the future of which the many covert believers in astrology are amiable examples, and of which all single-truth men and ideologists, whether of the parlour or parade-ground variety, are less amiable examples. The second represents the pride of the engineers – again, everything is method or technique (and there is, strange view, *a* scientific method). The third represents the man who suffers from the abstract tyranny of the concrete fact – everything must be demonstrable by 'the facts' and always 'the facts demand' that some particular policy must be carried out.

This third 'pseudo-scientist', while the most abstract and the least original, is perhaps the most dangerous, for he is the follower who gives power to the lonely theorist or to the unequipped technocrat – he is the man who is impressed with the fact that the trains ran on time in Fascist Italy: 'there's a fact' – and who has 'no doubt at all' that 'the facts must show' that free régimes are less efficient and less able to protect themselves than totalitarian societies. He is the person who is touched by Khruschchev's recent praise of an ideology which 'can be understood not only by the head but, so to speak, by the stomach and by one's whole being to be a more progressive system than capitalism'. The Soviet Union will win, he argued, 'not only by its possession of the most progressive and scientifically based theory, but also because of the ever-increasing material benefits of the people.' A contrast so arbitrary and absurd in economic terms, between a capitalist system and a communist system, is what has to be swallowed by the man who is impressed 'simply by the facts'. It may be a politically effective argument, but the 'facts' that are impressive are those of productivity, not of ideology.

Totalitarian ideologies are, in large part, a perversion of science. They could arise only in a scientific age, not because of the techniques of power hitherto lacking, but because the whole concept of remaking society utterly is a derivative from the idea of scientific law – applied to understanding society, and of a scientific method – applied to changing society. Ideology arises when science is thought of as the only type of human knowledge and is then misapplied to government in the name of some general theory of society. 'For an ideology,' wrote Hannah Arendt in her *Origins of Totalitarianism,* 'differs from a simple opinion in that it claims to possess either the key to history or the solution for all the "riddles of the universe".' Ideologies then are essentially pseudoscientific; they claim to do for history and society what the physicists are doing for our understanding of nature and the engineers for productivity. Indeed an ideology fuses understanding and action completely: an ideology is always a plan for action. The ideologist is the scholar-scientist become the engineer-administrator. The ideologist is very proud that his theory is not based upon ethical considerations, but upon an objective factor. Two 'objective factors' alone, as we have said, seem to be proved sufficiently plausible, sufficiently pseudo-scientific to have emerged as offering total explanations in powerful hands: race struggle and class struggle, blood and economics. The claims of Marxism to be scientific are famous and, strangely, even when doubted, are not thought improper, monstrous, or inherently implausible. But the Nazi claim for the scientific status of racialism has seldom been taken as seriously, though it was a genuine pseudo-science, not 'just' propaganda. For propaganda is never effective if it does not touch deeply held, even if furtive and illicit, beliefs. Perhaps racialism is not given its pseudoscientific due because, like nationalism, it is a category that fits neither Marxist nor liberal-capitalist ideologies. But men have often acted against their economic interests under the spell of racialism. It was once, even or particularly in Great Britain, an orthodoxy of historical explanation, as well as the operating creed of nearly every agent of imperialism. The memory of its respectability is almost deliberately repressed; it is more comfortable to treat it as simply the politics of the gutter, rather than what one finds when one opens the dust-covered sets of histories of three generations ago. Tocqueville could write to Gobineau that his theories of race 'are probably wrong and certainly pernicious'. But he did take them seriously as scientific hypothesis; for they were one of the dominant themes of nineteenth-century thought, one obvious and tempting way of linking the two new sciences of biology and sociology, of extending Darwin's theories to politics.

Let us call such perversions of genuine scientific activity, all attempts to apply science beyond its own sphere, 'scientism'. Scientism goes hand in hand with ideology in the size of their claims. A scientific law must apply to all instances of the thing treated as the object of generalization. A single contrary instance will refute a scientific theory. Totalitarian ideologies make claims to be the basis of a world order, to offer a comprehensive explanation of everything. They are nothing if they are not cast in uniquely large moulds. If the theory does not fit all circumstances, it is not true for any. The relativism of political theory is precisely what is wrong with it in the eyes of the ideologist. That one set of institutions may work better here than there, and that any form of politics at all may not be possible in all circumstances, these are damning admissions to the totalitarian. He is not interested in this kind of frustrating, piecemeal humility. He is not interested in understanding, but only in explanation. He has the scientific key to history and if he thinks in terms of immediate political issues at all, then they are simply tactics, indeed tactics of history, part of the grand strategy of the advance towards a fully rational world order. He is obsessed with size and with the beauty of universal generalizations. Even in fairly stable political régimes, such as Great Britain and the United States, one finds touches of this psychology among the academics and the young – people who are only interested in large issues. They have not yet embraced a comprehensive ideology, but they are rapidly deserting politics. These large issues are important issues – racial discrimination, the 'bomb', the 'war on want', 'the problems (which?) of the underdeveloped areas', the environment. But to be tackled at all, they must surely be tackled politically, simply because they are so large and call for so much coordination of effort and organization, and because they cannot, perhaps, all be realized at once. Many of the people who try to ride all these large issues at once say that they are bored and disgruntled with ordinary politics – though they have usually had little or no political experience themselves (demonstrations do not count); but whatever is said of politics by its actual practitioners, it is seldom called boring. Some politicians, indeed, are as little ashamed as some marchers of thinking the activity itself enjoyable. But those who lead the life of large issues only are never prepared to enjoy or even tolerate the present; like the ideologists, they attempt to live in the future and so prophecies, or the predictions of pseudo-science, play a great part in their lives. Always some huge catastrophe will occur unless you take my medicine quickly.

Scientism can also exist in free societies in the respectable disguise of academic social science. There are those who have no huge and elaborate programmes for the just society, unlike their nineteenth-century predecessors, and who may, as they say, *'qua* citizen', in their leisure time, non-academic capacity, act like normal political animals, but who none the less teach that a scientific investigation of society will have a kind of therapeutic effect which will eventually remove all serious political tensions. Politics is, to so many social scientists, a kind of disease: society is a patient ridden with tensions and political events are the unreal, neurotic fixations by which it tries to rationalize these contradictions. This is what Professor Lasswell has called 'the preventive politics of the future' which will exist in a world-wide 'techno-scientific culture'. 'The ideal of a politics of prevention is to obviate conflict by the definite reduction of the tension level of society by effective methods, of which discussion will be but one.'[2] If the causes of these tensions are exposed and are put before the patient, therapy will result. Here is, as it were, the underlying religion of the empiricists, those who think that each humble fact finds its place in some grand order and that it is possible or desirable to study society purely objectively. But such a 'politics of prevention' is not politics at all, it is the elimination of politics; and it is not science, either – it is ideology. Genuine understanding, true scholarship, pure science, the attempt to be as dispassionate and as disinterested as possible in understanding the situation we are all in, inevitably involves political values, the political relationship, however imperfect, with all its uncertainty, diversity, and freedom. The claim for objectivity can be a kind of arrogance which leads men to despise the slowness of improvement and reform by persuasion and discussion. Such scientism of the chair may not be directly dangerous to free societies; but it can indirectly undermine a true education in politics by studying things too small to be relevant, as if they are all examples of a general or total scientific theory of society too large to be plausible.

The debate among academic students of politics about whether or not their study can be made a science is notoriously sterile. The choice is one that need never be made. Political knowledge draws together the findings of many disciplines so as to understand how human purposes are realized in the activity of government. No 'objective' study of government is ever so stick-in-the-mud as to avoid, implicitly

---

[2]*Psychopathology and Politics* (New York 1930), p. 202.

or explicitly, grinding some political axe (human beings are, thank God, creatures of discontent as well as of curiosity); and no moralist is ever so lofty as not to offer us some evidence that his prescriptions might conceivably work (rewards in heaven are, alas, simply irrelevant to the mundane immediate responsibilities of governments). Both, unavoidably, deal in doctrines. Political doctrines state purposes which stand some chance of convincing people that they can be realized politically; or state generalizations about government worth making for political purposes. Every purported methodology of how to study the activity of government objectively, that is every prefabricated set of rules for the discovery of knowledge in advance of experience, is itself a doctrine – political or antipolitical. This will only disturb those who are disturbed at politics itself. All thinking about government and politics crystallizes into doctrine at some level of experience; and all advocates of doctrines, like the lawyer in court, offer evidence to try to convince those who sit in judgement. The evidence is shaped according to a lawyer's understanding of his own and his client's self-interest; he does not throw a packet of facts on the table and invite the judges to sort it out themselves. He, like any politician, attempts to prejudice the issue. But only incompetent advocates and incompetent politicians offer evidence which does not appear relevant and convincing, and which does not stand up to criticism. The student of government should, indeed, attempt to be more dispassionate than the advocate or politician; but he will not succeed in becoming passionless unless he becomes quite irrelevant to the life of a free society. (The student of government in a totalitarian state will not, of course, be allowed even to appear uncommitted.) If he is wise, he will be careful not to speak too often or too stridently on the issues of the day – his business is not the politician's; but he will not be studying politics at all if he does not find himself speaking on the issues of the age.

The belief that politics can be reduced to a science, both in understanding and action, is not, then, a product of scientific reasoning, is not by its intellectual failure and political ruthlessness anything to discredit science, but is simply ideology using pseudo-science to justify the application of technological thought to society.

Technology is really the master-concept running through Marx's great attempt to offer a scientific socialism to restore the unity of knowledge, to integrate fully thought and action. In an abstract but real sense, Marxism arose through the breakdown first of religion and then of 'reason' as single sources of authority. The world as revealed through Descartes and Hume, a world in which mathematical truths alone were objective and in which all moral truths seemed subjective or relative, can prove too much for the nerves of not only philosophers, but men of practical affairs as well. Many are disturbed with something like terror, with a neurotic inability to deal with reality, when they come to feel that they have senses whose evidence does not coincide with revealed religion, or with 'reason' or even with the mathematical order of the natural world. There has been a kind of panic before dualism – people crying 'how am I-in-here-so-passionate a part of all-that-out-there-so-remote?' Kant might speak of his never-ending wonder at two things, 'the starry heavens above and the moral law within', but to many this wonder is an awesome terror at the unbridgeable abyss between the two. Then they listen eagerly to any preacher of a single truth, rather than see that this initial separation of a world of science from a world of society, of an 'I' from an 'it', of the observer from an object, was only a separation for the limited purposes of science – a separation from a total flow of human experience which can be divided or distinguished in many ways which are not mutually incompatible, but which simply exist, for the purpose at hand, at different levels of abstraction. Science and politics, indeed art, history, and philosophy, are different ways of looking at a common reality for different purposes: they only conflict and contradict when the purposes are confused or are each regarded as limitless. No two men will draw the limits of these activities at the same point, but we are here dealing with claims that some particular activities, like science and politics, are the same and are limitless.

It was not really Hegel whom Marx turned upside-down in his quest for a single truth, but Aristotle. Aristotle, we have seen taught that politics was the 'master-science' in the sense that it controls and coordinates, without destroying, all other activities which may make a claim on the resources of society. Marx's scientific-socialism puts a science of sociology on top of a science of politics. Society is no longer viewed as a diversity of interests to which politics alone can give the necessary degree of unity, but as a natural unity which politics divides and disturbs. Scientific socialism makes a double claim: that the sociological dimension of experience is the only dimension of experience, and that science is inevitably technological – thus any understanding is a prelude to action and the laws of evolution show how society is to be changed, environment engineered. Marxist 'technology' is only an explicit case of a claim more often implicit. 'Technology' can furnish the theories of the untheoretical. Here are the vast assumptions about what is to be taken for granted held by those 'purely practical men' who take so much for granted. They take for granted that all problems are technical and that each advance in scientific knowledge somehow uniquely determines a new and proper sphere of application. This is not merely Lenin's famous 'Communism is socialism plus electrification', or Hitler's *Gleichschaltung,* linking all society to one grid, to the same source of electric energy (and how quickly dated does each such technological claim or metaphor become!); but it is also the sober, even a little dull-sounding, claim of many an American social scientist: 'Many of the problems now besetting the world arise from the fact that physicists and engineers know how to combine theory and fact more efficiently than do political scientists and political policy-makers.'[3] This has the same plausibility – both intellectually and politically – as Khrushchev's stomach as a judge of ideology. Truth is only what works and 'the system' which produces and distributes the most consumer goods will ultimately prevail. This is no small claim, and its realization might seem to reconcile perfectly the technocrat with the moralist, the engineer with the politician. As once it was said that ballots are better than bullets, now it is said that butter is better than ballots. But need we really make this latter choice?

There is now need to be a little brave – to risk inevitable misunderstanding – and to insist that however great and pressing are the problems of economic and technical aid for underdeveloped territories, such aid can never be an end in itself. To help other people avoid even the risk of starvation is a good action whatever the motives. To help other people attain some idea of a decent standard of living is a good action whatever the motives. But if making a living at all is a primary biological urge of man, this is very far from levels of civilization which have been and can be attained. The reality or memory of desperate poverty is no excuse for organizing people always to the maximum pitch of economic efficiency if that efficiency involves the suppression

---

[3]William A. Glazer, *The Types and Uses of Political Theory, Social Research* (Autumn 1955), p. 292.

of politics, of the canvassing of alternatives, and of free discussion; the killing of all spontaneity, play, and frivolity; and the forbidding of even occasional extravagances. It is terrible nonsense to presume that a richer, or a more productive society is necessarily a happier one for people to live in than a society poorer or less efficient. The price in terms of freedom of the rapid industrialization of an underdeveloped country may be rationally thought worth paying – but why should it be paid for ever? The price is then bound to be too high. Some would argue that totalitarianism simply arises from rapid industrialization – but then why need it be total? 'The revolution has no time for elections', Dr Castro was reported as telling a parade of more than a million Cubans on May Day 1961. Perhaps – but the price seems too high when: 'He asked: "Do you need elections?" and the crowd shouted "No, No".' For there is, after all, a difference between knowing that you are paying a price for something, and either not knowing, or thinking that you don't care at all. The difference is that if you know what you are sacrificing, you may want to return to it when prosperity is greater – if not, later generations may not even know what it means. There is a difference, once again, between denying freedom out of economic necessity and denying it out of principle; between persuading people that a price for progress is worth paying and deceiving them that they get it for free. 'When I see a Soviet oil-tanker, I think of Lenin. When I see a Soviet tractor, I think of Lenin. Whenever we get anything from the Soviet Union,' Dr Castro told K. S. Karol, 'I feel gratitude to Lenin.'[4] Lenin is thanked, Dr Castro made clear, because Leninism has no connexion with Stalinism. There are many who believe this. Ernesto Guevara, the 'theoretician' of the régime, tried to provide them with an extra argument. He reassured Karol that there was 'no danger we shall . . . slide towards what you call Stalinist totalitarianism'; Stalinism had the 'necessity to create, by its own unaided efforts, the basic industries required for its economic development'; but, he went on, 'we do not need to make such sacrifices to industrialize because we can get all we want from the other Socialist countries'. It is hard to tell whether these are the words of a morally stupid man, unable to see the enormity of such an unnecessary 'necessity', or of a cunning man trying to extort money

---

[4]Reported in the *New Statesman,* 19 May 1961, p. 778.

by threats of self-flagellation. There is every excuse, amid oppression and poverty, for the second motivation, but the first would exhibit a quality of reckless blindness which is more frightening for the future of humanity than almost any present oppression or poverty. There are no absolute necessities in politics. The language of necessity spells the death of freedom – and usually of men too. 'I now realize,' continued Guevara, 'that Marxism is not simply a doctrine, it is a science' – and such a science it is.

Certainly, technological achievement (or possession) is the modern symbol of sovereignty – the prestige of science gives majesty to mere power. Every small country like Cuba demands, at the least, its own basic industries – regardless of economics. And Sputnik did more for Communism than the spectacle, for instance, of a dozen Presidential or general elections can do for free countries. Quite apart from the prestige of technology, people do, after all, prefer a simple idea to a complex one. A man in space is supposed to be so much more tangible than the ability to conduct free elections. But technology threatens not merely politics, but science as well. Science has got to show immediate and spectacular results to bolster the prestige of the régime in power. Science is no longer a disinterested activity but is – as something called 'Darwinism' is taught in Soviet schools – the struggle of man against nature led by the party. Everything is to be turned to the manipulation of environment. It is a sad but perhaps a hopeful thought that if technology cannot in fact thrive without pure science, then freedom will stay alive, or re-create itself, out of the sheer administrative need for freedom for scientists – however inefficient, tentative, and extravagant some of their activities may be, like the 'irresponsible behaviour' of so many free men. An élite of engineers and managers may find itself blaming the politicians or the party *apparat* for not being able 'to produce' enough pure scientists. This, however, is speculative fantasy. But the growing power of technological thinking in politics is fact.

There is also a type of technological thinking which may have little to do with scientism: those who think that *administration* can always be clearly separated from politics, and that if this is done, there is really very little, if anything, that politicians can do that administrators cannot do better. This is a very familiar view. It is the view of the servant who would not merely be equal, but who would be master, or of the administrator who feels constantly frustrated in *his* work by the interventions of politicians whom he will often, oddly, call theorists. He means by this that his experience teaches him better than those who try to tell him what should be done without his experience: speaking without experience is thus theorizing. Government could be so much better carried on by those who do the real work of the state. 'For forms of government let fools contest, whate'er is best administered is best' is the hackneyed and subversive slogan of this disliker of politics. So far, this is the familiar view of the expert. There are many such who believe that there is some training to be had which can teach a science of public administration. The civil servant is then as much a technician as the engineer. He may not profess to think that all problems are technical; he may see himself as the 'means-and-methods' man of some superior 'democratic decision-making body' – the familiar language of the social scientists. But what it amounts to is not that *all* decisions of government can be implemented 'scientifically', or as if by a definite and preconceived technique; but that government should only do those things which can be reduced to such a technique. The Leninist vision of the 'administration of things and not of men' will take place only if men are treated as things; 'the state will become a mere filing cabinet' when men can be treated simply as the contents of files.

There is also a type of rather well camouflaged technocrat who claims very forcibly to have a great contempt for such 'expertise'. He may even make a cult of the well-rounded amateur, versatile and wise, setting experience against 'so called experts' as well as politicians. He may think himself so anti-technical that he will even oppose any form of special training for higher civil servants.[5] This viewpoint is really pre-political. He knows the truth that the first duty of a government is to govern – which he may feel, quite rightly, is often insufficiently realized by the reforming politicians. But he stays in this pre-political stage of government without politics. So, of course, in a political society, he should; the civil servant should not get deeply involved in politics; but he must not exaggerate his importance. 'The essential character of government, and so of the administration by which alone it is effective, is a process of maintaining the unity of a political group,' writes an English civil servant. How true for government in general but – our

---

[5]See, for instance, C. H. Sisson, *The Spirit of British Administrators* (London 1959).

whole theme – how inadequate for political rule. The civil servant, we are told, 'is a man who has been trained to a practical operation' which is 'nothing less than the preservation of the state. He is, no less than any soldier, a man who must give his life to the Crown. That is what gives his task a permanent sense amidst the mutations of party politics.'[6] This is the humble arrogance of the gentleman indeed. The servant of the state is the permanent element amid the mutations of party politics ('party' politics is presumably even worse than ordinary politics). What business has an administrator to pledge his life to the Crown when he is quite simply employed by a politically elected government? People rarely offer to sacrifice themselves to a fiction. They seize hold of the fiction to achieve some position which is not political, or politically tenable. It is not administration but government itself which maintains order in any régime; and in a political régime it is the activity of politics itself which provides something permanent amidst the mutations. The administrator blames politicians for the very thing they can do so well – allow diversity and change amidst order.

Why is this view technological? It is technological because its holder thinks he knows best what is wanted because, like the engineer, it is his task to do what is wanted. It does not matter that he may attack technique in the sense of learning how to administer from books or some pseudo-science of public administration; for he is still tempted to believe that, as the fruit of experience, he possesses a unique knowledge which can be applied and can govern without politics. He thinks he has a technique of rule which is not arbitrary and yet which is not political.

Both this Mandarin type and the social scientist can make absurdly unwarranted claims for their own impartiality and for the efficacy of their knowledge. Theirs is another instance of an activity needed within politics claiming to be the whole of politics – which is, as we have seen, in fact to deny politics. Because they sincerely claim to have no doctrine or ideology, but only the efficiency and the permanent interest of the state in mind, they are often trusted more than they deserve. We all deserve to be distrusted in politics. And it is the particular lot of the administrator to be more distrustable than anyone. In quite simple human terms, if a man cannot stand this, he should change his job, not create a mystique of technical indispensability.

---

[6]Ibid., p. 23.

'Technology', then, confuses the question of the application of resources with their allocation. This application may be a technique, but it can be applied only after authoritative decisions have been made as to both the allocation of the product and of the resources to go into it. People are deceiving themselves if they do not realize that over the months and over the years, even if not for each particular day's business in front of one on the desk, these decisions are essentially political. It may be thought in some free societies that these decisions are in fact made by 'the market' – that economics is a science, telling us what we may not do. But it is a science only in the very simple but important sense that it can calculate the price of any social demand in terms of relinquished alternatives. But it cannot comment on the legitimacy of the various demands – even ones that may be 'economically restrictive' or 'economic nonsense'. The study of economics furnishes us with evidence relevant to any political decision about the allocation of resources, may even be said to furnish evidence necessary to any rational decision; but it cannot predetermine any decision. All resources are not economic, all alternatives are not priceable; freedom, for instance, we may properly say is in the long run beyond price; the desire for knowledge – which can have, God knows, the most unpredictable consequences – is quite unpriceable. People in unfree societies which have abolished or forbidden the institutional means of making political decisions may think that the ideology – Marxian science, for instance – determines these allocations, so that everything remains simply a problem of application. But this, however much believed, is simply an error. It does not describe what in fact happens. What they are in fact doing, faced with all sorts of complicated choices and alternatives as to how to allocate scarce resources, is to make political decisions without the institutions and procedures which register actual social demands honestly – a place for people to speak without fear for themselves or the interests of their group.

So those in political societies who apply the technologist's style of thought to the business of government have, in fact, taken for granted the political devices by which some things emerge as problems, and some other things are submerged as irrelevancies. Politics defines what the inhabitants of a state think should be the problems to be solved. They may not all be capable of solution. But it is a pity that so many of the experts or technologists who are called in to attempt the solution of some of these problems feel that they know best what order of priority should be attached to these attempts, and feel that politics impedes, rather than clears the way for, their use of their techniques. So many problems are only resolvable politically that the politician has special right to be defended against the pride of the engineer or the arrogance of the technologist. Let the cobbler stick to his last. We have a desperate need of good shoes – but too many bad dreams. And as the French anarchists used to say, 'only the one who wears the shoe, knows where it pinches.'

Chapter 6

A Defence of Politics against False Friends

Politics may need defending against certain of its friends. They meant to be genuine friends. Even if they do not always like to admit how well they know politics, yet in ordinary times they act politically, they argue among one another with great heat, but they observe certain conventions which avoid violence. They are each proud of their own existence and fully self-confident, yet normally they will admit that the other friends of politics at least restrain them from excess. But if politics reaches some crisis, then each of these rival friends may try to force on it an exclusive and jealous attachment – the bane of politics as much as of ordinary friendship. Each then offers some drastic remedies which show more care that the cure should be known to be by their system, than that it should respect and leave unchanged the character of the patient. There are occasions on which elements in such normally respectable political doctrines as conservatism, liberalism, and socialism can show themselves unhappy, not just with any particular political order – as it is their proper, polemical business to be, but with political activity itself. These normal allies of politics can occasionally forget themselves, and act in the way that once made Wellington say of his troops: 'I don't know if they scare the enemy, but by God – they certainly scare me.'

The non-political conservative

Consider the man who claims to be above politics. He recognizes that it must go on among others, but he himself is above it all. He is conserving the essential order of the state against all those politicians, lobbyists, and careerists who exude self-interest and intrude into statecraft. He is, indeed, prepared to toss these dogs some bones, to make positive use of patronage as an instrument of government, in order to carry on government at all. He says with Dr Johnson that politics is but a way of 'rising in the world'. If he despairs of getting rid of these *parvenus* and pillagers, yet he is sure that he himself is firmly established above such politics and knows how to maintain the state on an even keel; he can manage these 'little dogs' so long as his nerve lasts. He is a man who is animated by the most trusting view of himself and his class, and the most cynical view of all others. His image of the state is that of a ship which needs firm handling by its captain, constantly threatened by rough seas and by the sloth of its crew; not the classic image of a city, long settled behind thick walls, whose citizens are civilized in their habits, eclectic in their tastes.

This conservative is not a tyrannical man – at least to his own people; if he values discipline, yet he hates arbitrariness, or any reputation for arbitrariness. He is not an intolerant man – ideas of any kind may be canvassed so long as they do not make the masses more restless than they are already. Censorship is a necessary method of social control, but it need not apply to gentlemen or to inherently unpopular works; and he does not care enough about any general ideas to persecute for the truth's sake. His dislike of any fanaticism may prepare the ground for politics; but he despises politicians. Even in England he once considered that all politics was 'factious' and all opposition disloyal – only the enemies of the King's Government had politics. He asked God in the National Anthem to 'Confound their politicks, frustrate their knavish tricks.' This type of conservative has much in common with the administrator who distrusts the expert, but himself lays claim to an intangible knowledge, or code of behaviour superior to mere political activity. He may also be a soldier – like General Groener, who described the German army in 1931 as 'the one element of stability in a world of political flux'. He may be the priest of a national church, again considering himself to embody the permanent interests of the state as something apart from politics. The atheist Gibbon spoke well enough for his devout fellow-Tories when he praised 'the usefulness of Christianity to Civil Polity'.

Above all else, however, the conservative wants to appear as the well-bred product of a landed aristocracy. Property is then thought of as outside politics, something which should never be touched by political enactments. He covers himself with a mystique of property: property, meaning primarily landed property, gives a man the experience and responsibility of the care of tenants – it can almost become 'the cure of souls'. And property alone allows a man that leisure which is the condition for knowledge and independence. The argument is perennial. 'Leisure,' said Hobbes, 'is the Mother of Philosophy.' 'The wisdom of a learned man cometh by opportunity of leisure; and he that has lithe business shall become wise . . .', Burke quoted *Ecclesiasticus*: 'How can he get wisdom who holdeth the plough . . .?' From this is drawn the consequence that any franchise, as Cromwell and Ireton said to the dissident Colonels of their army in the Putney Debates of 1647, must have an 'eye for property'; must be given only to those who have a 'stake in the land' and thus 'a permanent interest in England'. For 'if all men shall vote equally, many shall soon pass to taking hold of the property of other men.' There are tradesmen and craftsmen who work with skill by their hands, again says *Ecclesiasticus,* and 'Without these cannot a city be inhabited'; yet 'They shall not be sought for in publick counsel. . . .' But if this long familiar argument is pressed too far, if it is adhered to as a fixed principle when circumstances change and the skilled worker demands a share in allocating the fruits of his necessary labour, then the response becomes inevitably what Colonel Rainborough replied to General Ireton: 'Sir, I see that it is impossible to have liberty but all property be taken away.' The attempt to put property above politics merely provokes the attempt to take away property without politics. Any such fixed principle is inherently unpolitical. It did not need Marx to teach us that disputes about the property relationships of society are one of the great causes of conflict in any state – the great business of politics to conciliate. But there is no fixed line that can be drawn; the only thing that can be insisted upon is that 'the property question' be settled (unsettled and resettled) politically. So there is no reason for the conservative to appear surprised and pained when other interests sometimes fail to appreciate why his sense of ineffable property should deserve special non-political respect. Then there is the conservative who makes a shibboleth of the fact that the first business of government is to govern. This is not a bad truth. But as often as liberals need reminding that it is a necessary truth, conservatives need reminding that it is not a sufficient truth. When the choice is really between any order and all anarchy, then it is enough just to govern; but more often the task of preserving a state must be seen in terms of governing well. Governing well means governing in the interests of the governed and, ultimately, there is no sure way of finding out which these interests are, but by representing them in the politically sovereign body; and there is no sure way of convincing people that all their interests may not be realizable together or at once, but by letting them try, letting them see for themselves the conflict of interests inevitable in any state. Again, if the government is to be strong, such politics must reach down to involve the very base of society. No group which is powerful can be permanently excluded from the franchise without driving it into sedition or breaking its spirit utterly. If the government is to govern, there are no excuses for not governing well. Revolution, certainly, is the breakdown of politics, not an accelerated type of politics. But revolution more often takes place through the breakdown of an existing but negligent style of government, as in the American, French, and Russian Revolutions, than for the ideal reasons which the party who come to power in the resulting anarchy will then enforce as the official history of the pre-revolutionary era. If the conservative would tell us that politics is a matter of managing established real interests, then it is no use his flattering the doctrinaire that revolutions are caused by 'abstract ideas', 'restless innovation' and 'philosophical mistakes'.[1] For the most usual cause of revolutions, when all is said and done, is not that some band of zealots – who come to power during or after the revolution – has pushed the old government away, because they thought they knew all the time where they were going and what was going to happen next (as the historians of the revolution whom they afterwards commission will tell us); but just that the old government, probably for a great variety of reasons, simply ceased to govern. And the most usual cause of failing to govern is simply not knowing what the governed want or will settle for, through not giving them adequate representation. Too often the revolutionary is the man who must create order in the chaos left by failed conservatives. Similarly the 'doctrinaire' can simply be the man who offers us reasons and explanations when the conservative has exhausted our patience with appeals to be trusted in the business which he believes he knows best – and yet is in fact mismanaging.

---

[1] See Michael Oakeshott, *Rationalism in Politics* (London 1962), *passim,* and Kedourie, *Nationalism,* op. cit.

The conservative quarrel with the doctrinaire in politics is one, then, which often reflects too much credit on both sides. They can both claim more for the importance of certain slogans than these slogans may deserve. The conservative as anti-doctrinaire often needs to make up his mind whether he deprecates 'political dogmas' because they cannot work at all, or because they can be made to work too well. The case for 'equality' can be derided as a dogma impossible of realization, the product of a misunderstanding more than of a programme; but it can also be studied as a product of a particular history and shown not to be a rational, preconceived first principle at all, but the summary of the suppressed aspirations of – might one say? – underdeveloped social groups. If this is so, if the doctrinaire in power, the Danton and the Robespierre, in fact builds with old bricks more than he is aware – is completing tendencies towards centralization already afoot in France of the *Ancien Régime*, then what matter that he writes and speaks so pretentiously; let us see what he really does. Consequences may or may not flow from what a man says. We too often seek to explain things as a product of reason and doctrine which can only be explained as a product of history. And, as for the doctrine itself, a political doctrine is 'doctrinaire' only if it excludes other alternatives, the possibility of changing course at all, by the scheme it proposes – or, of course, if it is simply impractical. The conservative is himself doctrinaire if he thinks that a particular order or connexion can or should be always maintained, if only the rulers remain (or become) just and merciful and the people trusting and deferential.

The conservative as anti-doctrinaire may appear to be on firmer ground when he treats of politics as a purely practical activity, as an enterprise which is purely empirical. Events are reacted to as they occur; theories are avoided, experience is everywhere and alone sought after (or, at least, praised). Here is a would-be practical man who does not pretend to even the apparent qualifications of the technologist in politics, but only to 'character' and 'intimations'. What even Edmund Burke called 'this cant of men and not of measures', is held to be the supreme political value. But, of course, no one is purely practical or purely empirical by any self-sufficient standard. To be practical at all, to drive a nail into a piece of wood, is to presume that it serves some purpose (even if the purpose is only play), is to have some prior idea of what hammers and nails can do and how wood reacts. To be purely empirical in politics is to presume to operate within a closed system of presuppositions and expectations. But the salient thing about the *practice* of politics is that no door is ever completely closed, and about the *theory* of politics is that it arises when closed societies are found unworkable or intolerable.

The man who claims to be purely empirical in politics – indeed in the study of politics too – is simply preserving uncritically the established order, is simply a conservative without doctrine. 'Empiricism' in this sense could be justly called 'the English fallacy'. The English empiricist is a blinkered horse grazing in a well-ordered island garden. There may be, perhaps, some general reason for thinking that there is little that needs doing urgently in this garden; but it is a strange way of not looking at the actual importance of new ideas and general ideas in terrain so much more rugged elsewhere. This blinkered empiricist deplores the fact that other peoples take doctrines so seriously.

Not all conservatives place this reliance on empiricism. Some are aware of its intrinsic capriciousness. Professor Michael Oakeshott tells us that: 'From a practical point of view . . . we may decry the style of politics which approximates to pure empiricism because we can observe in it an approach to lunacy.'[2] (Presumably only the lunatic without memory really tries to react, or has to react, to each event as it occurs as if it were a completely unique thing in itself.) Something is needed, he says, 'to set empiricism to work'. And that something is dependence 'upon a traditional manner of behaviour'. Politics is, then, as it were, a 'conversation with tradition', something we simply carry on with as part of the human condition, neither an argument nor a method for making new discoveries. We think that we are acting on first principles, but a little history can make us aware that they are neither first nor principles, but have their roots in actual political experience, however partial an abridgement they may prove to be of what is always a larger and more complex theme. We may think that we have high ulterior purposes, but we may in fact simply be enjoying what we are doing at the moment – like the pregnant girl in William Faulkner's *Light in August* we may not, really, be looking for the fled or future lover at all, but 'just travelling' – for the sheer joyful hell of it. 'Freedom,' Oakeshott tells us, 'is not a bright idea,' but something 'which is already intimated

---

[2]Oakeshott, op. cit., p. 115.

in a concrete manner of behaving.' Now there is much to be said for this view. It is plainly superior to an ideological understanding of politics, to any attempted 'pure empiricism' as well, and it chastens the over-zealous claims of any particular political doctrine. But it has the difficulty of being too true in the pleasant circumstances it fits and of scarcely fitting some other circumstances at all. It is too true in the sense that it purports to be a general characteristic of political activity – and it is. But it is so general as to be, if not vacuous, yet a truism, no possible guide to political conduct. Now, of course, the holder of such a view will claim, with a large measure of justice, that he does not mean to offer any vulgar guide to conduct. He may, with scornful modesty, say that it is 'impertinent' of academics – for this is a very academic view – to offer advice to politicians. Politics is simply politics. So it is. But it depends on what one means by politics. And it is simply not true, as we will see, that politics is always so intimately aligned with tradition. Tradition may be, in some sense, a necessary condition for politics, but it is very far from being a sufficient condition.

Tradition itself, however, furnishes the biggest obstacle to seeing much significance in this view of politics – beyond a poetic perception that a thing is what it is. For political tradition is to be considered not as a uniform, but as a coat of many colours. It is not even to be seen as a ship, but rather, to adapt a well-worn metaphor, as a convoy sailing together for mutual protection. Their business is plainly not, as the rhetoricians of *the* ship of state tell us, simply 'to keep afloat on an even keel' – even granted that with some neglected ships it is an achievement to stay afloat at all. For the ships' masters have not merely a memory of from whence they came, but they will usually have some idea of where they think they are going – and they may not merely change their course while at sea if the winds veer, but they may, thanks to modern technology, receive authoritative orders to alter their destinations entirely in response to some change in the terms of trade. And at every point of this noble metaphor of politics, the fact has to be stressed that we are dealing with a convoy. One reason why the idea of treating politics as tradition is misleading is that, far from there being no conscious goals in any political order, there may be too many; each ship has to be restrained, for the period of common danger, from trying to steer its own course.

There are always several traditions in any advanced or complex society. There is the tradition in England of the conservatives; but there is also the democratic tradition of what Mr Raymond Williams calls the 'Long Revolution', or of that ancient alliance of religion and political nonconformity which Algernon Sidney on the scaffold called 'That OLD CAUSE in which I was from my youth engaged, and for which Thou hast Often and Wonderfully declared Thyself'. In France there are the many traditions of the Revolution itself, anti-traditional in substance though they all are. And in America the traditionalism of anti-traditionalism, fed from a dozen tangled roots, is flagrant: American political tradition is, in substance, liberal. The traditionalist is right – too right. The most crazy, the most far-gone and far-left, the most inventive of theories and ignorant of history *youth* – even – can hardly help relive, to an astonishing degree, the style of long, long forgotten political saints and martyrs. Politically, for instance, it is often a weakness of Left Wing parties in free states that they neither understand nor claim how traditional they are – just as they are shy of even patriotism as distinct from nationalism. But the conservative's choice of being traditional or anti-traditional is meaningless – something one need never make up one's mind about, for the result is the same either way. The conservative scholar may think that he is simply making a point of general intellectual warning, with little direct relationship at all to political decisions: that we must always remember that all thought and action falls into some tradition of behaviour. But this argument is banal in the extreme. Indeed, if thus stripped down of all content and simply advocated as a method of studying politics, then the argument is circular, merely stating an identity: if everything is tradition, everything is – indeed – tradition. Then we need some other criteria to reduce the total flow of experience to recognizable and usable dimensions. More often, this academic conservatism is a great smuggler of content and substance under the guise of talking simply about method, education, and philosophy. 'Tradition', when left so undefined as being all tradition rather than particular traditions, becomes a concept very close to ideology. One offers a way of understanding everything; the other a way of explaining everything. Because everything is interrelated, both traditionalist and ideologist agree that nothing significant can be changed without changing everything. They simply draw different conclusions from the same inflated premise.

The conservative as traditionalist only rescues himself from the obvious plurality of tradition by talking about *the* tradition, usually a 'concrete' tradition of political behaviour – a word that is the mark of a Hegelian in trouble. But this only becomes an argument to show that there is a correct and good tradition which blends the 'above politics' kind of conservatism with the claim to have mysterious antennae which pick up intimations from the general will or the common good with insufferable prescience and sensitivity. The plain truth, however, is that what holds a free state together is neither general will nor a common interest, but simply politics itself. Through the rough-and-tumble of politics the varying traditions in a country, each with its own memories and purposes, strive for power with only a politic restraint. Politics is not really as subtle as the traditionalist would tell us – it is something much more rough-hewn and hard, more easily made and more easily marred. So the traditionalist would tell us that, since all is vanity, politics is simply a conversation with tradition. But in the unfamiliar mode of Oakeshottian irony we hear, in fact, a familiar hortatory voice telling us that for any politics there *should* be one dominant tradition. Otherwise the identification of political conservatism with traditionalism is little more than a pun. If all politics is traditional, then an actual conservative party or doctrine has to be understood, like any other party or doctrine, as the advocacy of particular social and economic doctrines in a particular time and place. *The* tradition then becomes seen as simply the tradition of the governing class.

The conservative is usually the last to deny the amount, after all, of sheer accident in the practice of politics and the history of states – all that which can suddenly, like a river in flood, upset the most settled policy and the most careful plans, all that Machiavelli meant by *'Fortuna'.* But the conservative has a quite unfounded optimism that tradition will usually be able to absorb such shocks; or, if not, he simply shrugs and says: *'après moi le déluge'* – a morbid realism that things may not work anyway which is often sloth and lack of imagination about how to try to shape events. The concept of tradition gives a poor picture indeed of the amount of inventiveness, innovation, and conscious dexterity which is necessary for any state to survive at all. The anthropologist can teach the political philosopher a great deal. There are very few communities, however primitive, in which the anthropologist does not find that custom serves a creative function of providing responses to new challenges to the survival of the community. Custom is a clearer concept than tradition to explain the relationship between the primary need of survival and the growth towards something fit to be called civilization. States survive only by constant adaptation to changing circumstances. Events may force us to choose. We may not be able to justify all of our choices, but we do not just sit back and enjoy the flow of experience. Tradition may be a guide, but alone it is a poor stimulus for survival – for survival at all can often demand a highly conscious degree of change, whether in agricultural techniques, in military strategy, in the pattern of trade, in the ownership of industry, or in the framework of governmental institutions. The traditionalist's polemic against the rationalist and the doctrinaire is almost always a valuable corrective; but it is not something sufficient in itself. The rationalist does at times have to insist that there is a limit to the number of patches that can be put on an old suit of clothes. Neither doctrine nor tradition are sufficient in themselves. The relationship between them, and between the many forms of them which may exist at any time, is politics itself. Let us be bold in our claim that politics is the 'master-science'; it espouses habit for security, but it must also love lively inventiveness so as to deal with what fortune may offer.

There is then a time of politics when it is not merely necessary 'to reform in order to preserve' as Burke's great maxim had it, but actually to create in order to preserve. John Adams once looked back with ironic justice to the debates of the Continental Congress in 1775:

> I knew that everyone of my friends . . . had at that time no idea of any other government but a contemptible legislature in one assembly, with committees for executive magistrates and judges . . . I answered by sporting offhand a variety of short sketches of plans which might be adapted by the conventions. . . . I had in my head and at my tongue's end as many projects of government as Mr Burke says the Abbé Sieyès had in his pigeon-holes, not, however, constructed at such length, nor laboured with his metaphysical refinements. I took care, however, always to bear my testimony against every plan of an unbalanced government.

Here is the real politician in a circumstance where tradition alone gives little help. There are rival plans. One simply has to choose the best there is; plans cannot be avoided. Experience has to be distilled into some abstract principles, some criteria at least for the judging of plans. Small wonder that the English conservative has usually had to treat American politics as if they did not exist. When everything has been said about how very traditionally minded were the American Founding Fathers, in correction to some earlier American myths about themselves, yet it is still crystal clear, contrary to the conservative myth of tradition, that the deliberate invention of institutions took place and had to take place, but by political means and for the sake of political order.

Then it is not always possible to preserve a political connexion without reforming or altering the basic framework of government to a degree which conservatives have often found intolerable. There are times when prudence and prescription fly apart. How often have Burke's great pleas for prudence in dealing with the American colonies been taken as truths of politics and tone of real conservatism? Do not stand on pride or points of law, he argued, but conciliate and be magnanimous: 'Again, and again, revert to your old principles – seek peace and ensure it – leave America, if she has taxable matter in her, to tax herself. I am not here going into distinctions of rights, nor attempting to mark their boundaries. I do not enter into these metaphysical distinctions; I hate the very sound of them. . . .' But how easy to forget that this kind of appeal to lay aside legal right is also an appeal to the governed simply to trust without guarantees. And it is flagrantly clear that by 1775 this simply would not work: the trust has disappeared entirely. The Americans required guarantees that they could not be taxed but by their own representatives, not simply that if better men were in the saddle in Westminster they would be spared. The dogma of Parliamentary sovereignty lay in the way – as much to Burke as to Lord North; the reluctance of the conservative to think of Federal solutions obstructed any possible political solution. Written constitutional guarantees would not have meant the end of politics – only of one type of politics. And the only other way of maintaining the connexion with America failed because, after all, the degree of military strength required was not possible while England itself was politically divided on 'the American question'.

Conservatism is thus a doctrine of politics like any other. It is almost always partly true, but its precise truth will vary from circumstance to circumstance. It may profess to be anti-doctrinaire, but it will in any particular formulation contain pieces of arbitrary dogma – like Oakeshott's 'tradition' and Burke's 'sovereignty'. If it merely counsels us to consult experience, then it is true for all types of politics, and does not carry us very far. Where it can carry one far is in circumstances which are far from universal. This good friend of politics has deserved special care simply because he so often claims to know politics in the sense I defend better than any other doctrine – so he often may, but he may often exhibit a too jealous and too narrow attachment. The conservative contributes to politics like anyone else by trying to gain or maintain his interests – but his claim to be non-political only invites the suspicion that he does not always act in a political manner. He likes to be thought above politics. He prefers to settle public matters privately.

The a-political liberal

If there is a conservative who expects too little, there is a liberal who expects too much. He wishes to enjoy all the fruits of politics without paying the price or noticing the pain. He likes to honour the fruit but not the tree; he wishes to pluck each fruit – liberty, representative government, honesty in government, economic prosperity, and free or general education, etc. – and then preserve them from further contact with politics. He may treat certain things as natural rights – thus by definition outside politics – or he may think that politics is simply the acts of political parties and politicians – thus narrowing the scope of politics drastically and unrealistically. This liberal is somewhat close to the technocrat in that he believes in a clear line of distinction between politics and administration, indeed between the state and society. But steeply though he draws such lines, he always leaves some place for politics. He merely tries to scrub it down, clean it up, and tether it firmly until this terrier becomes a fairly lifeless, if respectable, lapdog. He overestimates the power of reason and the coherence of public opinion; he underestimates the force of political passions and the perversity of men in often not seeming to want what is so obviously good for them. He is not fond of political parties – when he joins them he sternly resists the corruption of principle by practicality. He tends to think in terms of an enlightened public opinion working on clear and simple representative institutions. The politician gets squeezed out; he is a mere intermediary, not a creative force; indeed the very word 'politician' in American English has retained its invidious meaning of the eighteenth century. The politician is a 'fixer', and this is somehow thought bad even by businessmen. This liberal will join in political crusades to clean up this or that, but he abhors the political regular. If he has a party at all, as in England at the moment, then it is a party of anti-party. He praises a man for saying that he would rather be right than President, quite failing to see what a dangerous and irresponsible attitude that can be. Here is a political type, in other words, whose besetting vices are self-righteousness and prudery. 'We are all here on earth to help each other,' W. H. Auden ironically remarked, 'but what the others are here for, God only knows.'

The varieties of political experience are too great for such prudery. Politics involves genuine relationships with people who are genuinely other people, not tasks set for our redemption or objects for our philanthropy. They may be genuinely repulsive to us, but if we have to depend upon them, then we have to learn to live with them. The liberal tries to ignore these unpleasantnesses – at the cost, so often, of failing to govern at all. The liberal is a man who would govern, or would be a member of a responsible political party, if only every issue did not float up into his mind as an issue of first principle. This can lead to a dangerous incapacity for action – a refusal to use force, even in the defence of political values. The tragic fumbling of the French Assembly in face of Louis Napoleon and, a century later, in face of De Gaulle; the incapacity for action of Asquith's Liberal Government faced by Conservative sedition in Ireland; the fear and legal formalism of the Weimar Republic faced by the Nazis; and the terrible slowness, in terms of world politics, of the American executive to ensure the legal rights of coloured citizens, these are all classic examples of liberal squeamishness and prudery. The great liberal *Manchester Guardian* in 1931 solemnly counselled Hindenburg that it would be undemocratic to exclude the Nazis from the government since they were the largest single party. And plenty of 'naive liberals' and 'decent conservatives' in Germany believed that somehow the exercise of legal power would *inevitably* make the Nazis act in a normal political manner.[3] The liberals' narrowness of vision supported their dislike of themselves using power to defend 'mere politics'.

The prudery of liberals about politics can also lead to failure to understand the needs of the less respectable elements of society.

[3]See Brigitte Granzow, *A Mirror of Nazism: British Opinion of the Emergence of Hitler, 1929–33* (Gollancz 1964), *passim*.

There were some things they simply did not like to look at: trade unions in Great Britain; the new immigrants in the United States. The English liberal editor, W. T. Stead, once found his deckchair during an Atlantic crossing next to Boss 'Tiger Dick' Croker. Stead expounded, no doubt, the usual views of honest men on Tammany, but was honest indeed to record Mayor Croker's reply:

> 'What is the one fact which all you English notice first of anything in our country? Why, it is that that very crowd of which we are speaking, the minority of cultured leisured citizens, will not touch political work – no, not with their little finger. All your high principles will not induce a mugwump to take more than a fitful interest in an occasional election. The silk stockings cannot be got to take a serious hand continuously in political work. They admit it themselves. Everyone knows it is so. Why, then, when mugwump principles won't even make mugwumps work, do you expect the same lofty motives to be sufficient to interest the masses in politics?'

> 'And so,' I said, 'you need to bribe them with spoils?' 'And so,' he replied, 'we need to bribe them with spoils. Call it so if you like. Spoils vary in different countries, here they take the shape of offices. But you must have an incentive to interest men in the hard daily work of politics, and when you have our crowd you have got to do it in one way, the only way that appeals to them. . . .'[4]

This is a remarkable passage. For it reminds us that politics has to be taken as it comes, or else abandoned. But even when it comes like Croker's, it is serving some good purpose. Here was a way of bringing the Irish immigrant poor into the national life, a way of giving them some power so that they could shape as well as be shaped by those already long arrived in America. Politics was the way of advancement of the socially excluded – a way of gaining respect for them, crooked or not, out of respect for their power. The corrupt democratic politician like Croker seems a hard case of politics to defend, though his kind deserve thanks from the American liberal for at least helping prevent the rise of a political labour movement – England de-classed its Crokers too

---

[4]Quoted in M. T. Werner, *Tammany Hall* (New York 1928), p. 449.

quickly. But he must be defended against both the liberal prude who shies away from real political problems – him to whom class and ethnic discrimination 'do not really exist' – and against the man who would rather have honest autocracy than corrupt politics. Most liberals, one suspects, would prefer autocracy to corruption, because it is tidier and because it may honour personal virtues more – like honesty and sincerity (in which the liberal places an excessive trust: 'if men were honest and sincere, all politics would disappear' – says the liberal). But corruption is at least a human value, at least a loophole of choice or chance, compared to the awful inflexibility of an unchangeable government by dedicated moralists. The real objection to corruption in politics is not that it is an immoral act in itself – so is killing a fellow creature, even if we are dressed in uniform to do it; but that it may distort the representativeness of politics so that effective, responsive government becomes impossible or exceedingly hard. In a totalitarian state, corruption can actually preserve a germ of freedom.

The liberal, then, wishes for the ends of politics, the reconciliation of freedom and order, but he is often unwilling to will the means. He piously wishes in 'the interests of the individual' to take the politics out of – oh – local government, the schools, the trade unions, business associations, newspaper ownership, churches, indeed pretty well everything except the Parliament or National Assembly. And there are even now worried idealists who would like to take the parties out of politics, or rather to make all elected representatives independent of party. This last demand is little more than a device to avoid the clear absurdity of asking to take the politics out of politics (unless he becomes, at this point, the autocrat or technocrat meaning to take politics out of government). The Member of Parliament, he says, should make up his own mind freely as an individual – though it is not always clear why anyone actually in politics should be required to imitate the anarchist or the anchorite.

The liberal, then, has been fertile in devices for putting politics at one side. His jealousy for the purity of liberty is so great that he tries to keep such a man-of-the-world as politics away from her. His love of liberty can be superb and confident in every respect, except in relation to politics itself. For in liberalism as a doctrine, the goals are worthy but it offers a description and understanding of politics which is inadequate. The liberal rightly protests at every persecution of a person for his political opinions. But these opinions are seen as valuable because they are personal – as if political opinions exist on the same level of experience as moral or religious opinions. The fact that they derive, if they really are political, from some group interest or ideal, is deplored. 'Individualism' becomes not just a false description of political behaviour, but a dogma – a completely illicit inference from the empirical fact that each human being is unique. The liberal asks a man to consult his own self-interest – as did the utilitarians – or to try to will the common good – as did the later liberals; but he wishes to take away the corporate means by which these views in fact arise. Strictly speaking, there is no political self-interest, and no political common good. Politics arises only because neither accidental self-interest, nor some arbitrary idea of the common good, provides a sufficient warrant to govern a free community. Individualism is not by itself a political doctrine. A man is a man because he is not something else. His self-identity is part of the human condition. Politics does not give him this, so it cannot take it away. Politics must respect individuality, rather than try to dissolve it away, as the ideologist attempts; but no particular style of politics follows from the great and simple fact of self-identity. Politics itself does depend on some assertive self-identity, but simply because all acts are acts of individual men. The differing interests which create politics, however, are group interests within a known area which cannot be treated as a total moral and social unity. This many liberals have never faced. For obviously the interest of a group is a far more rough and ready thing than the niceness and preciseness with which some people, so they tell us, can read the book of their own conscience. The liberal, as we said, likes the smooth fruits without wishing to care for the gnarled tree.

There is a sense, of course, in which we are nearly all liberals – we love liberty and we try to be tolerant; just as there is a sense in which we are nearly all conservatives. But liberalism has been a far more precise doctrine of politics than many are now prepared to remember. And much of the dogmatic lumber which liberals would like to abandon is concerned with this very business of trying to put things outside politics. The liberal is more personally modest than the conservative, but more publicly inventive; he has always sought to put some laws of nature or constitutional laws outside politics, to bind even himself. At one time he believed, with Locke, that 'life, liberty, and property', or with Jefferson that 'life, liberty, and the pursuit of happiness' were natural rights outside politics and government. Every known government must in fact legislate in ways that, to some degree, take away the lives of subjects, their liberty, and their property. The liberal might reject the idea of natural rights but put in its place some idea of a natural order – an economic system which if left substantially free from state intervention would lead to such increasing prosperity as to make politics become almost unwanted. The liberal's picture of economics existing independently of politics only paved the way for Marx's assertion of the primacy of economics over politics. Or he might believe, as in the radical liberal break from *laissez faire,* that there were simple electoral arrangements which could guarantee social harmony. At all times, the liberal has placed very great stress on the idea of a written or at least a fundamental constitution. For liberty to exist there must be some things which the government is legally prevented from doing. Liberals have defeated themselves in constant attempts to make final reforms – of the franchise, or fixed legal definitions of the scope of government intervention in economic life. But while it is of the essence of politics that everything cannot be treated politically at once, yet it is quite arbitrary to try to remove definite spheres of human activity from any possibility of political intervention or influence. Indeed, it is quite impossible to do so. Politics, as we have said, is the predominant but not omnipotent social activity; yet this predominance must be free to turn in any direction if the need arises, either in terms of survival, or in terms of a clash of interests which cannot be ignored, which must be conciliated somehow. Religion, the liberal says, should be taken out of politics. The United States Constitution built a great 'wall of separation' between Church and State. But can it go so far as to prevent people making religious issues in politics? Obviously not, without destroying liberty. It can prevent the State giving direct aid to a church, but it cannot prevent co-religionists from giving direct aid to particular politicians – from whom they may not expect material favours at all, but only representation, ethnic or religious justification. If the Catholic Church and Catholic politicians in America campaign for Federal aid to parochial high schools, no amount of saying that this is unconstitutional can prevent it from becoming a political issue which then has to be dealt with in political terms. And if any group so large is frustrated in all its ambitions, though it might have ambitions more easily settled or granted than the schools question, the risk arises that it will cease to act politically. So much of politics is the ability to turn impossible demands (in a given circumstance) into possible substitutes.

The arbitrage of politics is made much easier in advanced or complicated societies by the fact that few people are members of only one group, and the political interests of their groups may clash. This reflection adds to the absurdity of the traditional liberal picture, still alive in liberal rhetoric, of the state as the servant of society and of society as composed of isolated individuals all in a direct relationship with the state. Marxism here merely stands on the shoulder of liberalism in prophesying the eventual reign of (economic) society itself, finally emancipated from the meagre (political) state apparatus required by the great liberal philosophers and economists. There is, of course, no such thing as society in this sense. It is an abstraction expressing the fact that there is some relationship between various group interests in a given territory. It is not itself a group like other groups and in so far as it assumes a general relationship, this relationship is a product of politics or some other type of rule. The liberal has an antipathy to group interests which makes his theories of society inferior descriptions to those of the conservative or the socialist. His wide canvas of 'society' obscures the social question. And his claim that society is logically prior to the state begs the entire question of how politics holds divided societies together without destroying diversity.

The liberal's distrust of the State frequently leads him to neglect the public sector of interest and expenditure. If the totalitarian ideologist forces public power into every private issue, the liberal tries to cut down all public power except where it serves private interests. The liberal neglects the public sector and inevitably stirs up those in need of public help and public care to distrust and resist the whole political system. As Professor Galbraith has argued, the liberal builds an affluent society on private splendour and public squalor. The liberal is so much in love with liberty that he can too easily neglect to make use of the public power of politics to maintain the external social conditions in which abstract liberty becomes meaningful to the many.

Politics, then, the liberal is right, is a limited activity. But he is wrong to think that these limits can be expressed precisely in any general rule; such rules are themselves political attempts to compromise and conciliate rival forces in a particular time and circumstance. Politics cannot embrace everything; but nothing can be exempted from politics entirely.

The anti-political socialist

Socialism as a theory of politics is never less than a strong criticism of the narrowness of conservatism and of the generalities of liberalism. It is significant that conservative parties stay in power, as in Britain, by assimilating socialist measures – 'conservative men and socialist measures' is a potent political formula. And socialists have themselves assimilated liberalism and speak more often of fulfilling liberalism than of destroying it. Liberties, it is held, have meaning only if they can be exercised; liberties are meaningless while poverty limits the life of the majority to the narrow toil of mere survival; they become significant only amid some broad equality both of opportunity and condition. For political régimes to be stable, the opportunity for the habits of freedom has to be extended from the few to the many. Indifference to human suffering discredits free régimes; and if people are prevented by protective dogmas of 'property' or 'free enterprise' from expanding production and attempting a more equitable distribution of goods, then they will seek other dogmas which promise these things. All this, in the belief of this writer, is good. But the characteristic danger of socialist parties and thinkers is an impatience which breeds a quest for certainty and a contempt for politics. They can become impatient with the slowness of political methods and they rediscover the tempting Marxist position that politics is but a sham or conspiracy by which the bourgeoisie tries to pervert or delay the advance of equality. J. S. Mill in his *Representative Government* wrote:

> It is not much to be wondered at if impatient or disappointed reformers, groaning under the impediments opposed to the most salutary public improvements by the ignorance, the indifference, the intractableness, the perverse obstinacy of a people, and the corrupt combinations of private interests armed with the powerful weapons afforded by free institutions, should at times sigh for a strong hand to bear down all these obstacles, and compel a recalcitrant people to be better governed.

The actual record of social democratic administrations has been remarkably free from utopianism or from vast assaults on liberty in the name of progress. This actual record is, admittedly, a very small one, almost entirely confined to countries of Western European experience or influence: the Scandinavian countries, one majority government in Great Britain, the strong case of New Zealand, the precarious case of Weimar Germany, and some short-lived episodes in the French Third Republic – apart from some régimes in Latin America about which it is very hard to generalize. An Englishman has some excuse, however, for attaching peculiar importance to the case of the British Labour Government of 1945–51. For it was the strongest socialist government there has ever been in a leading industrial power. It arose, like the other social-democratic régimes, in a context already political. Social democracy has been, as it were, an extension of existing political habits and values, not a reversal or a sudden challenge to non-political régimes. The exercise of power in a free society is a great teacher of responsibility. The leadership of the British Labour party, though it did not lose all sense of vision, had certainly acquired by 1950 a remarkable sense that politics is the art of the possible. The main source of wonder about that administration was not that they went as far as they did in great acts of nationalization, but that they were so uninventive in social reforms, particularly in relation to education.

Socialist rhetoric, then, has been more frightening (to those who cultivate their fears) than socialist practice. Rhetoric is the great sword of opposition. But this is not to deny that long oppositions incubate anti-political spirit. 'Oppression maketh a wise man mad'; prolonged opposition makes a good man desperate and fanciful. The rank and file of the British Labour movement is rich indeed in 'saints'. The 'saint' is someone who wishes to find principles worth sacrificing himself for. He may think that he has them already, but more often he will admit that he is still 'a seeker' after some new and blazing light. He likes to sound tough-minded and realistic about politicians, but somewhat like the non-political conservative with his intimations, the 'saint' can only live in the hope of future illuminations in which all things, from the first to the last, will be made plain. And this psychology – which has its own history and tradition – even breaks right outside the actual organizations of Labour movements. As in the so-called 'New Left' in Britain at the moment, it can reject all such real political attachments as corruptive of the pure spirit of socialist principle. Not until the Labour Party is reborn will the saints condescend to enter into its Kingdom. So, cutting themselves off from real hope of actual political experience or influence, they tend to scorn political methods and indulge in what they call theoretical thinking which is, in fact, mainly visionary thinking. 'Realism' thus becomes the conviction that it may be necessary to suppress liberty, to destroy opposition, on a vast and violent scale, before anything of real good can come. They brood upon revolution like a fond nightmare and think themselves realists when they repeat, in constantly reinvented forms, Robespierre's aphorism that one cannot make an omelette without breaking eggs. This is not to deny, particularly in their conduct (which is fresh, cheerful, and delightful), their passionate love of liberty; but they pretend that revolutions, 'transitional periods', 'worlds in the making' are the normal state of affairs for which their talents are uniquely suited. They leap too quickly to the defence of every politically unnecessary injustice and bloodshed committed by the Soviets and, best of all, by an armed bohemian like Castro, with the *a priori* claim that such acts are necessary for economic progress. They are not themselves aware how much they distrust actual politics, so they are being for ever taken in by ideologists whose hatred of politics and freedom is quite genuine. They think in terms of stark contrasts of good and bad, moralizing every political issue so that every bad act ennobles someone – *because* the British attack on Suez was to be condemned, therefore the Dictator Nasser had his praises sung; *because the* American connivance in the unsuccessful invasion of Cuba was to be condemned, therefore Castro was beatified.

Theirs is the tradition of 'that stubborn crew of errant saints', as caricatured long ago by Samuel Butler in *Hudibras,* the puritan knight:

> Such as do build their Faith upon
> The Holy Text of *Pike* and *Gun,*
> Decide all Controversies by
> Infallible *Artillery*;
> And prove their Doctrine Orthodox
> By Apostolic *Blows* and *Knocks*;
> Call Fire and Sword and Desolation,
> *A godly-thorough-Reformation. . . .*

Much of this violence is purely rhetorical; but it does leave some mark on their conduct. If they are not complacent like the conservatives, or prudish like the liberals – they will go everywhere and look at every stratum of society, their sympathies are keener and wider; yet their attitude becomes pharisaical. If people will not live up to their standards and principles, so much the worse for the people. 'Better,' one hears, 'that the Labour Party never win another election than that it abandon socialist principles.' I do not need to press my argument too far; the point is very simply that such an attitude is not political. They pursue, in the terms of Max Weber's distinction, an ethic of ultimate ends rather than an ethic of responsibility. They scorn 'purely political' considerations: the fact that there are, in any political community, a variety of different interests and moral ends which must be reconciled, if one is to act politically at all; if not, then ignored for a time, or destroyed for ever. They do not believe in political action – which is, indeed, compromise, even though it can be creative compromise: to build a better future out of a wide and discriminating sympathy for all the best elements in the past. They believe, instead, in moral gestures and demonstrations. They appear before the people, but they are not of the people. The ethic of ultimate ends in politics is, at its best, the phariseeism latent in pacifism; at its worst, it is the ruthlessness of Stalinism. They judge things by what is said more than by what is done – thus they appear almost irredeemably sentimental about the Soviet Union. 'Where there is no vision', indeed, 'the people perish.' But the vision needs to be a persuasive vision, not a strident, intolerant, denunciatory vision. The vision must be of people as they are, so hard to love, not the perverse desire to offend and denounce them in favour of a vision of an abstract people who will gamble, telly-view, and motor-mortgage themselves no more. They wish to build People's Palaces, but not homes that actual people wish to live in. They indulge themselves in love for humanity, but are embarrassed by men.

The ultimate absurdity of this kind of political anti-politics is a style of behaviour which I do not think it too parochial to call 'student politics'. It is a style recognizable in other lands and in other times. It is the style of the amateur (who avoids real political work) joined to that of the enthusiast (who wants a doctrine and 'a cause' more than he wants criteria for judging between doctrines and causes). It is the style of those who think more of building 'New Jerusalem in England's green and pleasant land' than of the more humdrum, limited but immediate benefits which actually winning an election might bring to the electorate. 'Student politics' is the politics of affirmation. Groups must be got, typically student groups themselves, whatever their nominal purpose, to affirm certain principles or 'their stand' on each and every great issue of the day. If necessary, groups must be invented to do just this. Such a process of affirmation is quite endless. A judgement has to be delivered on everything of any conceivable importance. This affirmation usually carries with it a certain arrogance that they – as youth – have a particular right to be heard – as youth; for they are the next generation, or through the positive power of *in*experience they have the innocent-eye, a Rousseauistic purity in a corrupt and artificial age – or some such nonsense. And all this usually goes with a complete forgetfulness that such politics is not really politics at all. Their attitude to political involvement is like that of the coy maid of the story towards marriage; they dart between fears too deep and hopes too high. There is almost nothing that can do less harm or good to man or beast, or which has less political power, than students' politics. They can, indeed, occasionally pass from affirmation to demonstration, thus setting some real problems for the police and striving desperately – almost as an end in itself – to 'catch the public eye', that is to get a paragraph in an evening paper. The making of gestures becomes an end in itself. From this type of political education politics becomes seen as a series of great moral occasions on which one lends one's voice to a protest, or – in societies more dull but righteous – to a valedictory address to one's leaders or to some foreign delegation of similar affirmers. Thank God and alas, politics is not really like that. Here then, once again, is the pseudo-politics of large issues. Only large issues are considered worthy of attention – *the* bomb, *the* race question, *the* problem of the underdeveloped areas, etc. – a state of mind generous, beyond doubt, but precarious and quite unpolitical. The politician must insist, whether he risks being thought boring or just immoral, that precisely because all these issues are important, genuine advance or control will take time, patience, and even pain at choices of where effort must be made at any moment, always at the expense of something else, since we do live in a world, as yet, where time, energy, and resources are limited, but where demands seem infinite.

The voice of student politics in Britain, for instance, says 'Ban the Bomb', with fantastic disregard of a level of scientific and technological knowledge in nuclear physics which makes 'banning' about as sensible as urging the abolition of all hemp, steel, and electricity in order to make capital punishment impossible. The problem of the military use of atomic power is a problem of *control,* not of all or nothing. But control is a complicated political problem – so abandon politics and 'Ban the Bomb', indeed unilaterally, just to make no mistake that one is not interested in politics or diplomacy in any form. It is characteristic of 'student politics', of this whole type of anti-political socialism, that its followers do not use their skills, as one might expect, in ever drawing up plans or schemes of control, or even in simply discussing criteria for priorities in action among so many real alternatives; rather, they tend to treat each issue as it comes up as a matter of 'principle', beyond political compromise – and then drop it and pass on to the next act of affirmation. They are as suspicious of anyone who professes to study 'weapon systems', their use and control, as is the non-political conservative. This unnatural alliance is strengthened by the fact that most of the apostles of 'strategic studies' are American (here is only one of several points, indeed, on a great circle where the anti-political socialist and the non-political conservative seem to join hands as a matter of principle to deny any middle ground of actual political responsibility).

The man who treats everything as a matter of principle cannot be happy with politics. The man who says 'we cannot compromise until we have gained "x" or "y" ', or that' "a" and "b" must never be given up' is acting unpolitically, even though he may be playing a part in a political system. Whoever says 'we must never compromise our ideals' is either dooming himself to frustration or pledging himself to authoritarianism. Ideals are valuable as ideals and not as plans for a new order of immediate things. And ideals should not be confused with the means to their attainment. By all means let us never compromise a genuine ideal – 'true equality' or 'social justice' indeed. But let us not then say that 'more nationalization' or 'democracy' are first principles which can never be abandoned or modified. For these things are only relative means to what we may take to be absolute ends (there is no need, as we shall see, for the defender of politics to take sides on whether such absolute ends or ideals are meaningful or not); their applicability must vary with time and place. The man who speaks the language of absolute demands – say 'a guaranteed living wage' or 'the right of property' (or of compensation for property taken) – should at least be expected to realize that these things are gainable or relinquishable in a multitude of different forms. They are, in a word, negotiable – political, not total, commitments. To entertain politics at all is inevitably to enter into a world of morality in which one is aware of sacrifice as much as of aspirations (and at times 'absolute principles' may have to be sacrificed as much as material goods and personal pleasures – for some worth-while purpose); and in which one is aware of public responsibility as well as of private conscience. It is said that someone asked Lincoln once why he looked 'so sad and so wise'. He replied: 'because I know I can't get everything I want.'

To descend to a more immediate political level, to consider for a moment a precise politics, rather than to continue to attack the enemies and the false friends of politics, may be pardonable since by so doing we can begin our praise of politics. The British Labour Party after its electoral defeat in 1959 was thought to be in the midst of a unique crisis.

Week after week for almost two years members of this party seemed to be tearing themselves to pieces with very little need for outside help. Quarrels continued – and still do – between those who spoke of going back (or forward) to 'first principles' of socialism and those who talked about revisionism and modernization. Both sounded as doctrinaire as the other, both talked in terms of *the true* constitution of the party, and both claimed to express the true nature or history of the movement. And 'both' has been itself a simplification of many rival factions forming on this and that principle, one moment in alliance with other factions, another moment opposed, as the argument has shifted to different ground. The curious thing was that few commentators disputed with the journalists that this was, indeed, a unique crisis. In fact, the smallest degree of historical perspective should convince one that the British Labour Party and the Labour movement has always been very much like this. There is something almost comic in the belief that there is a 'Left' or a 'Right' of which either one or the other must and can win a clear victory if the party is to survive or to win elections. For the Labour Party has found its support in all sorts of different places. It has never been a party of a single doctrine. And even if that single doctrine is called socialism (there are in fact many socialist doctrines), it should be obvious that this is only one part of the actual Labour movement. The main motivating power has always been the desire, as it was when the party was founded, simply to get more representation of organized labour in Parliament – organized labour including some very unsocialistic trade unions. The Labour movement in Britain has been a remarkably wide coalition, both of interests and of ideals, held together by a common sense of injustice arising from the monopoly of power once held by the Conservative and Liberal Parties and by their lack of sympathy or response to working-class needs and working-class prestige. At no time was the Labour Party ever 'truly socialist' – a party of a single doctrine. The many voices of nonconformist and anti-establishment England joined together in the coalition of the Labour movement.[5]

To think of the growth and survival of British Labour is to be impressed not with the efficacy of a single doctrine, but with the wonder of politics. It was acting politically that bound these forces together into a party of which, all too obviously, an intellectualized socialism was only one part.

---

[5] I leave this passage exactly as I wrote it in 1961 – foresight, not hindsight, or rather a simple application of thinking in political terms.

It was an essential part; it may well have been and could be again, the driving force; but it was not the whole of the machine. And most political machines or parties are rather like that; certainly in the eyes of an ideologist, they are coalitions – always insufficiently unified. (And much of the misunderstanding about political parties arises from the natural tendency of the parties themselves to try to discredit each other by picturing each other as far more doctrinaire than they can possibly be.) Coalitions need ruling politically. This is the truth of politics which a profane old doctrinaire, Jimmie Maxton, once recognized, but was apparently ignored not merely by the 'saints' but also by the late Hugh Gaitskell: 'A man who can't ride two bloody horses at once has no right to a job in the bloody circus.' Politics has rough manners, but it is a very useful thing.

*

We have criticized here certain styles or tendencies in conservative, liberal, and socialist doctrines. The entire doctrines do not stand condemned. And even where they might seem, when considered alone, to challenge the political way of rule, yet they rarely in fact appear alone. None of them has a permanent tendency towards that real hatred of politics which characterizes ideological thought and totalitarian doctrines. They seek to persuade or exclude opposition, but not to destroy it. They are normally content to work in a political system with other parties or doctrines pulling and pushing them, perhaps only a little but still some, this way and that. A political system may be sufficiently well grounded in history, habit, and belief to withstand much unconsciously unpolitical or even anti-political behaviour. (A statesman may even think that he is acting according to some ideological principles; but if he is subject to political pressures, his actual behaviour may be more reasonable than his rhetoric.) Political doctrines are products of time and circumstances; there are occasions when elements of them all seem needed. But this does not make it sensible to try to synthesize them into some perfect political packet; for they do represent different interests and their common acceptance of political methods does not in the least imply agreement on anything more fundamental than that. This, perhaps, is our whole argument.

Chapter 7
In Praise of Politics

And every man that striveth for the mastery is temperate in all things.

ST PAUL

In the prison of his days
Teach the free man how to praise.

W. H. AUDEN, In Memory of W. B. Yeats

Politics deserves much praise. Politics is a preoccupation of free men, and its existence is a test of freedom. The praise of free men is worth having, for it is the only praise which is free from either servility or condescension. Politics deserves praising as – in Aristotle's words – 'the master-science', not excusing as a necessary evil; for it is the only 'science' or social activity which aims at the good of all other 'sciences' or activities, destroying none, cultivating all, so far as they themselves allow. Politics, then, is civilizing. It rescues mankind from the morbid dilemmas in which the state is always seen as a ship threatened by a hostile environment of cruel seas, and enables us, instead, to see the state as a city settled on the firm and fertile ground of mother earth. It can offer us no guarantees against storms encroaching from the sea, but it can offer us something worth defending in times of emergency and amid threats of disaster.

Politics is conservative – it preserves the minimum benefits of established order; politics is liberal – it is compounded of particular liberties and it requires tolerance; politics is socialist – it provides conditions for deliberate social change by which groups can come to feel that they have an equitable stake in the prosperity and survival of the community. The stress will vary with time, place, circumstance, and even with the moods of men; but all of these elements must be present in some part. Out of their dialogue, progress is possible. Politics does not just hold the fort; it creates a thriving and polyglot community outside the castle walls.

Politics, then, is a way of ruling in divided societies without undue violence. This is both to assert, historically, that there are some societies at least which contain a variety of different interests and differing moral viewpoints; and to assert, ethically, that conciliation is at least to be preferred to coercion among normal people. But let us claim more than these minimum grounds: that most technologically advanced societies are divided societies, are pluralistic and not monolithic; and that peaceful rule is intrinsically better than violent rule, that political ethics are not some inferior type of ethical activity, but are a level of ethical life fully self-contained and fully justifiable. Politics is not just a necessary evil; it is a realistic good.

Political activity is a type of moral activity; it is free activity, and it is inventive, flexible, enjoyable, and human; it can create some sense of community and yet it is not, for instance, a slave to nationalism; it does not claim to settle every problem or to make every sad heart glad, but it can help some way in nearly everything and, where it is strong, it can prevent the vast cruelties and deceits of ideological rule. If its actual methods are often rough and imperfect, the result is always preferable to autocratic or to totalitarian rule – granted one thing alone, that sufficient order is created or preserved by politics for the state to survive at all. Praise, in politics as in love, beyond the early days of idealization, can only hearten if it paints a picture plausible enough to be lived with. It must be asked, when is politics possible at all? It is possible when there are advanced or complicated societies, societies with some diversity of technical skills and which are not dependent for their prosperity or survival on a single skill, a single crop, or a single resource. Not all societies (or people) are in this position. Some primitive societies may be so near the margin of survival, so dependent on constant toil and on the precarious success of harvests or trade in a single commodity, that they never amass any capital, hence no leisure, no margin for tolerance, and hence no possibility of political culture. Diversity of interests, which creates a speculative recognition of alternatives, may simply not exist, or if so, be a luxury endangering sheer physical survival. Advanced states in times of war or emergency revert to this condition; if everything depends on the military, then everything is subordinated to military considerations. But, of course, a people who have known politics will be more reluctant to accept this condition on trust; they will take some chances with survival in order to preserve liberty.

Diversity of resources and interests is itself an education. Men living in such societies must appreciate, to some degree, alternative courses of action – even if just as speculative possibilities. There is then not just a technique of doing some one thing, but an abstract knowledge of how other things are done. Some division of labour exists and this, of itself, creates attempts at seeing their relationships: abstract knowledge. The Greek *polis* was perhaps the first circumstance in which a division of labour went together with a division of interests (or speculative alternatives) to a sufficient degree to make politics a plausible response to the problem of ruling such a society. Politics is, as it were, an interaction between the mutual dependence of the whole and some sense of independence of the parts. Obviously the small size of these cities helped to make politics possible. The idea and the habit of politics stood little chance of administrative survival in an Empire as large as Rome, when so many parts of the Empire were entirely dependent on their immediate crops and on the military power of the centre. In an Empire politics must expand from the Mother City, or perish under the burden of the struggle for sheer survival and the habits of autocratic rule which it is forced to create in the true citizens. Part of the price of the Commonwealth's remaining a British Empire would almost certainly have been autocracy in Britain itself – as France came at least so near in the attempt to keep Algeria. And the Romans did not even have the fortunate necessity of having to negotiate politically with other independent powers – the quasi-politics of international relations.

Thus diversity of resources and interests is itself the education which is necessary for politics. There is no *a priori* level of education – even literacy or any such test – which can be laid down as necessary for politics. The level of education will be relative to the level of technological development. The unique modern problem arises when advanced, Western industrial technology is suddenly introduced into a hitherto colonial or underdeveloped area. Then there will almost inevitably be a time lag, at least, between a country's ability to handle these particular skills itself and its ability to develop or recognize a speculative sense, even, of the alternative uses to which these skills and this capital can be put. The simultaneous introduction of Western ideas, including that of free politics itself, may help; this is also a resource and a skill. But politics has to strive against an initial sense that the introduction of scientific and industrial technology is one unified and overwhelming good. Industrialism becomes at first a comprehensive slogan. The fact of new machines is confused with the doctrine of 'technology': that technology solves everything and that all problems are technological. Perhaps only time can show that not merely are real choices of policy called for at every stage of industrialization, but that new and real differences of interests are created.

Here is, of course, the great hope of many that freedom will grow even in the Soviet Union, even in China. The complexity of industrial society, it is argued, will force genuine negotiation first between the party and the managers, and then with the scientists and perhaps even the skilled workers. At least the managers and the scientists, it is argued, because of their function cannot be prevented from meeting together, from developing corporate interests divergent from those of the party and the party ideology. This is a reasonable hope, but it is only a hope. Certain conditions of the modern age work against it. There is the power of bureaucracy. One of the great conditions for, and achievements of, the process of state consolidation and centralization in the whole modern period has been the growth of centralized, skilled bureaucracies. The idea of a rational bureaucracy, of skill, merit, and consistency, is essential to all modern states. Like democracy, as we have seen, bureaucracy is a force that strengthens any state – political, autocratic, and totalitarian alike. The bureaucracy, like the priesthood of medieval Christendom, can become more than an intermediary between the scientists, the managers, the workers, and the seat of power; it can become a conservative power on its own acting in the name of whoever controls the state at the time when these great changes begin. This ambivalent factor of bureaucracy, necessary to all states, strengthening free and unfree alike, has then to be seen in the context of a second obstacle to the hope that industrialization by itself creates freedom.

There is also, as part of industrialization, as we have been at sad pains to insist, a genuine revulsion from, hatred of, and theoretical attack upon, politics. Politics itself is attacked for dividing communities, for being inefficient, for being inconclusive and – with a completely false but powerful idea of science – for being anti-scientific. Political thinking is replaced by ideological thinking. The force of abstract ideas is not to be ignored – though it is the academic fashion of today to do so. So if we ask when is political rule possible, we must also add – far from formally – that it is possible only when at least some powerful forces in a society want it and value it. And it follows that politics is not possible when most people do not want it. The element of will is not independent of circumstances, but it may often and has often weighed the scales one way or the other. Certainly, there is little doubt at the moment which of the two great fruits of Western civilization – politics and technology – is in greater demand in the non-Western world. If Western history demonstrates that they did emerge together, this is no guarantee that in their migration they will always be received together.

Skilled manpower is itself a crucial factor for the possibility of politics in underdeveloped areas. The demand on educational resources, on the very small skilled talent available at all, for scientists, doctors, and engineers, may make the vocation of politics seem either an unjustifiable luxury, or else seem a refuge for not merely the second-rate, who anyway are the bulk of steady representative figures in free societies, but for the utterly third-rate. In this dilemma it is worth noticing that the lawyer often holds a key position. In Nigeria, for instance, and in most of the present and former British colonial dependencies, the profession of law is highly esteemed and sought after. It was almost the only avenue of social advance for the educated, and the most likely springboard for politics. The supply of lawyers is already greater than the demand, at the moment, for strictly legal work. This can mean that political values are kept alive – when politics becomes the arena of the talented underemployed. But, of course, it can also mean that if political opposition has been silenced out of principles or alleged necessity, the supply of skill for a despotic bureaucracy is ensured. Hope and fear spring, once again, from precisely the same factors.[1] The decision depends, once again – in large part at

---

[1]Perhaps it is not merely pride which has made several 'national leaders' recently cancel the scholarships of students studying abroad, who are reported, amid the heady freedom of London or New York, to have expressed even slight doubt that their leader has all the virtues of, shall we say, Mohammed and Lenin combined. Such men depend on the skills and the support of such youths. One knows the cost and the risk, but such youths may be in a stronger position than they think – if they are in earnest with their scepticism.

least, on a conscious affection for politics or disaffection from it. Closely related to this decision is what some writers mean by praising 'political ethics' or 'constitutional ethics' as a condition of free societies: simply that people must agree to, or accept, the solution of social problems by political and legal means. Problems can always be attacked by autocratic means. There was a time, as we have seen, when liberals had a profound distrust of party and faction. James Madison argued in the great Tenth Paper of *The Federalist* (one of the masterpieces of political literature) that factions were, indeed, selfish and divisive. But he argued that they were inevitable (he said 'natural') and could be eliminated (which they could be) only at the cost of eliminating liberty; they could and should be restrained, but not destroyed. Indeed, as the state has grown larger and more complex, we go beyond this and say that such organized factions – better still, parties as things which are capable of forming responsible governments – are essential to free politics in the modern state. They should pursue their 'selfish' ends, for they are devices, whatever their doctrines or lack of doctrine, by which an electorate may hold a government responsible for its actions; and they are gauges by which a government may learn what it can safely and properly do. But they must be forced to pursue their aims in a way which does not endanger public order and their aims should be limited, if they are to be worthy of support by free men, to things which can be done without destroying politics. However convinced men are of the rightness of their party, they must compromise its claims to the needs of some electoral and legal framework, at least so far that the only way of removing it from power does not have to become revolution. Political compromises are the price that has to be paid for liberty. Let us not delude ourselves that we are not paying a price; but let us summon reasons to think that it is normally worth paying.

Political power is power in the subjunctive mood. Policy must be like a hypothesis in science. Its advocates will commit themselves to its truth, but only in a manner in which they can conceive of and accept its possible refutation. Politics, like science, must be praised for being open-minded, both inventive and sceptical. One is not acting politically if one pursues as part of a policy devices intended to ensure for certain that it can never be overthrown. This condition embraces both the well-meaning but futile attempts of constitution makers to put something permanently above politics (though it may be part of politics to make the gesture), and the autocratic attempt to forbid or destroy opposition. The true activity of scientists, not the myth of 'scientism', should give some comfort – if only by analogy – to politicians. When anything is deemed to be fixedly true by virtue of the authority who pronounces it, this thing can be neither politics nor science. Everything has to be put to the test of experience – though some men are better at framing hypotheses or policies than others. If all boats are burnt, if assertions are made categorically, as in a totalitarian party, then the pace of the advance can only be intensified and made desperate. Politics is to be praised, like science, for always retaining a line of retreat.

For independent positions in society to survive there must be some institutional framework. And this framework can be thought of as guaranteeing these independencies. There is a long tradition of Western political thought which sees the essence of freedom as the cultivation of constitutional guarantees. The laws or customs which define the framework of government and representation must be put on some different footing to ordinary customs or acts of legislation. There must be, it is said, some fundamental law, something entrenched against the momentary caprice of government or electorate – something at least made more difficult to change than ordinary laws. Some writers, then, properly aware of the difficulties and dangers of calling free régimes 'democratic', call them 'constitutional-democracies' and speak of 'constitutionalism' as the key to free politics. This view deserves praise – but a qualified praise.

Let us simply realize that this is desirable but impossible to ensure. Some political societies survive without such a strengthening of their foundations. Constitutionalism is itself a doctrine of politics. Like any doctrine of politics it says that something is the case and that something *should* be. It says that political government is limited government: that governments cannot do everything we or they may want. This is true. But it also says that we should guarantee that they should not try – and this is impossible. There are no guarantees in politics. Guarantees may have to be offered as part of politics. But while guarantees stop short of giving independence to a former sub-group or dependency, they remain themselves things subject to change, negotiation, and, even in the most rigid-seeming written Constitution, interpretation. Constitutionalism is vitally important to politics. It is one of the great themes of Western thought and a fruitful concept in that it leads us always to see abstract ideas as needing institutional expression, and to see existing institutions as existing for some purpose. But the praise of politics as constitutionalism needs to be realistic; it needs to be seen that it is the belief itself in fundamental or constitutional law which gives this law force. No law can survive the withering of the belief. No law can survive the growth of new needs and demands; if the fundamental law is not in fact flexible, it can hinder more than help free politics. Constitutions are themselves political devices. They may be viewed as self-sufficient truths in the short run; but in the long run it is political activity itself which gives – and changes – the meaning of any constitution. When we praise a constitution we are doing no more than praise a particular abridgement of a particular politics at a particular time. If the abridgement was a skilful one and circumstances are kind, it may last into a long middle period and help to give stability to a state. But, in the long run, though the words are the same and formal amendments to it may be few, the meaning of it will be different. Even the old Anglo-American Whigs, the arch-constitution-makers, used to say that no constitution was better than the character of the men who work it.

Certainly, at any given time a settled legal order is necessary for freedom and politics. Law is necessary in any society at all complex and people should be able to find out what it is fairly precisely and to use it fairly cheaply. (Litigation, not politics, is the necessary evil of free states.) The autocrat was, indeed, an arbitrary ruler – making laws without any process of consultation or litigation. And the totalitarian leader thinks of law as policy: people are judged not for specific breaches of the law, but for not living up to the general ideals of the régime. Certainly politics should be praised in procedures. Since the business of politics is the conciliation of differing interests, justice must not merely be done, but be seen to be done. This is what many mean by the phrase 'the rule of law'. The framework for conciliation will be a complexity of procedures, frustrating to both parties, but ensuring that decisions are not made until all significant objections and grievances have been heard. Procedure is not an end in itself. It enables something to be done, but only after the strength behind the objections has been assessed. Procedures help to stop both governments and litigants from making claims which they cannot enforce. Procedures, legal or Parliamentary, if given some temporary independent power themselves, tiresome, obstructive, and pettifogging though they may be, at least force great acts of innovation to explain themselves publicly, at least leave doors open for their amendment if the government has misjudged the power of the forces opposed to it. More praise, then, for politics as procedure than for politics as constitutional law, since, while there is no doubt that procedures are necessary for politics, there is also no doubt that every particular procedure is limited to time and place. Justice Frankfurter once asked the interesting question whether one would rather have American substantive law and Russian procedures or Russian substantive law and American procedures. Every essay should be pardoned one enigma.

Some common views about constitutions are more helpful if restated in political terms. Some claims for necessary legal elements in political order need seeing, by just a shift of perspective, as themselves parts of political order, or as possible but not exclusive types of political order. Consider the view that free government depends upon legally instituted checks and balances and the division of powers. People at times have felt extremely certain about this.

Alexander Hamilton wrote in the Ninth Paper of *The Federalist*:

The science of politics, however, like most other sciences, has received great improvement. The efficacy of various principles is now well understood, which were either not known at all, or imperfectly known to the ancients. The regular distribution of power into distinct departments; the introduction of legislative balances and checks; the institution of courts composed of judges holding their offices during good behaviour; the representation of the people in the legislature by deputies of their own election: these are wholly new discoveries, or have made their principal progress towards perfection in modern times.

But these are not 'principles' at all. They are already the summary of an existing political practice in which power was divided, indeed to an extraordinary degree; and in which legislative checks and balances already existed in most of the separate Colonial or Provincial Assemblies as the procedural products of a long struggle between the Royal Governors and the Assemblies, indeed between factions in the Assemblies themselves. The American Federal Constitution was an invention intended to summarize and synthesize an existing division of powers into a Federal Union which had itself only the minimum power necessary to ensure common survival. (Federalism has been a practical response to divided power more than a way of dividing it as a matter of principle.) And in America these divisions had been astonishingly political in nature. They were predominantly the separate interests of thirteen existing fully political units. Only through these political units could 'national' and sectional economic and social differences express themselves.

This is not to say, however, else our praise would be but faint and local, that Hamilton's 'principles' (even if not strict principles) had relevance only to American Colonial conditions. As we have argued, there already exist in certain advanced societies divisions of power, group interests with independent strength from the state itself – independent at least in the sense that the central state is not willing to risk destroying them, but is conscious that it must conciliate them. It is these divisions which make the Constitution necessary; they are not created by it. The constitutional principle of the division of powers only affirms the reasons for which politics arises at all, and attempts to make them secure amid the need for strong government to maintain both internal and external safety. The constitutional principle of checks and balances only affirms the need for organized participants in politics to remember that their will is not the only will. Even when this will does seem to be in fact the only will, typically in the first generation of some colonial Liberation, it affirms the need for this unified majority to set obstacles against itself developing illusions of infallibility and permanence. In the constitutions of many of the American states there was, indeed, the praiseworthy spectacle of a unified majority willing to bind itself against itself. The binding can never be permanent, but it can set up sufficient obstacles for second thoughts to follow any initial impetus for great innovations.

So the relativity to time and place of all constitution-making does not mean that we are driven back merely to the maintenance of order as the only clear criterion of good government. Mere order is not enough to satisfy men as they are. Politics will fail if it cannot maintain order, as at the end of the French Fourth Republic; but it is a counsel of despair to think that all that can be hoped for is public order and 'merciful and just rulers'. We live in a democratic age whether we like it or not. And if none of the devices for limiting power and for subjecting governments to control, even when they extend their control of the economy vastly, are permanent or sure, yet we have learned more about such devices, even about constitution-making, than the tired or despairing conservative will usually allow. Politics, again we insist, is a lively, inventive thing as well as being conservative. We can use it for good and deliberate ends.

*

Political rule should be praised for doing what it can do, but also praised for not attempting what it cannot do. Politics can provide the conditions under which many non-political activities may flourish, but it cannot guarantee that they will then flourish. 'One cannot make men good,' said Walter Bagehot, 'by Act of Parliament.' No state has the capacity to ensure that men are happy; but all states have the capacity to ensure that men are unhappy. The attempt to politicize everything is the destruction of politics. When everything is seen as relevant to politics, then politics has in fact become totalitarian. The totalitarian may try to turn all art to propaganda, but he cannot then guarantee that there will be art as distinct from propaganda – indeed by his concern to destroy or enslave the abstract speculation of the philosopher or the creativity of the artist, activities apparently quite irrelevant to mere political power, he demonstrates that these irrelevancies are necessary to free life and free society. The totalitarian, like the autocrat, may try to make use of religion until he is powerful enough to destroy it, but he is driven to degrade men in order to try to prove that there is no soul which need not fear the body's harm.

To ensure that there be politics at all, there must be some things at least which are irrelevant to politics. One of the great irrelevancies to the total-politician is simply human love:

> How can I, that girl standing there,
> My attention fix
> On Roman or on Russian
> Or on Spanish politics?

– the poet rightly asks. The girl, of course, may happen to be involved in politics – Yeats had his Maud Gonne and Zhivago his Larissa – but the value of the involvement between the poet and the girl is not political. Yeats called this poem 'Politics' and headed it with a remark of Thomas Mann's: 'In our time the destiny of man presents itself in political terms.' Would Mann, one wonders, have disagreed with this splendidly contemptuous criticism, or would Yeats have made it, were either sure that the other was using politics in the narrow sense which we have striven to show is its best sense, and not as standing for all forms of power and authority? If man has a destiny, politics is obviously incompetent to legislate about it; but it can keep him alive and free to seek it. If artistic activity is an end in itself, then it is the denial of politics to start laying down laws about art. No wonder poets and writers have constantly explored the theme of the clash between political values and art and love. The independence of art and love, it is some comfort to think, are not merely the sure signs of a free society, but have a deep influence in making men think freedom worth while amid the temptations there are to surrender ourselves to the sense of certainty offered by an ideology. Politics does not need to defend itself against the anarchy and irresponsibility of the artist and the lover; it does not need even to claim that it is necessary for everyone to be involved in and to support politics. (It can withstand a lot of apathy; indeed when the normally apathetic person suddenly becomes greatly interested in political questions, it is often a sign of danger.) But if the politician, too, has a little proper pride in his vocation, he can at least ask such critics whether they are not sometimes confusing state power in general with political rule in particular, or, more subtly, are not accusing political régimes of being purely democratic – democracy, again, as the belief that because men are equal in some things, they are equal in all. It is this belief against which the very existence of the philosopher, the artist, and the lover is a unique testimony.

Even in true politics, however, there is no guarantee that there will not, in some unhappy circumstances, be a clash between the public interest and private conscience. Indeed the paradigm-case of political philosophy, the point at which this new thing began, was Plato's picture of the trial of Socrates as just such an event. Plato, of course, leaves us in no doubt that love of wisdom – *philosophia* – should be put before love of country; and he was condemning a particular democratic régime. But – the mark of the great artist – he could not help but give us enough of the other side of the case to show that Socrates really could be thought a danger to the state, by corrupting the most able youth of the city with a technique of self-doubt at a time when the city was struggling in war for very survival, and needed every ounce of military ability and civic patriotism available. Certainly Plato's Socrates himself saw no way out of the dilemma but death. He could not promise, as an inspired philosopher, to hold his tongue for the duration of the hostilities. Nothing can guarantee us against genuine tragedy – that moral virtues can lead to disaster in certain circumstances – except belief in an ideology which abolishes tragedy by making every sacrifice a pragmatic calculation towards gaining future benefits for the collective cause.

One of the great disappointments of modern liberalism, made possible by democracy, was the need and the ability to introduce military conscription, first in time of war, and then even in times of the mere threat of war. Conscription taught liberals a sad lesson in the primacy of survival over personal liberties. But how great and praiseworthy was the fact that even in the Second World War, even in genuinely total war, Great Britain, and to a lesser extent the United States, solemnly made provision for conscientious objection to military service. Let one be as critical as one likes of the bizarre concept of 'conscience' which arose in the tribunals. Let one be as Machiavellian as one can and call it a mere gesture, something which would never have been tolerated if the numbers involved, or the example, had proved in the least bit a hindrance to the war effort. But the gesture was a gesture towards the kind of life which a political régime thought it was trying to preserve. If someone's sense of self-identity was so deeply bound up with feeling it impossible to kill a fellow human being, then that sense of self-identity had to be respected. Perhaps pacifism as a social force did not matter very much. And a pacifist was just as useful – as some of them sadly realized – replacing an agricultural labourer for service in the infantry as he would have been serving himself – probably more so. But it is the mark of political régimes that they do not, as ideological régimes do, condemn even ineffective opposition out of sheer arrogant principle. It is the mark of freedom that, even if ideas may have to be prevented from achieving institutional and powerful form, the ideas themselves are not forbidden and hunted down. We cannot always get what we want, but if we lose the ability to think of wanting other things beside what we are given, then the game is lost for ever.

Political activity is important not because there are no absolute ideals or things worth doing for themselves, but because, in ordinary human judgement, there are many of these things. Political morality does not contradict any belief in ideal conduct; it merely sets a stage on which people can, if they wish, argue such truths without degrading these truths into instruments of governmental coercion. If the truth 'will set you free' and if the service of some ideal is held to be 'perfect freedom', let this be so, so long as the advocates are prevented from involving others in the fraudulent freedom of coerced obedience. The view that the belief in absolute ideals (or what Professor K. R. Popper has called 'essentialism') is dangerous to political freedom is itself intolerant, not a humanistic view of society but a gelded view, something so over-civilized and logically dogmatic as to deprive many of any feeling that anything, let alone free institutions, is worth while. Freedom and liberty are not ends in themselves, neither as methods nor as substitute moralities; they are part of politics and politics is simply not concerned, as politics, with absolute ends. It need neither affirm nor deny. And when sceptics or true believers are in fact acting politically, it should teach us to take with a grain of salt the 'purely practical' or 'the purely ideal' construction which they put on their own involvement. Political morality is simply that level of moral life (if there are other levels) which pursues a logic of consequences in the world as it is. To act morally in politics is to consider the results of one's actions.

Lincoln once set out to define the position of the new Republican Party on the slavery question. He said (in a speech of 15 October 1858):

The real issue in this controversy – the one pressing upon every mind – is the sentiment on the part of one class that looks upon the institution of slavery *as a wrong*, and of another class that *does not* look upon it as a wrong. . . . The Republican Party . . . look upon it as being a moral, social, and political wrong, and while they contemplate it as such, they nevertheless have due regard for its actual existence among us, and the difficulties of getting rid of it in any satisfactory way, and to all the constitutional obligations thrown about it. . . . I repeat it here, that if there be a man amongst us who does not think that the institution of slavery is wrong in any one of the aspects of which I have spoken, he is misplaced, and ought not to be with us. And if there be a man amongst us who is so impatient of it as a wrong as to disregard its actual presence among us and the difficulty of getting rid of it suddenly in a satisfactory way, and to disregard the constitutional obligations thrown about it, that man is misplaced if he is on our platform. We disclaim sympathy with him in practical action.

This is true political morality – indeed political greatness. If anyone is not willing to walk this kind of path he might be happier to realize that he has in fact abandoned politics. He may abandon them for the lead of the benevolent autocrat who will promise the end of slavery tomorrow, or he may simply do nothing because he is not willing to muddy his conscience with such 'terrible compromises' or equivocation. As regards the greatness of a man who can sharpen the issue so clearly, I admit that there is always an alternative interpretation of such words – hypocrisy. Someone may just be offering excuses for not doing something which he does not believe in anyway. This is a matter of judgement – and perhaps the motive does not matter if the right public actions follow, except to the man's own soul and to his biographer. 'Hypocrisy,' said Swift, 'is the tribute that vice pays to virtue.' What matters in politics is what men actually do – 'sincerity' is no excuse for acting unpolitically, and insincerity may be channelled by politics into good results. Even hypocrisy, to a very, very small degree, keeps alive something of the idea of virtue. Certainly on an issue such as slavery, some people must keep a pure moral vision alive, but such visions, perhaps held only by 'saints', fanatics, reformers, intellectuals, will be partially fulfilled only when there is an attempt to realize them in terms of public policy. There is little doubt in Lincoln's case that he did truly believe that slavery was a 'moral, social, and political wrong'. But it is rare good fortune for the leader of a state himself to combine absolute ethics and the ethics of responsibility. And these are things only to be reconciled through time.

The politician must always ask for time. The hypocrite and the enemy of reform uses time as an excuse for inaction – literally the 'time-server' or the slave to time, he whose vision is entirely limited to the immediate. But 'eternity', said the poet Blake, 'is in love with the products of time'. 'Eternal values' cannot be treated as immediate values; but time in itself is nothing but a tedious incident on the way to death unless in it and through it we strive to achieve – what the Greeks looked for in the public life – 'immortal actions', ever memorable reforms, monuments to the belief that civilization can advance. In 1955 the United States Supreme Court declared that racial segregation in all American schools supported by public funds was unconstitutional. It enjoined the responsible authorities to integrate, not immediately – which would have been impossible, without the use of force incredible to imagine in a free society – but with 'deliberate speed'. This was an act not merely of great moral (and presumably legal) significance, but of political wisdom. *The law* is now known. That is as far as a Court or a moralist can go. But it will be an act of political cowardice if the Federal executive cannot now constantly nudge the unreconstructed time-servers to implement the law. Time by itself solves nothing; but time is needed to attempt anything politically.

Now let us continue to praise Lincoln as a great politician on even harder grounds, which may scare away still more fairweather friends of politics – or men who would do good if it did not mean walking, like Bunyan's Pilgrim, through both Vanity Fair and the Valley of the Shadow of Death. In the middle of the hardest time of the American Civil War, Horace Greeley, a militant abolitionist, challenged Lincoln to commit himself to immediate emancipation as a matter of principle. Lincoln replied:

> My paramount object in this struggle is to save the Union, and is *not* either to save or destroy slavery. If I could save the Union without freeing *any* slave, I would do it; and if I could do it by freeing *all* the slaves, I would do it; and if I could do it by freeing some and leaving others alone, I would also do that. What I do about slavery and the coloured race, I do because I believe it helps to save the Union, and what I forbear, I forbear because I do not believe it would help to save the Union . . . I have here stated my purpose according to my view of *official* duty, and I intend no modification of my oft expressed *personal* wish that all men, everywhere, could be free.

Lincoln put preservation of the Union, the political order itself, above everything else, not because he did not care for Negro suffering and exclusion – he did; but because only if there was a Union again, a common political order again between North and South, could any of these problems be tackled. Suppose I will risk the case of politics on even more unhappy grounds than Lincoln actually had to face – that a man in his position could have felt confident of winning the war and preserving the Union only by promising *not* to use his emergency powers as Commander-in-Chief to emancipate the slaves. Would this have been justified? I think the hard answer is obviously – yes. The first responsibility of a leader is to preserve the state for the benefit of those to follow. Suppose such a leader had privately believed that after his making such a promise the legislature would, immediately after the war, overrule him. This is no deceit; he could not have been held responsible for their actions – or if so, it would have been an agony for the private conscience faced with the primacy of public responsibility. Suppose even the darkest situation of all, that he had privately believed that once his promise was made and once his war-time powers were gone, the legislature would not emancipate the slaves. The personal agony of such a position as this cannot be evaded, and it would be hard to blame a man who would abandon politics in such a situation in the sense of resigning from office. But even then such a man as Lincoln would probably not have abandoned power, for the true political statesman knows that while there is *political* power at all, while there is a representative assembly, nothing is really certain, no single aspect of policy is not negotiable somehow, realizable in however small a part in the flexibility and management of a free assembly.

The example of Lincoln is not too bad a one on which to rest this case for politics – however much pietistic myths have obscured the grosser human tale of political action. He offended beyond reason many responsible men of his day by rarely being willing to talk seriously in private, by his infuriating retreats into badinage and the telling of old jokes. His dignity was a very variable quality. He seems to have been an indifferent administrator, disorderly, inconsistent, and even slothful; his relations with Congress were often inept and usually bad. But, for all that, he is as great an example of a mere politician as can be found. If this claim actually sounds more odd to American than to English ears, it is because American English, or rather American liberalism, has debased the word 'politician'. True, he preserved the State as a statesman; but he sought to do it, even at the height of the emergency, politically. (It is not helpful to inflate, as is done in American vernacular, every small but honest politician into a 'statesman'.) Lincoln, before his death, made it quite clear that he would oppose Congress if they sought to treat the South as a conquered territory without constitutional rights. The task, he said, was that of 'doing the acts necessary to restoring the proper practical relations between these States and the Union'; he scorned 'deciding, or even considering' whether these States had ever been out of the Union; he ironically suggested, almost parodying his own best style, that 'each for ever after, innocently indulge his own opinion whether, in doing the acts, he brought the States from without, into the Union, or only gave them proper assistance, they never having been out of it'. Politics, as we have seen, is indeed a matter of 'practical relations', not of deduction from higher principles.

Lincoln had little dignity, but he had enough authority and he did not have pride. Pride is an easy vice for any whose business must be in the public eye. But a true politician cannot afford it. The politician lives in a world of publicity, calumny, distortion, and insult. He is often looked down upon by polite society as being a mere 'fixer' and an 'opportunist' (though it is puzzling why this last word always has a bad meaning); and he is mocked by intellectuals for rarely having ideas of his own:

a politician is an arse upon
which everyone has sat except a man

– which is the whole of an easy poem by e. e. cummings. And, indeed, the politician, beneath his necessary flexibility, will rarely be a man of less than normal pliability and ambitions. He will provoke such cheap mockery from spectators. But he will not take these things to heart. The successful politician will learn how to swallow insults. The successful politician keeps in mind the English nursery proverb:

Sticks and stones may break my bones
But names will never hurt me.

He does not store up memories of insults and nor does he, when in power, take opposition personally, making a matter of principle or of *lèse majesté* of every ungenerous suspicion hurled upon him. A politician, like any of us, may not be above such pettiness; but he has no need for it, so he must not show it. The temptation is great, however. It is now an offence in Ghana's criminal code, punishable by up to three years in prison, to defame or insult President Nkrumah. This law is a sad monument to a man who showed such zest and ability for politics when in opposition himself. It is sad to think that this tender soul may not even have enjoyed such politics. Lincoln once remarked, with pragmatic humility: 'A man has not the time to spend half his life in quarrels. If any man ceases to attack me, I never remember the past against him.' He told one of his generals: 'I wish you to do nothing merely for revenge, but that what you may do shall be solely done with reference to the security of the future.' The politician has no more use for pride than Falstaff had for honour. And if when suddenly dismissed from favour, he then invokes pride and asks for employment and honour, he is just kicking against the terms of his trade which he, like any of us, had ample opportunity to study. Politics as a vocation is a most precarious thing, so we should not grudge the politician any of the incidental rewards he can pick up. But we must always beware that he does not grow bored or frustrated with 'mere politics' – that all this need for compromise stops him from doing what is obviously best for the nation. The price of politics is eternal involvement in politics ourselves.

The political leader, as we have seen, may have to take risks with liberty to preserve the nation. He may have to invoke 'sovereignty' and, at this point, the leader who cannot lead is not worth having. But he will lead so that politics can survive. Lincoln wrote to General Hooker: 'I have heard, in such a way as to believe it, of your recently saying that both the army and the government needed a dictator. Of course it was not *for* this, but in spite of it, that I have given you command. Only those generals who gain successes can set up dictators. What I now ask of you is military success, and I will risk the dictatorship.' Free politics is a risky business, though not so risky as dictatorship. And 'free politics', as I have sought to show, is really a pleonasm – either word will do. If a politician has pride, it must be, as Aristotle distinguished, a 'proper pride' – in his skill at his conciliatory vocation, not hubris, the attempt to be more than a man, which commonly makes a man less than a man.

*

Conciliation is better than violence – but it is not always possible; diversity is better than unity – but it does not always exist. But both are always desirable. Perhaps it all comes down to the fact that there are two great enemies of politics: indifference to human suffering and the passionate quest for certainty in matters which are essentially political. Indifference to human suffering discredits free régimes which are unable, or which fear, to extend the habits and possibility of freedom from the few to the many. The quest for certainty scorns the political virtues – of prudence, of conciliation, of compromise, of variety, of adaptability, of liveliness – in favour of some pseudo-science of government, some absolute-sounding ethic, or some ideology, some world-picture in terms of either race or economics. Perhaps it is curious, or simply unnatural, that men who can live with dignity and honour in the face of such endemic uncertainties as death, always so close in the normal possibilities of accident and disease; as love, its precariousness and its fading, its dependence on the will and whims of others, yet can go mad for certainty in government – a certainty which is the death of politics and freedom. A free government is one which makes decisions politically, not ideologically.

There is no end to the praises that can be sung of politics. In politics, not in economics, is found the creative dialectic of opposites: for politics is a bold prudence, a diverse unity, an armed conciliation, a natural artifice, a creative compromise, and a serious game on which free civilization depends; it is a reforming conserver, a sceptical believer, and a pluralistic moralist; it has a lively sobriety, a complex simplicity, an untidy elegance, a rough civility, and an everlasting immediacy; it is conflict become discussion; and it sets us a humane task on a human scale. And there is no end to the dangers that it faces: there are so many reasons that sound so plausible for rejecting the responsibility and uncertainty of freedom. All that we have tried to do is to show why political activity is best seen as only one form of power relationship and political rule as only one form of government; and then to advance some arguments to show why the political solution to the problem of government is normally to be preferred to others. The only end to such an incomplete essay of defence and praise is to repeat drily what it is we have been describing.

Aristotle repeated his definition in almost the same words as we quoted at the beginning:

> The object which Socrates assumes as his premiss is . . . 'that the greatest possible unity of the whole *polis* is the supreme good'. Yet it is obvious that a *polis* which goes on and on, and becomes more and more of a unit, will eventually cease to be a *polis* at all. A *polis* by its nature is some sort of aggregation. If it becomes more of a unit, it will first become a household instead of a *polis*, and then an individual instead of a household. . . . It follows that, even if we could, we ought not to achieve this object: it would be the destruction of the *polis*.

A Footnote to Rally the Academic Professors of Politics (1964)

Ther bith ij kyndes off kyngdomes, of the wich that on is a lordship callid in laten dominium regale, *and that other is callid* dominium politicum et regale. *And thai diversen in that the first kynge may rule his peple bi suche lawes as he makyth hym self. . . . The secounde kynge may not rule his peple bi other lawes than such as thai assenten unto.*

SIR JOHN FORTESCUE, *The Governance of England*, ed. Charles Plummer, London 1926, p. 109

The political system

That while politics is probably present to some degree in all systems of government, that some systems are usefully differentiated as 'political systems'. The political system is both an 'operative ideal' and the most scientific standard of comparison available.

Engraved on the ring of power there are two primal curses upon all who profess to study the types and ways of Government. One is the curse of separation: that walls of fire flare up between the study of 'institutions' and the study of 'ideas'. The other is the curse of identification: that when we ask in the common tongue for the market-place of 'politics', students are quite happy to direct us to any old castle called 'government'.

While both government and politics are all but universal phenomena, yet the most useful distinctions for any theories which would explain governmental activity are between degrees of political activity; and there are societies whose systems of government do not merely contain some political activity, but normally depend on political activity to function at all. These are properly differentiated as 'political systems', what Aristotle meant by 'polity', Fortescue's *dominium politicum et regale,* what the Whig translators meant by 'mixed government', or what Machiavelli, the European inhabitants of Free Cities, and the American patriots meant by 'republican'.

Political science, or the study of politics, is, of course, concerned with all types of government. And there are many classificatory schemes or typologies which inhabit the text-books – for different purposes (but all for some purpose, consciously or unconsciously). But it is unnecessary to deny that political science has a peculiar commitment to political rule or the political system, if only for the obvious but important reason that as an activity it exists only with great difficulty in non-political systems, and does not exist at all as a free science in anti-political régimes. The term 'politics' is ambiguous, but only in two ways, both easily distinguished. In *the Politics,* for instance, we see Aristotle using the term to stand for the general study of all systems of government, but also to point to what he regarded as a peculiar system of government, and the one that was normally the best. He even says, as we have seen, that Plato would press the idea of moral unity – as being the essence of good government – so far that 'a *polis* . . . will cease to be a *polis'*.

Basically there are three styles of government which arise in societies of any degree of complication, that is, in societies which recognize that there are deeply rooted conflicts of interest (whether moral or material). There is the *tyrannic* or *autocratic* way where it is attempted to solve the problem of diversity and order (the problem of government) by the authoritative enforcement of one of these interests as a compulsory *consensus.* There is the *political* or *republican* way where it is attempted to conciliate these differing interests by in some manner letting them share in the business of government. There is the modern *totalitarian* way where it is attempted to create a completely new society, such that conflicts would no longer arise, by means of the guidance and enforcement of a scientific ideology whose claims, both for knowledge and allegiance, are total. The most common form of 'politics' in the first type of society is passive obedience (usually worship); in the second is individual participation or citizenship; and in the third is mass enthusiasm (the pie is always in the sky).

When Aristotle called politics 'the master-science', he simply meant, not that it explained all other 'sciences', activities, or interests, but that it was the one that gave the others some reasonably acceptable mutual priority in their claims on the scarce resources of any known community. Certainly if the fundamental problem of society is that demands are infinite and resources are always limited, politics, not economics, is the master-science. Decisions as to the allocation of resources are ultimately political; and they are *political,* not just governmental, if they are in a manner which is rational in the sense that all relevant factors are considered – by having political devices of public consultation and (in varying degrees, of course, but always some) 'free speech'. And this process of political consultation and conciliation obviously depends both on peculiar institutional arrangements, some form of representation, and on a peculiar tradition of speculation about policy (neither of which are universal phenomena – like science and technology, they have been products and exports of Europe). Politics is the master-science, both as an activity and as a study (and it will be argued that neither the activity nor the study can exist apart from each other). The 'political system' is *both* the 'operative ideal' of normal politics and the most scientific standard of comparison available to us. That this is neither arrogance nor tautology becomes clear if we consider, first, both a type of popular distaste for politics at all and the theoretical assault on its explanatory primacy as a theory of how societies hold together. The political system is not necessarily part of all social systems since it is meaningful to deny that one wants it.

Anti-politics

That there are meaningful attitudes and theories which reject politics, thus showing its unique character.

Sometimes those who dislike or hate politics have a better understanding of the specificity and importance of the political system than do those who take it for granted. Even in régimes obviously both 'political' and 'democratic' there are those, as David Riesman wrote in *The Lonely Crowd,* who 'hate politics even though they would insist that they only hate bad or corrupt politics'. Certainly we need more studies of such attitudes and the movements associated with them. For the moment, may one just appeal to common experience? One meets many people to whom it is the first test of a new acquaintance's sensibility that he despises politics, politicians, and political speculation (even occasionally among those who profess 'the subject'). He may be allowed to press a handful of good causes on one, but he must then make clear that their fulfilment is thwarted by politics; or he may complain that the rational planning of his private industry or of the 'public interest' is prevented by the intrusion of politics.

It would be easy if such people's views were based on a complete misunderstanding of the nature of political activity. On the contrary, they may understand it better than some academic students of politics. They object to its most characteristic features – compromise, conciliation, uncertainty, conflict; to its necessary ambivalence or tension between preservation and creation; and to its curious movements between bureaucratic anonymity and the magnification of personality in politicians. To some, the politician is a standing insult to personal idealism, because in the practice of his vocation he has to treat deep divergences of values as natural and as mere differences of preferences or opinion. To others, the politician is a barrier to efficiency because he compromises particular interests instead of making total plans.

Even those who admit that politics as an activity is a 'necessary evil' may deride any attempts at formulating theories of politics. Politicians themselves commonly believe that they are 'purely practical men', and many historians flatter them in the strange (and usually partisan) belief that this means they neither need nor are influenced by theories. Then there are intellectuals who have no time for political theory since it does not try to discuss aesthetic matters – fortunately; and this often tempted the unpolitical towards the seeming comprehensiveness of Marxism.[1]

Others formulate theories which make all politics something inherently irrational or subsidiary, something to be 'explained away' by religion, psychology, economics, sociology, or even biology. There is a lot to be said in favour of inter-disciplinary zeal – and even more in favour of refusing to take much notice of the conventional pedagogic boundaries of subjects; but we want to make use of many bodies of knowledge

---

[1] Witness the former fad for that torturous trimmer, George Lukacs.

precisely because government and politics are the social activities which most affect both the stability and worthiness of all aspects of society.

Marx at his most dogmatic, unlike when writing about actual politics or history, would denounce the political state as a bourgeois state (accepting the concepts but rejecting the values of Aristotle and Machiavelli), but then as a system of coercion and deceit: politics was a trick of the State to prevent the reign of Society. He spoke in the *Communist Manifesto* of the need to deprive the 'public power' of 'its political character'. This had been explicit in an article in *Vorwärts* in 1844: *'Political* thought is really *political* in the sense that the thinking takes place within the framework of politics. The clearer and more vigorous political thought is, the less it is able to grasp the nature of social evils.'[2] And in *Die Heilige Familie*: 'Only *political superstition* believes at the present time that civil life must be held together by the State, when in reality the State is upheld by civil life.'[3] If priorities must be assigned in such terms Marx was surely wrong. There can be no complex 'civil life' without politics. But the point to be made here is that the proper advice that political science should broaden its perspectives into political economy is often confused with a demand that politics must be reduced to sociology or economics. The whole of Professor Talcott Parsons's *The Social System* (1952) could be quoted as an example of this, but the point is made more simply when such systematic theories come to life as anti-political doctrines – whether of Right or Left. The hero of Joseph Goebbels's novel *Michael* remarked that 'Political Parties live off unsolved problems. That's why they are not interested in their solution'. A multitude of the enthusiastic and the embittered have spoken of 'mere politics' and the need to get rid of 'the politicians'. And Proudhon had spoken of the 'irksome situation' of his times as being due to: 'Une certaine maladie de l'opinion . . . qu'Aristote . . . a nommé POLITIQUE'.[4]

---

[2]See T. B. Bottomore and M. Rubel, *Karl Marx: Selected Writings in Social Philosophy* (London 1956), p. 217.
[3]Ibid., p. 220; see also p. 100: '. . . That England is a *political* country' – which is the very trouble, he argues.
[4]Quoted in Sheldon Wolin, *Politics and Vision* (New York 1961), p. 415.

Political rule

> That political rule sees politics as the activity by which differing interests within a territory are conciliated.

Now there is much point in blaming Aristotle if one does not like politics, or if one doubts the utility of treating political activity as a variable whose strongest manifestation is one type of government – political rule (the government of a political system). For Aristotle first made clear how specific an activity it is: 'There is a point at which a *polis* by advancing in unity, will cease to be a *polis*. . . .' And he saw that politics was not a 'pure form', like Monarchy, Aristocracy, or Democracy, but was a blending of elements – *élites* based on wide consent. It will be said that this is all too Greek, and that, anyway, the unstable *polis* was giving way to the (unstable) Empire. But the contingencies are irrelevant: the point is that Aristotle provided a theoretical definition which, based on a true generalization, transcended the particular form of *polity* of his day. There is simply one type of governmental system which is inherently concerned with conciliation based upon a recognition (both sociological and ethical) that civilized communities are internally diverse. Politics can then be defined as the activity by which differing interests within a given territory are conciliated. It presumes that there are already organized states. It is concerned with the government of organized territories. But it is only one type of government. Its enemies, as has been said, recognize this more readily than its friends. And it presumes the existence of active and self-reliant individuals (the Greek man of *arete,* Machiavelli's *virtu,* or the Republican 'citizen') and of a multiplicity of organized groups – both of which concepts, it is interesting, have been challenged by the two great anti-politicians, Hobbes and Rousseau.

Most governments try to suppress politics – though the widespread emulation of the form, at least, of a political system is remarkable. Few succeed entirely, but some succeed sufficiently to make the distinction clear between political régimes and nonpolitical régimes. Totalitarian régimes, indeed, are explicitly antipolitical. This does not mean that there is not some politics in such régimes: but it is palace politics, not public politics. Such régimes cannot sensibly be regarded as 'political systems', as working by or for politics. The existence of such 'politics' even as these (for which words more ordinary and apt can be found – 'rivalry', 'intrigue', 'conflict', 'bargaining', etc.) is a measure of their incompleteness, not of their stability; it is not thought to be, and it is not, their normal method of rule. Some politics exist in most types of régime. But most régimes are not organized for politics: politics need be neither the normal method of government nor a widely shared ideal for practical conduct.

Semantic depression

That there is a tradition of using 'politics' in this sense.

All right, but why use 'politics'? Well, what else? It is obvious why 'democracy' is wrong: there are political régimes which are not democratic in any sense (eighteenth-century England, for example, to go no further); and then another word for 'democratic' would be needed to express the fact that *all* strong governments since the Industrial and the French Revolutions depend upon mass support to govern at all. Common usage may not always make the distinction, but learned usage can, for it always did. Consider the famous passage from Fortescue at the head of this Footnote. Granted that Charles McIlwain uses this passage in his *Constitutionalism; Ancient and Modern* as part of his theory that 'constitutionalism' explains the peculiarity of Western government: he lays stress on the word 'lawes'. But surely Fortescue, like Bracton before him, was pointing to the manner in which the law was declared? In England it was declared politically, by consultation with the magnates and the *optimati* at least. In France of the 1560s, those Catholic noblemen who came to see that the pursuit of absolute principles was wrecking the State, were called – naturally enough – *les Politiques.* Machiavelli in his *Discourses,* perhaps the clearest analysis of the conditions for free government ever written, frequently describes a Republic as being *'uno vivere civile e politico',* even just *'vivere politico',* and on occasion he uses *'politico'* and *'libero'* interchangeably. His fundamental distinction was between personal or princely rule, relevant to times of crisis – the best way to save corrupt old states or to create new ones; and republican or political rule, relevant to normal conditions in states with a large middle class – the best way to preserve states through time. One can read how Henry VIII pondered between these two alternatives in relation to Ireland, and finally decided not to use (expensive) military force, but to try to govern by 'sober ways, politic drifts, and amiable persuasions'.[5] And the distinction is vivid and colloquial enough when Thomas Mann railed against his brother, even in a book called *Betrachtungen eines Unpolitisches*: 'It would be a misunderstanding to believe that our politician is concerned with politics, that is reform, compromise, adaptation, mutual understanding between reality and spirit . . . and not rather with the grand gesture of the world turned upside down, the destruction of the state, permanent rebellion of the mob, revolution.' Examples could be multiplied; but the point is that when ordinary people talk of someone 'being political' they do not mean that he is either administering or making (or acting in response to) a command.

The political system as fact and value

That the political system rests on an empirical generalization and on an ethical commitment: that there is diversity and that this is normally good.

Politics thus rests upon an empirical generalization and an ethical commitment. The sociological generalization is that territory organized under a government is normally 'an aggregate of many members', that established, advanced, or civilized societies contain a diversity of interests – whether moral, social, or economic. The ethical commitment is that there are limits beyond which a government should not go in maintaining or creating unity. No specific fixed limits can, of course, be demonstrated. They are all relative to time and place. But the *principle* of limitations is general and the empirical distinction is usually clear between systems which strive to limit power and those who strive after total power. A political system occurs when and if it is believed by enough people that government, though it is the predominant social institution, yet neither can nor should be omnicompetent or omnipotent.

[5]Edmund Curtis, *A History of Ireland*, 6th edition (London 1961), p. 167.

Totalitarianism is in fact a distinct and destructive aspiration, but not a literal possibility.

Thus politics, as a working system, exists in relatively few countries (though lip-service is paid to it in more), still fewer of which appear very stable, even though in some degree it must exist in all countries. But this difference of degree defines whether the system of government is itself political or not. In fact, there is seldom much doubt about saying whether a régime is political or not, either by commonsense general judgements, or by the application of various criteria, such as we all from time to time draw up. We argue about specific items and formulations, but we do draw up some criteria in order to explain the admitted crucial difference – whether we couch it in terms of political and nonpolitical systems, democratic and non-democratic systems, constitutional government, representative government, etc., etc. . . .

Probably the most useful criteria common to such lists are – once again – the existence of individualism, of voluntary groups with – in any sense – political effect, and of publicized opposition. Direct attempts to say that some things are inherently beyond the reach of government have all proved fruitless; and even more subtle indirect attempts lead us to doctrinaire absurdities of the type we attack in others.[6] But it can be said that when all things are thought relevant to government at once, there is no politics. Anything *may* prove a proper subject of governmental intervention in a political system; but it is not a political system at all if there is a single authoritative source for the allocation of all values and for the determination of all policies.[7]

Again this comes back to what Aristotle meant by calling our study 'the master-science'. He did not mean that it explained everything else scientifically. This arrogance has either been religious, or else the modern concept of *ideology* which has stemmed from Marx's claim that everything is a product of the economic system (or the far more absurd, but vastly influential, claim that everything is a product of ethnic composition). He meant that without politics all the other 'sciences' or interests would be left either without any ordering principle, without anything to establish

---

[6]For instance, Professor Michael Oakeshott's flesh-creeping account of 'collectivism' in his 'Political Economy of Freedom' which he reprinted in *Rationalism in Politics* (1962). See my 'The World of Michael Oakeshott', *Encounter,* June 1962.

[7]And if this sounds like a version of 'pluralism', it is – subject only to the function of the state to preserve order at all.

priorities in every different time and circumstance for their rival claims on the limited resources of any given territory – which is anarchy; or else the advocates of some one science or interest would be established above all others – which is tyranny. The political system deals in priorities – by what is, after all, a fairly rational procedure for discussing alternatives. Tyranny, Absolutism, Kingship, and Empire are systems which assign priorities in an arbitrary manner. Totalitarian régimes believe in a final and lasting absolute allocation of resources and values.

The present decay in the status of the master-science (both in its achievements and in its academic prestige) is due, above all, to a widespread failure to recognize both its specific and limited nature, and, at the same time, its overwhelmingly valuable nature – its obvious and inseparable connexion with freedom. Certainly political theory concerns a wider class of phenomena than political activity alone. But this is not to descend into a crippling relativism. Political theory does show that political rule is the most preferable type of government in any but times of desperate emergency. Political doctrines, even, however various, do assert that the very problem of government arises from the fact and apperception of diversity, not from any ideal or material drive towards complete unity; and that conciliation is more part of the human condition than the violence which is necessary to achieve unity.

All conciliation and compromise is not, of course, justifiable. Only those compromises which preserve politics and social justice are justifiable. The argument *is* circular. At times we suffer from a rather over-civilized sense of relativity: free and unfree societies alike are accepted as simply the products of different histories and sociologies. Some sense, certainly, of what was once called 'the relativity of morals' is necessary for the tolerance which is the political manner of living together in cities. But it is inhuman coldness, or a false chastity of intellect, to push this so far that all distinctions are obliterated, so that all systems of government and all political judgements simply reflect different circumstances. Politics embodies an ethic and a conscious purpose which cannot be reduced to sociology. Some systems of government plainly thrive on constant violence and a perpetual sense of crisis; some others are able to keep violence and coercion as a final and exceptional reserve to defend the state itself. There is no necessity in government. Can one still not be simple enough to think that the fundamental reason why socialist dictators and reactionary generals repress opposition is because they do not like it? They enjoy power, believe they are using it rightly, but hate politics.

The conditions of the political system

That it is possible from the existing political theory to reach substantial agreement about the conditions for political stability.

It is one thing to define political rule; it is another to explain the occurrence of political systems, or to understand the likelihood that they may or may not prove viable in different circumstances. Surely the most important task of political studies, both scientifically and morally, is to understand and explain the conditions under which political systems prove stable?

In one sense, everything we do has some kind of relevance to this problem. We cannot study a single institution, be it the House or Lords, an election, the Parliamentary question, or a pressure group, without commenting (explicitly or implicitly) on its effectiveness in maintaining the system of which it is part. But we are hindered by the pedagogical distinction between ideas and institutions, and also by methodological preoccupations which always disguise, and sometimes inhibit, actual generalizations. (The function of 'methodologies' is, at best, the testing of actual generalizations, not their formulation.)

Much of the professional debate on the nature of 'Comparative Government' is really concerned with this problem. But it tends either to draw up shopping lists of possible relationships, conceived *a priori,* as in Macridis[8] and in Almond,[9] which were so general as to be finally tautologous (extended definitions of 'system' with a dash of political colouring); or else, as in Lipset,[10] though far more fruitfully, to be too specific by treating all politics as if it were democratic politics.

---

[8]Roy C. Macridis, *The Study of Comparative Government* (New York 1955), esp. Chapter VIII.
[9]Gabriel A. Almond and James S. Coleman, *The Politics of the Developing Areas* (Princeton 1960), Introduction.
[10]Seymour Martin Lipset, *Political Man: the Social Base of Politics* (London 1960).

In fact there is more knowledge about this problem in the traditional writings of political theory than self-consciously 'modern' social scientists often recognize (Machiavelli's *Discourses,* Montesquieu's *L'Esprit des Lois,* the *Federalist,* Mill's *Representative Government,* and the second volume of Tocqueville's *Democracy in America* are obvious examples). From these, and from many piece-meal modern studies, there is a great deal of knowledge to be had about the conditions for political rule – far more than we normally suppose.[11] Some such generalizations as those which follow might be widely accepted. But their mutual priority and their inter-relationships are vastly complicated and variable. Alas, here is no general theory of the conditions for political rule – this argument only seeks to identify the political system; but if it exists at all, it has these elements. Plainly they all condition each other to some extent, but obviously it is only possible by discussing actual cases to gain any sense of their relative importance.

The political system is stable when these conditions exist:

1   A society which recognizes itself to be complex (that is, a plurality of interests and a division of labour).

2   A society which recognizes itself to be composed of individuals (that is, some assumption that individuals are more real than groups, and as real in this life as in any next).

3   A society in which there are institutions representative of some of the governed which are capable of being broadened to include more of the governed (that is, there appear to be no cases of original creation or spontaneous combustion of free institutions).

4   A society in which the ruling *élite* is not exclusive of penetration from other groups (that is, in which the *élite* is not exclusively religious, hereditary, ethnic, or even learned or 'expert').

---

[11]I can only think of two modern studies, both with severe limitations, which approach the comprehensiveness of these older books: Hannah Arendt's *Origins of Totalitarianism,* and William Kornhauser's *The Politics of Mass Society.* Only one chapter of Seymour Martin Lipset's *Political Man* is really relevant.

5   A society in which there is a large middle class (that is, to provide, in conjunction with Condition (2), a citizen body – but this does not imply the impossibility of a classless society; such a society would have the better attributes of bourgeois society).

6   A society in which government is deemed to be predominantly a secular activity (that is, Christian dualism can fortify politics, but if government is simply a part of a known divine order, then priest-kings or holy-men but no politicians).

7   A society in which some conflict of interests is recognized as normal and is institutionalized (that is, Madison's account of faction in the *Federalist* No. 10, or Machiavelli's account in the chapter of the *Discourses* (1, 4) headed: 'That Discord Between the Plebs and the Senate Made This Republic Both Free and Powerful.'[12]

8   A society in which there are no extremes of wealth (this is formal and always subjective – but to a degree: political equality is impossible amid great inequalities of wealth – the unemployed are the clearest instance).

9   A society in which there is economic growth (at least in the long run – see Max Weber's *Capitalism and the Protestant Ethic* and Ernest Gellner's *Thought and Social Change*).

10   A society which can normally defend itself (whether by diplomatic or military means), but which can control its own military (historically the relations between militias and republics have been close).

11   A society in which a distinction is recognized, in law, custom, and speculative thought, between 'public life' and 'private life' (that is, the foundation of much of what is now meant by 'civil liberties', but with the proviso that neither 'private' nor 'public' can be defined except in terms of the existence of the other. See Hannah Arendt's *Human Condition* Part II).

---

[12]And in that chapter: 'Every city should provide ways and means whereby the ambitions of the populace may find an outlet, especially a city which proposes to avail itself of the populace in important undertakings.' And 'Hence if tumults led to the creation of tribunes, tumults deserve the highest praise'. Conflicts about the transference of power and the succession of governments will, of course, be the most important to institutionalize.

12   A society where there is a tradition of political speculation (that is, alternative policies are canvassed in the belief that 'progress', betterment, or reform can be made possible through political action and debate).

13   A society in which the governing élite have the will to act politically (that is, Israel fulfils every classical condition for 'liberty having no relevance to a city in a state of siege', Ghana few; yet one is a political system, the other is not – it seems hard to avoid the conclusion that deliberate intention enters into it).

Consensus

That consensus is not among those conditions.

To the above list there might have been added a negative condition: 'a society in which there is no universal consensus (beyond a pragmatic agreement, derived from the other conditions, to do things politically).' This will take some arguing: for 'consensus' is a favourite magic formula both of the simple and of the over-subtle. It would have been easy enough to exclude consensus from an account of the political system on grounds of ambiguity. Most of us can define it – differently; and we all know what it means.

But if its hard-core of meaning, derived from Cicero's *consensus juris* (which he thought a necessary condition of a Republic), is something like 'agreement about fundamental values', then it fails on empirical grounds. Where is the consensus in Canada, for instance? Or anywhere, between Catholic, Protestant (High or Low), Muslim, Hindu, Jew, Sceptic, Agnostic, Freethinker, Atheist, and Erastian, who commonly share some common political allegiance – if they take their fundamentals seriously and take them to be directly applicable to politics? Either this *consensus* is *very* fundamental – 'a man's a man for a' that', or 'a rose is a rose is a rose',[13] which probably *is* a necessary assumption of any civilized governmental order, indeed of any legal or political judgement;[14] or else it is simply, in our sense, narrowly political.

---

[13]Or G. Marx's existentialist *cri de cœur*: 'Take care of me. I am the only one I've got.'
[14]See H. L. A. Hart, *The Concept of Law* (Oxford 1961), pp. 189–95.

But such a *consensus* about individual human autonomy is not in itself an ethical system; rather it is the presupposition of any possible ethical system. The *consensus* is not some systematic, external and intangible spiritual adhesive, not some metaphysical cement or something mysteriously prior to or above politics; it is the activity of politics itself. In a political system the 'public interest', 'the common good', and 'the general will' are simply pretentious or partisan ways of describing the common interest in preserving the means of making public decisions politically.

Those who say we desperately lack a *consensus* of values, and have such a thing to offer (usually a 'fighting faith for democracy', or else monotheism), are in fact simply trying to sell us a particular brand of politics while pretending that they are not, as it were, in trade themselves (our own island reputation for empiricism commonly hides the fact that we are a nation of metaphysical shoplifters; the weirdest prejudices stick to the hands of those who believe themselves to be purely practical – such as monetarism).

Where such an articulate and systematic *consensus* does seem necessary is in an autocracy. A government whose legitimacy is not maintained by a public adhesion to method, means, procedure, and participation will need the propagation of a myth of a single, true, substantive *consensus* as a kind of teleological 'final-cause' for society. And perhaps there are still societies in which the existence of such a *consensus,* drawn from religious foundations, hinders the development of a political system of government.

If *consensus* is simply taken to mean that a high degree of agreement in fact exists about social values – all right; but this is more likely to be a product of politics than a condition.

It does, of course, make things very much *easier* if one builds *consensus* into one's definition of politics. Elsewhere I have attempted to show that this is common in purportedly 'scientific' theories of politics. It is the metaphysics of the social engineer. If one takes 'certain basic axioms for granted', then one can be scientific, or rather technological, about their implementation. That is why Professor David Euston's *Political System* has the same defects as the cruder types of 'scientism' he criticizes. 'My point is,' wrote Easton, 'that the property of a social act which informs it with a political aspect is the act's relation to the authoritative allocation of values for a society' (p. 134).

What authoritative allocation? Why 'values'? He is plainly thinking of a particularly democratic type of society which in fact had an abnormally high degree of agreement about what may perhaps be called 'values', but which are more likely to be habitual socialized attitudes rather than autonomous judgements.

The political system and order

That politics presumes that order already exists, both as a historical condition and as a potential – called 'sovereignty' – to be reasserted in times of emergency.

More important than consensus, even in some minimal sense, there is an assumption about the political system which must be made explicit: the fact of government at all – the primacy of government, or the prior success of government in establishing order. The political system is partly a response to the problem of government; it is a way of maintaining order without the use of more violence than the ruler is able to stomach or willing to risk – if the outcome would be uncertain – in certain ethical traditions. Realism from above is as necessary as clamour from below in the acceptance of great political reforms – the history of the British franchise shows this. Clearly political rule is the best form of government, in many circumstances. But it is a *form* of government. It is subject to many of the same conditions as government in general: *politicum et regale* said Fortescue, but the King must act *'regale'*, or absolutely, to defend the realm and enforce the laws (and this had to be so even in the American Federal Constitution of 1787). The fact of government must exist, both historically and logically, before the condition of politics. The horse does go before the cart – even though he can never quite shake it off. And it is necessary to say this, since much – most? – specifically democratic and liberal theory has it the other and the more difficult way round: that government is a response to the demands and the needs of the governed. It should be. It may come to seem so. It may be most stable when it is. But the picture is unhistorical and is always subject to refutation in times of emergency. Consent can be simply a need of strong government. If a government is to do great new things, it will need more support. If a government is to change the world, it will need mass support. This is one of the great discoveries of modern government. Napoleon Bonaparte once said: 'The politics of the future will be the art of stirring the masses.'

Political rule can only succeed in a political system. But political systems may need to suspend political rule and may survive such periods of suspension. 'Those republics,' wrote Machiavelli, 'which in time of danger cannot resort to a dictatorship will generally be ruined when grave occasions occur.' This reminds us that 'dictatorship' was, in its original signification, a device of republican and constitutional politics. The first way that political systems try to cope with states of emergency is to recognize in a legal sense that they exist. This again has been a field but sparsely explored[15] (perhaps because it falls between 'institutions' and 'ideas', while purely legal accounts are plainly inadequate). The trouble that the Weimar Republic had with the Emergency Powers provisions of the Constitution has been often examined, but have we a coherent account of how Britain was able to convert herself for time of war into an autocracy which achieved a degree of mobilization of resources and of planning more 'total' than any of the totalitarian powers?

Most of those who have espoused the concept of sovereignty as a necessary aspect of any governmental order have surely, in fact, been following Hobbes in *abstracting* a state of emergency (or a natural condition of society without government) from normal political conditions. In this light, there is no theoretical conflict between the concepts of 'political rule' and of 'sovereignty' – however much the political invocation of the doctrine to cover a failure of political prudence, as in the American question in British politics, may make the very doctrine seem a synonym, as to the American Whigs, for tyranny.

There is no necessary contradiction even between the theory of sovereignty and the theory that power can be (or is) federal. Most Federal States have, in fact, constitutional provisions to enable the concentration of coercive power in time of emergency. The problems are great, but they are practical ones. Lincoln said: 'It has long been a grave question whether any government not too strong for the liberties of its people can be strong enough to maintain its liberties in great emergencies.' But he knew that it was at least possible. He was not asking a genuine and open question; he was simply trying to get

---

[15]But see Clinton Rossiter's interesting *Constitutional Dictatorship* (Princeton 1948).

a free people used to the idea that there would be some diminution of their liberties for the duration of hostilities. Similarly it will take the sovereign power of both the British and Irish governments to resolve the Northern Ireland question, but it cannot be resolved at all, not merely if they both continue to claim a sovereign jurisdiction, but even if either does. Sovereignty is most relevant to the formation of states and to their preservation in emergencies, less so to the difficult government of them day-to-day. Since Northern Ireland does face two ways, the most probable form of stable political order will be one that recognizes this: institutional connexions with two states, in some sense government by two states. If the link was more exclusively with the Republic of Ireland, it could only take (without extraordinary coercion) a confederal form, not even federal. Some people object to the Economic Community because it violates state sovereignty when seen as a doctrine or principle; but its very existence shows that the need for governmental order to be sovereign is not universally true as a theory.[16]

'Sovereignty' as a theory was a response to the rise of an early modern form of government, 'the State'. Before such a highly centralized institution and symbol arises it is clearer simply to speak of order, and of those types of order which are characterized by government. But if we hope to learn much from the earliest or very simplest instances, anthropologists will disappoint us more than we are often led to believe by the great prestige of their discipline. The recent discovery of the existence and importance of organized government in even the most 'primitive' societies has not been without, once again, some considerable confusion between government in general and political systems in particular. This unfortunately makes much of the evidence advanced by anthropologists hard to integrate into political and social theory.

Max Weber was concerned with types of order; but he too can be confusing. He defined politics in *Politik als Beruf* as the 'striving to share power and striving to influence the distribution of power, either among states or among groups within a state'. Thus politics, to Weber, can hardly be a universal phenomenon; at least its existence

---

[16]For example, the famous passage in Blackstone's *Commentaries* does not merely say that Parliament is sovereign in England, but that 'there is and must be in every state a supreme, irresistible, absolute, and uncontrolled authority, in which the *jura summa imperii,* or right of sovereignty, resides'.

will be highly marginal in some states. But immediately before he had defined the state as that 'human community that (successfully) claims the monopoly of the legitimate use of physical force within a given territory'. Thus politics 'among states' where this force – this prepolitical condition of statehood – is lacking, must at least be a very different kind of activity than that within a state. This is not just a matter of words (or of subjective preferences). It is a matter of historical and sociological knowledge – of true theory: distinctions need to be drawn to describe accurately two radically different kinds of situation. Politics is one form of human activity; diplomacy or the conduct of international relations is another. The political system exists within a prior framework of order. International 'society' is not a political system. It is a proper subject for the study of government; but because it has no common government at all, sadly it can not exhibit normal political behaviour.

The political system and knowledge

That knowledge of politics only thrives in political systems.

There is something else implicit in any formulation of the conditions for a political system: the importance of knowledge, or simply of truth. One peculiarity of the political system is that it is the only system of government in which telling the truth about how the system works does not endanger the system. Particular governments may – fortunately – be harmed by truths being discovered; but political systems *can* be completely open systems (though this does not imply that they will be). It is no platitude, however, that authority in primitive and tribal societies necessarily depends in large part, at least, on religious myths whose claims to be true cannot always be taken too seriously. Punishment for blasphemy is an essential institution in most such societies. It is no platitude that autocracies can never allow the free and public canvassing of theories of politics, or even the accurate reporting of political events. The censor is an essential institution in any autocratic society. Those who talk about the tolerance shown by some autocrats are merely kissing the boot that does not kick themselves.

This is the answer to those who doubt the connexion of political theory to political action; and it is the caution to those who admit but deplore the connection. Theirs is a theory of human action which actually works against politics – or at least each case of theory-lending-to-action needs to be publicly weighed on its merits, to see whether it excludes future modifications or allows for them. Political knowledge is always tentative and hypothetical; it cannot hope to find scientific laws without excluding politics. (Machiavelli, even in the *Prince,* even in his most deterministic mood, introduces the concept of *'Fortuna'* – something highly empirical; and *if* Fortune is to be overcome, it can only be by heroic force. But there is no guarantee that such force will always work.) But political knowledge cannot simply be a matter of 'intimations' or 'experience' either; there is in fact often a will to do things politically where politics has not existed before, and considerable knowledge about how to make the attempt – emulation is not always disastrous as, in their heart of hearts, disciples often know.

The academic study of politics depends on certain conditions. These are, at the best, precarious in even the most enlightened despotism; they are non-existent in totalitarian régimes. The most important of these conditions is plainly that truths can be discovered and may be told. The Russians, for example, were as concerned as the rest of us to understand the reasons for educational choice; why do, for instance, so many schoolchildren and students of high intelligence try to choose 'non-productive' subjects? Western sociologists asked their colleagues at a conference in Moscow in the old days whether this might be connected with social class. They received the answer, of course, that there are no social classes in the Soviet Union. Conceptual blocks limit political inquiry quite as much as direct controls.

We often take for granted the great amount of sheer information that is readily available in a political system. Government statistics are usually reliable, because they are open to public rebuttal. Government statistics are available both because people want to know why such a policy is thought desirable, or very often just want to know; and because the government itself feels under a political compulsion to offer such information. Oddly, we take this very much for granted, though true information and publicity for it are perhaps institutions quite as important for political government as, for instance, electoral arrangements. There may not be enough electoral studies, certainly from some sociological approaches, but it is hard to think of any studies which have seriously tried to assess the amount and kind of information about governmental activities which is or is not available, and to try to establish criteria to explain why some information is not released (or is perhaps never sought for), and why perhaps some should not be. Some of the points would be very obvious; but not all. There is an atmosphere, we all know, about information in Whitehall and Westminster which, by comparison with Washington, looks quite pro-political – if one aspect of politics is the ability to tell the truth about the operation of government without endangering the State. The ineffability of *Raison d'État* only exists in a political system in time of emergency.

Politics as freedom

That where there is politics, there is freedom.

Where there is politics there is freedom. There is some freedom, even if limited to contesting aristocratic clans, wherever government recognizes by institutional means the need to consult with conflicting interests on some regular and known basis – whether, as we have said, through prudence (being unable to predict the outcome of coercion), or through principle (when, in some sense, the equal freedom of individuals or of other groups is part of the moral culture).

'Freedom' was not included in the list of conditions for a political system because, in a minimal sense, it is almost a pleonasm for politics; and because, in a more elaborate sense, it is a derivative of an already existing political system or culture. If consultation and compromise are to be effective, if the government is to find out accurately what groups want or will stand for, or what is their relative power, then people representative of these groups must be free to speak the truth. Aristotle remarks that it is very difficult for a tyrant to find people who will tell him the truth. If this is to be done, which surely contributes to the efficiency of any government, the penalties of mistaken or unwelcome advice must not be too drastic. Governments need some spheres of independent thought and action (if only, at the very least, the court-jester: in tyranny only the licensed simpleton tells the truth).

A political system is a free system – though the order is thus: freedom depends on politics as politics depends on government. The activity of politics is a public activity between men who have the legal status of freemen. Much purely semantic debate would be spared if we reminded ourselves more often that the original signification of 'freedom', and its Greek and Latin cognates, was always that of a status. The Greeks felt themselves to be the *eleutheros* because they governed themselves among themselves. The character of the free man was contrasted to that of the slave – the free were generous, expansive, above all public-spirited (liberal?); the slavish were mean, narrow-minded, and selfish. Certainly freedom has a history as a cultural phenomenon coterminous with politics long before philosophers and publicists came along to speculate to such absurd extremes – we are told – as that freedom 'really means' either the absence of all restraint (freedom from government and politics), or liberation from all error ('In thy service is the only perfect freedom' or Rousseau's '. . . must be forced to be free'). Such definitions are really attempts to limit arbitrarily or transcend politics. Freedom only has a contextual meaning – if it has any relevance to government at all.

It is heartening that political régimes will often consciously run risks with their very stability rather than curtail particular freedoms. Only anti-political régimes are for ever preparing the individual to sacrifice his freedom of action for the collectivity, or trying to persuade him that freedom is not the positive experience of diversity, but is the euphoria that comes from making the right choice in good company. Yet people who are reborn are seldom reborn free.

Some freedom in a negative sense may exist in autocracies, between the gaps of the laws, the indifference of the ruler, and the inefficiency or corruption of the bureaucracy. But in totalitarian and ideological societies not merely are fields of free activity hunted down, even in things irrelevant to the mechanisms of control of traditional autocracies – like art and music, but, as is well known, free actions are deemed to be impossible. Everything, in theory, is sociologically determined. But political societies neither enshrine such fabulous theories, nor do they even imagine the need to claim that all human actions should submit to the test of public policy.

Freedom depends both on some distinction and on some *interplay* between private and public actions, for it is neither isolation from politics (as the liberal often wants to believe), nor is it loneliness (as the concept of 'the intellectual' often involves). Freedom and privacy both thrive when government is conducted publicly in the manner called political. Freedom, then, is neither isolation nor loneliness: it is the privacy of men who are committed to maintaining, even if not personally participating in, public politics. Privacy is itself a social relationship and freedom is an activity. Men who cease either to identify or to value politics lose or threaten freedom. Politics are the public actions of free men; free men are those who do, not merely can, live both publicly and privately. Men who have lost the capacity for public action are not free, they are simply isolated and ineffectual. Again Aristotle reminds us, in a terrible phrase for all times, that the man who seeks to dwell outside the political relationship 'is either a beast or a god'.

Freedom, then, is the manner in which political action is conducted. 'To scour the universe for possibilities of freedom other than those given by the organization of human groups for the carrying out of specific purposes, and the production of desirable results,' wrote Malinowski, 'is an idle philosophic pastime.'[17]

Theory and the political system

That political theory is an essential part of the political system and is itself political – both descriptive and normative.

But to return to more academic preoccupations. Academics are often the first to say that the spell of political theory has declined, indeed all but vanished. So it is not surprising that other people believe this too. But political theory is, in practice, an essential part of any political system. There are no cases of political systems which have not contained a tradition of political speculation. Such a tradition explains rationally why power always exists in the form of authority. Quite simply, there is always need to explain *what* we are doing, and also to provide some reasons (though they will never be conclusive) why we are doing it in a particular way.

Political theory is itself political. If a political system is fundamentally a descriptive recognition of diversity plus an ethical recognition that this should be normal, then a political doctrine will display the same characteristics (a political doctrine is simply a more partial and specific, hence less general, theory).

---

[17]Bronislaw Malinowski, *Freedom and Civilisation* (London 1947), p. 95. His Chapter 2, 'Analysis of the Multiple Meanings', is the clearest and most neglected treatment of the problem in modern literature.

A political theory will always assert both that something is the case and that something should be the case (institutions *and* ideas?). And political theory has not in fact declined (its function is necessary to any political system); it has simply been disguised as *method.* Philosophers have demonstrated to us the inherent ambiguity and contestability of political concepts; and, most unsurprisingly, have shown that 'value' assumptions are contained in any attempt at descriptions of political processes. Some professional students of politics in the universities – indeed this is a malaise of the social sciences generally – react to such criticism from the analytical philosopher by redoubling their efforts to appear 'scientific' and purely factual, to purge themselves of value assumptions, and to emasculate themselves politically.

However, if one asks why these views are held, one can come to see that political theory has not declined, but has been disguised. It has been disguised precisely because it is an embarrassment to the prudishness of academic philosophers, since it *is* committed to value statements; and because it is an embarrassment to the promiscuity of amateur idealists, since it is also based on descriptive theories which help to tell us what is possible. 'The ethically desirable must be the sociologically possible,' said Hobhouse. Neither analyst nor idealist can live without it, even though it refutes their strange division of the world between fact and value. The logic of master-science is not that of the natural sciences – the observer is necessarily a part of his observations. Through politics men strive to realize public purposes realistically. Political judgements subsume the theoretical distinction between 'fact' and 'value'; political theories assert the unity of ethical and practical life. It is impossible to think of any political doctrine which does not claim that something *should* be done, or not done; but which does not also contain a positive description of the circumstances from which the policy arises.

Method as doctrine

That all methodologies are disguised doctrines, and doctrines only differ in emphasis or degree from theories.

The true claim of the master science and the inevitability of political theory can be made clear if we study the most flagrant case of the attempt to take politics out of politics – to avoid the purposive element in political theory. The academic study of politics has tried to do just this in its aspirations to be neutral, scientifically objective, and 'value-free'. Nothing illustrates the present malaise of true politics more vividly than to see how some of those whose profession it is, one might naïvely think, to defend the authority of the master-science, have in fact come near to destroying it. They have done this either by false scruples about what is 'academic', or else by a sense of 'professional propriety' which can be plain political funk. But these scruples and fears are unnecessary and the refuge they offer is, in any case, illusory.

Now in recent years the growing tendency in the university study of politics has been to make the criteria for research and study not political importance, but various notions of methodological impeccability. Political *doctrines* are felt to be biased, subjective, or purely relative things, *therefore* political theory must be based on some methodology. But there is no absolute difference between theory and doctrine (theories are simply the better doctrines), and every methodology is itself a political doctrine. It is a case of *Erst kommt die Politik: dann kommt die Methodologie.* (Certainly this puts the study of politics on a somewhat different footing from some other traditional subjects in universities; but this is no reason to think it inappropriate as a study at all, unless in the name of some spinsterish concept of 'objectivity' one turns one's back on the whole tendency of Western civilization to be an improving, reformist, ameliorative, not simply a contemplative, culture – as a contemporary school would do!)[18]

A methodology I take to be a set of rules and procedures for the discovery of knowledge. A political doctrine I take to be a coherently related set of proposals for the conciliation of differing social interests in a desirable manner. Probably there is no situation so simple that the number of possible resolutions will not be infinite (though they all have in common their political character and their openness to change). And a political doctrine is thus necessarily both evaluative and predictive. It will

---

[18]See Michael Oakeshott, *Rationalism in Politics* (Methuen 1962), Elie Kedourie, *Nationalism* (Hutchinson, 2nd ed. 1961), Maurice Cowling, *The Nature of Political Science* (Cambridge 1963), and Kenneth Minogue, *The Liberal Mind* (Methuen 1963).

offer an account in terms of anticipating the future; but other theories might also work, other policies might fit, so reasons are put forward why a particular doctrine *should* be adopted. The holding of political doctrines, both as scientific theories and as guides to action, is thus, at some level of explicitness, unavoidable.

Let us consider two types of methodology which claim simply to study, with pure lenses unground by any doctrinal axes, what they call 'political behaviour' or 'political behavior'. There is the 'non-U' U.S. scientific sort and the quite O.K. U.K. 'U' empiricist sort. (Students of literature and psychology might think that behaviourism is a pretty dead wild duck, but they would be interested to see how it functions as a political doctrine.)

The first type is that which is referred to, for instance, by David Butler in his *The Study of Political Behaviour*: 'In America "political behavior" is used by some writers in a restrictive and technical sense to cover studies designed to produce scientifically verifiable propositions about conduct in political situations.' And political behaviour, in the O.K. U.K. sense, is then presumably everything that depends upon, I quote from Butler again, 'what people actually do and say'. The idea of a value-free science of politics has dominated the thought of American students of politics in this century. The Americans have aspired to generalize and the British have remained content to describe, but they are as one in their dislike and distrust of political theory.

I have discussed the American example at length in my *American Science of Politics: its origins and conditions*. This sought to show not so much that the claim to be a true science was false, but that the real meaning of the claim lay in the doctrinal assumptions made by the advocates of this science: a type of specifically liberal and democratic political doctrine of far more limited applicability than the authors supposed. Values were taken for granted amid the enervating unity of belief of American liberalism, so it was believed that the mere discovery of facts would create a kind of spontaneous national therapy.

In Britain political behaviour research has blossomed less luxuriantly as pseudo-science than in the United States because empiricism or 'descriptivism' was already a long-established attitude in British historical and political writings. There was a rich, broad, often vague but much-tilled middle-ground of 'common sense', sir, from which we could 'refuse to be torn' to the excesses of either positivism and scientism, or of academic and vulgar idealism. But descriptivism or 'common sense' always reflected as calm and unthinking an acceptance of certain peculiar things as 'natural' as ever did American political science. How often is Lord Bryce's notorious dislike of 'theory' still taken at its own faceless value, as if the fact that he was not consciously theoretical could protect him against theoretical assumptions. (His complacent claim, in the Introduction to his *American Commonwealth,* that he would 'simply present the facts of the case . . . letting them speak for themselves', might have been more impressive had it not been in the context of criticizing Tocqueville for simply advocating 'somewhat speculative views of democracy'.) Bryce, in every sense, was a liberal. His methodology is perfectly attuned to the assumptions of politics from 1860–1914, but put his kind of questions – and apply, for instance, his rational treatment of public opinion – to European politics in the 1930s, and the result is sadly inadequate.

Consider a more contemporary example of the dangers of a descriptivism or empiricism which lacks self-consciousness about its own assumptions: the late Robert McKenzie's *British Political Parties.* Its purpose, he said, in the Preface to the First Edition, 'is not concerned with party ideologies' but only with the distribution of power. (By 'ideology' he plainly meant what is here called a 'doctrine'.) But the book in fact develops into a strong and very plausible case against attaching much importance to doctrinal factors. He does not simply make an author's division of convenience between 'doctrine' and 'power structure'; he tries to show how little can be attributed to the mere words of a doctrine. This may, perhaps, in *some* circumstances be true (though there is no reason to see why it should be true at all), but it is at least interesting that, in the time of Hugh Gaitskell's leadership McKenzie was among the leading advocates of the view that the future success of the Labour Party depended on its being able to shed from its formal constitution some words about 'nationalization'. This was not the kind of methodological importance that he attached to ideas in the book. Might not one think that the book, then, was to be seen not simply as an attack on doctrine in politics, but as an attack on a particular doctrine by another? And why not? He may have been poorer as an objective political observer, but richer as the proto-Social Democrat.

Britain has the distinction of possessing some academic doctrinaire anti-doctrinaires to whom all theoretical knowledge of society is either a fallacy – 'rationalism', or else a threat to the working of those unconscious intimations and habits on which true political order depends, etc., etc. Even when they choose to earn their living as students of politics they spend their time, in fact, mixing frivolity with malice, trying to retard or sabotage the advance of knowledge. For they are quite sure – and quite right – that knowledge leads to reform (though reformers should know that no reform is ever total or final – if its manner is political at all).

Now the most common self-characterization of British political scientists is, of course, 'empirical' or 'empiricist' – one is not always quite sure what this means, but this is what people say. Those who make a cult of 'empiricism' may appear to be of two quite different schools – but in fact doctrinally they are the same: the 'working empiricists' and the 'literary empiricists'. There is an almost mass-produceable kind of research which simply gets stuck to the facts – whether of parties, pressure groups, public administration, or electoral behaviour. There is a corresponding type of more bookish factory-writing which relates the abstract views of some foreign theorist (or literary traitor), taking every silliness seriously and concealing or disparaging every empirical element, and then ends up by demanding yet another healthy dose of good old British empiricism. And empiricism is clearly meant to be, not a substantive doctrine, but – though some empiricists have an inhibition about the word – a methodology. One hardly dares to offer a formulation of it, for however one does so it will seem to be identifying it with a particular political doctrine. 'Caution', 'habit', 'the virtues of experience', 'being anti-doctrinaire', 'a respect for tradition', 'facts as one finds them', these are the kind of characteristics usually given. Oakeshott claimed that his famous polemical inaugural lecture at L.S.E., *Political Education,* was simply an essay in 'the indicative mood', something purely descriptive; and he affects dismay at those who see it as a brilliant restatement of conservative doctrine.

Conservatism is, as it were, the affair of the politicians ('poor fellows – someone has to do the donkey-work we praise as the only reality'); whereas empiricism is the affair of the philosophers. Such philosophers talk of the virtues of 'experience' or tradition but they are usually extremely ignorant about actual politics; they never write from or about actual political experience (or even make use of historical writings); they always write logical critiques of other books which equally don't. They praise 'concrete actions' and 'actual situations' rather than abstract ideas; but they do so themselves in a purely abstract manner. They make a banal cult of the actual but they distrust social science. Thus there is, as it were, among the students of politics, a 'British school' of preposterous *a priori* empiricism. Students of political behaviour, on the other hand, while sharing the assumptions of philosophical empiricism, are at least curious about the present world and are energetic.

Two historical points must be made. First, empiricism and behaviourism both assume a very high degree of contentment with scepticism about the effect of general ideas on politics, which recent events in the world suggest is empirically false, or, if ever true, then only for short periods in unusual circumstances.

The inevitability of doctrine

That the holding of theories or doctrines is inevitable and that most doctrines, even, contain a high empirical element.

So here we have it. In political systems that take their politics too much for granted, the 'master-science' can only be disguised, put in some mask of method, one still cannot live without it. Anyone who attempts the most simple description of society is in fact involved in, as Butler says, 'constant ordering and classification'. The principles of such selectivity are those of some political doctrine, whether half-baked or well-baked. The most down-to-earth, practical politician will in fact act according to some understanding of what he is doing and what effect his actions or inactions will have on other things. These prejudices will be summed up or described in some political doctrine. Much of the study of politics is, in fact, the uncovering of, in Justice Holmes's words, 'the inarticulate major premises' both of the nominally unreflective (whether they are infamous statesmen or famous historians) and of institutional procedures. The empiricist dwelt on the surface-level of how people reacted to and tried to resolve those real problems which are seldom stated – what R. G. Collingwood called the 'presuppositions' of practical activity; political theory is concerned both to clarify and to resolve such presuppositions and problems.

There is no absolute distinction between the study and the practice of politics. All politicians hold some doctrine consciously, or act according to them unconsciously; all academics find their researches or very words used or torn to some purpose, so it is only responsible for them to make their purposes explicit and reasonable. The element of untestable evaluation in political theory need worry only those who dislike the diversity of political life itself. But the scientific should in fact be heartened to see that even such common-or-garden political doctrines as liberalism, conservatism, and socialism contain a strong empirical element. They all contain a certain picture of society; and to act according to these pictures may plainly be more or less reasonable and successful in different circumstances, times, and societies. To 'expose' much pseudo-scientific methodology as in fact types of liberalism or conservatism, as one could also show that much sociology is, indeed, socialism, is not to invite despair at the subjectivity of these doctrines, but rather to show how inevitable it is that they should be held and *how strong an objective element* they each contain. Each is scientific enough to make it plausible, but false, to try to elevate it above politics. The truth is that there is nothing, in this world at least, above politics. Politics is freedom. And for the same reasons there is no final distinction between the study of political ideas and the study of political institutions – except that of a conventional misleading pedagogy. All ideas seek institutional realization; all institutions embody purposes. There is no fact which is not pointed to for some purpose. Even this is an intellectual abstraction of what is in fact a unity: the experience and activity of the political system itself.

Certainly the academic student of politics should be committed to truth without compromise and to saying things from the head that the heart might wish were otherwise, whereas the politician can be pardoned, indeed sometimes praised, for compromising utterance and action with time and place. But since the distinction between theory and practice is not absolute, far better that the main subjects of study have an acknowledged relevance to politics than that students either deceive themselves that they can be fully objective or wallow in trivialities. They should not be so committed that their ability to give a true account of other doctrines is affected (but then neither should politicians, else their tactics will fail if they have no true knowledge of their opponents); but they must be committed both to political relevance and to political institutions. What can be political, however, is wider than is sometimes supposed.

A Footnote to Rally
Fellow Socialists (1982)

*Centralized ownership has very little meaning unless the mass
of people are living roughly upon an equal level, and have some
kind of control over the government. 'The State' may come to
mean no more than a self-elected political party, and oligarchy
and privilege can return, based on power rather than on money.*

GEORGE ORWELL, *The Lion and the Unicorn: Socialism and
the English Genius*, London 1941

*Régimes which depend on the suppression of all opposition
and the stifling of all civic freedoms must be taken to
represent a disastrous regression in political terms from
bourgeois democracy. . . . But the civic freedoms which,
however inadequately and precariously, form part of
bourgeois democracy are the product of centuries of
unremitting popular struggles. The task of Marxist politics is to
defend these freedoms; and to make possible their extension
and enlargement by the removal of their class boundaries.*

RALPH MILIBAND, *Marxism and Politics*, London 1977

Evolution and revolution

That politics as an activity is not merely compatible with what could
prove to be a revolutionary form of egalitarian society but is its

essential precondition, and that political means are essential if one is to move towards socialist ends.

By 1918 Rosa Luxemburg was warning Lenin after the Revolution, just as she had warned him thirteen years before, that freedom must be the means not just the eventual end of the party's strategy; and though the time traveller, H. G. Wells, visited Russia in 1920 and at first had good words to say for the Bolsheviks, he was under no illusion that Lenin's 'dictatorship of the proletariat' was either temporary or anything other than rule by a small party oligarchy. A 'fairy story' or fable written in 1944, George Orwell's *Animal Farm* was not untimely but created an astonishingly belated popular recognition that the revolution, based on cries of 'Liberty, Equality, Fraternity', had, once again, been betrayed. He did not argue that the fault lay in any inevitable growth of power-hungry élites (the 'pigs'), but rather in the excessive credulity and trust of the other animals in their leaders; 'all animals' must be the basic power behind long revolutionary changes as well as the objects of 'the revolution' led by those who unhappily can become 'more equal than others'.

Great confusion has arisen between the myth of 'the revolution' as a climactic event and the reality of 'the revolutionary process'. The opportunity for reshaping societies towards greater social justice may only come either through the sudden overthrow or more often the breakdown of repressive autocracies, but the revolutionary opportunity does not guarantee the revolutionary outcome: a benign outcome needs restraint and tolerance, as well as skill and will, exercised through decades and generations. If the classical Marxist critique of capitalism was broadly correct, its theory of inevitable stages was wrong; for it failed to reckon with and guard against nationalism, bureaucratization and above all the pure power-hunger and desire for self-perpetuation among new as much as among old élites. At the least, the theory of stages needed restating in terms of possibilities, and even diluting to allow for the overlapping of the various stages. This would seem a less misleading model of the post-revolutionary world, and hence a model more open to variety and to influence by popular debate, rather than one depending on belief in laws of history wholly determined by social structure or modes of production. These always condition but they never determine human action.

Thus the debate in the first part of the century between 'true Marxist' revolutionaries and revisionist evolutionary Austrian and German Marxist 'Social Democrats' (in the sense then current) was perhaps never as contradictory and unbridgeable in theory as it seemed to the passionate protagonists. They differed about means, not about ends. And there is no inevitability about progress either through revolution or gradual change, such as German socialists and British Fabians used to argue for in the 1900s and 1920s. They both thought that by governing with the right values and by deliberate stages of economic and social planning, a socialist society could be achieved. In this they differed utterly from the new Social Democrats, either the present West German S.P.D. or the new British Social Democratic Party. They, whether from wisdom, class-interest, exhaustion or fear, no longer believe that an egalitarian society can be achieved – or should be achieved, even; they hope more modestly, if somewhat vaguely, simply to manage a mixed economy benignly with the interests of the welfare of the disadvantaged strongly in mind. They aspire to civilize, perhaps to inject a few socialist values into, not to replace, the economic dynamic of that competitive, individualistic ethic of Western capitalism which intrudes so systematically and unasked into so many aspects of social, cultural and personal life.

The social democrats are right about the primacy of liberty but they are wrong to think that it is always threatened by equality and to believe that a proper sense of individualism must always be linked to the competitive acquisition of private property. Their own project is perfectly possible, given favourable economic growth such as Anthony Crosland assumed in the 1950s and 1960s in his book *The Future of Socialism.* The philosopher should lament and not mock that their hour of electoral opportunity seems to come at a time of unique difficulty for their theory; whereas it is the decline of the economy in Great Britain that could also give an opportunity to the Left of the Labour Party, as seems to have happened in France and Greece.

My real intention is not, however, to debate policies or argue for causes, whether local or international. There follows not a systematic argument for true socialism but simply an argument that there is no *necessary* incompatibility between revolutionary and evolutionary varieties; and that, if socialism is to occur at all, it must be pursued and consolidated through political means. Ralph Miliband, whose views on politics and civil liberties I quote at the head of this chapter and whose views on this point are not untypical of many modern Marxist intellectuals in the West, the Third World and even in Eastern Europe, wrote an earlier book on *Parliamentary Socialism.* In it he argued that the acceptance of parliamentary conventions and evolutionary socialism had emasculated the alleged revolutionary spirit of the early British Labour movement. Apart from the fact that this no longer seems to be true (if ever it was historically), his theses can at best only apply to specific contexts. It would be a massive *non sequitur* to say that, because of some past experiences, socialism cannot proceed by parliamentary means; or to identify all forms of republican assemblies with the specific conservative conventions of a particular phase of the British parliamentary tradition.

Determined political socialists, however revolutionary their long-term aims, have to build up *popular* support if their measures are to work. When they resort, as in Eastern Europe after the Second World War, or in many contemporary states in Africa and Asia, to dictatorial coercion and control, not merely is liberty destroyed, which is obvious enough, but even mere welfare is grievously limited. The evidence is now overwhelming in the Soviet world that productivity suffers both through the sheer inefficiency and often corruption of unchallengeable centralized bureaucracies and through a massive indifference, sullenness and propensity to go slow when workers can neither change their jobs, form free trade unions, strike, nor even – if driven to that pitch – hope to revolt with any chance of success. The very working masses, as in Poland or Czechoslovakia, whose productive power is essential to progress are rendered impotent.

George Orwell once reviewed F. A. Hayek's *The Road to Serfdom*:

Professor Hayek is probably right in saying that in this country the intellectuals are probably more totalitarian-minded than the common people. But he does not see, or will not admit, that a return to 'free' competition means for the great mass of people a tyranny probably worse, because more irresponsible, than the State. The trouble with competitions is that somebody wins them. Professor Hayek denies that free capitalism necessarily leads to monopoly, but in practice that is where it has led, and since the vast number of people would rather have State regimentation than slumps and unemployment, the drift towards collectivism is bound to continue. . . . Such is our present predicament. Capitalism leads to dole queues, the scramble for markets, and war. Collectivism leads to concentration camps, leader worship and war. There is no way out of this unless a planned economy can somehow be combined with the freedom of the intellect . . .[1]

Consider the many one-party States who claim to be socialist but whose dominant ideology is, in fact, nationalism. This nationalism often enables rulers to take the support of the masses for granted. But there is a world of difference between such States which can, like Tanzania, at least tolerate criticism and public debate about policies among the ruling élite and the intelligentsia, and those more common one-party States in which no public dissent is tolerated. The moral differences are the most important today because of the growing number of developing countries claiming to be 'Socialist'; and they will become ever more so the further back into history the original struggle for national liberation fades: nationalism cannot remain for ever an off-the-peg justification for each and every arbitrary act of party, leader or President. The differences in economic efficiency may be less obvious and may be affected by a hundred and one contingent factors; but in theory (that is, in long-term tendency), other things being equal, it is unlikely that uncriticized planning can be more effective than plans that are open to public debate and which may even have arisen out of such debate. Plans that can be criticized can be modified. People who tolerate criticism are more likely to change their minds. If the plan may neither be criticized nor modified and it does not work as expected, then little is left but to impose it with coercion, suppress evidence of failure and discontent, and imprison all those who say that the Emperor has no clothes. Such desperate anti-political measures have even been dignified by a name: 'permanent revolution'.

In multi-party régimes there may well be a consensus, indeed, which can hinder or delay the realization of socialist goals. But socialists, like anyone else, must realize that great enterprises take much time. Rome was not built in a day. If we are trying to liberate humanity and perfect human nature, we are unwise not to see this as the work of generations and to recognize the need to carry people with us, slowly, patiently, definitely, step by step. Socialists must distinguish between a consensus of values (which is extraordinarily rare in any society) and

---

[1]George Orwell, *The Collected Essays, Journalism and Letters,* Vol. III (Harmondsworth 1970), p. 114.

the need to reach a consensus about procedures (which is common in parliamentary democracies). These rules or conventions of the political game may be biased, quite naturally, in support of the existing system. But socialists cannot hope to modify these rules except by the rules, by persuasion or by demonstrating good fruits from political power gained by socialist parties observing these very rules. Socialists should not be surprised if their criticism of these rules is sometimes taken as a threat to ignore them; and if the very people they want to reach and uplift often reject them and suspect them of being not merely anti-establishment but anti-political. Even such a mild and democratic business as the British Labour Party's plan to abolish an appointed and hereditary House of Lords needs balancing simultaneously with measures which appear to ordinary people to check the powers of the Government in other ways. Intellectual socialists cannot have it both ways: to hold that the mass of the people have been 'socialized' into conservative constitutional beliefs is not to ignore such constraints, but to demonstrate that it is in these terms that the argument has to begin and has to be won. All politics, indeed, must deal with people as they are.

The potential political and the actual productive power of the people is, indeed, more essential to socialist theory (this is the minimal core of truth in the original labour theory of value), than it is to contemporary capitalist theory. While popular capitalist doctrine still preaches the individual work ethic, that workers should work as hard as they can for necessarily disproportionate rewards and that there are jobs to be had for those who *really* want to work, liberal economists favour a more technical argument about the inevitability of capital-intensive industry and of uncontrolled 'free trade' in finance and international investment, whatever the cost in unemployment. Full employment is no longer seen as economically possible or as politically crucial: free-market theorists now gamble on the passivity of the masses if the marginal rate of mere subsistence can be found and funded coupled with investment in a type of mass-communications designed, quite literally, both to take peoples' minds off things that matter and to create unfree illusions of helplessness (which was the satiric intent of Orwell's 'prolecult' in *Nineteen Eighty-Four,* aimed at the contemporary mass media not at a distant future). 'True conservatives', or old-fashioned tories, however, while believing deeply in natural hierarchy and in maintaining inequality, yet are genuinely paternalistic: they have a sense of community and would draw the line, if they knew how, at any economic doctrines that result in mass unemployment.

The 'new conservative' faith in the universality of the market mechanism could well founder on the bitter, dehumanizing effect of mass unemployment. But equally socialist leaders must show sensitivity to a complex industrial world in which the workers and managers, if not persuaded freely and given time to adjust, simply will not work or will not work well, and will prove unwilling to adjust themselves to new technologies and changing social priorities. Even an advanced industrial power which attempted genuine socialist programmes all at once, too quickly and without a broad prior basis of support stretching far beyond party activists, could face some of the same problems as in African and Asian socialism: the danger of alienating élites from the masses. Chairman Mao Tse-tung's 'Cultural Revolution' was no answer to such a problem, but the move towards a managerial bureaucracy in China is neither socialism nor the glimmering of liberalism that some Western observers imagine.

Coercive government by party bureaucracy all too often is the crowning achievement of revolutions pursued by non-political means. The apostle Paul was right to say that 'every man that striveth for the mastery is temperate in all things', if he is serious about the 'mastery'. And coercion by mass unemployment, in Western industrial societies, also marks the failure of 'mastery', not its typical or most efficient mode. 'Mastery' involves patience with men and women as they are, as well as an ability to persuade them of what they or their children could become.

Put in simple terms, one does not, as I think Miliband now agrees, throw out the baby with the bathwater. Liberty is not hopelessly tainted by capitalism, nor is the idea of 'liberty as we know it' purely bourgeois, a product of the rise of capitalism – as both Marx and Hayek have argued, the one rejoicing, the other lamenting, but agreeing on this essential point. On the contrary, the tradition of free politics and of republican government long preceded the capitalist era: it was both an ideal vision and an occasional imperfect practice from the time of European classical antiquity, the memory of which, among scholars and humanists, even among fearful tyrants, never died. There could come in time a revolutionary 'transformation of values', certainly of the priorities we give to our many different values; humanity could discover 'the dignity of work' as William Morris hoped, and reject its alienation, and a common culture could arise in place of an impersonal division of labour which both separates and cripples culture and citizenship; but all this will not, except in religious myths and their ideological substitutes, come suddenly or at once. The ideas and the sense of direction already exist, but the recruitment has hardly begun, detailed maps and plans for provision along the route are not to be found, nor has thought been given about how to keep up the spirits of the army on the march – still less about what should happen if it decided to stop or turn round. Transitions are never easy. Deliberate ones have been rare. But the enterprise is possible, if conducted by free men in a freely chosen way. Personally I am a 'moderate Socialist', no longer a 'moderate' in newspaper senses: my goals are extreme and therefore I moderate and measure my means.

The socialist theory

That the basic empirical theory of socialism is both more coherent and yet more conditional than is often supposed; and the moral doctrine of socialism is wholly consistent with the theory: both modify each other even if the roots are not always the same.

Let us grant that there are many varieties of socialism, even without each newly independent nation claiming a uniquely national form. Many, but not all, of these divisions are variations on Marx's themes, some of which, however, would be quite unrecognizable by and uncongenial to their founder. Some claim to possess 'true Marxism' and interpret the texts with scholastic zeal as direct guides to action. Others more subtly and sensibly claim that Marxism is a 'living method' – hence prone not merely to growth, but presumably to unforeseeable accidents as well. However, there is also the decentralist, syndicalist and cooperative tradition of socialism that stems from Proudhon: this rejects the economic theory of determinism and the historical theory of stages and holds that capitalism can be destroyed from within by forming cooperative communities for production. Then there is the managerial or mixed economy version of socialism which emerged from both the German revisionists and the British Fabians: that the capitalist state can be permeated and controlled for the general welfare. Not to forget what I technically call 'British socialism' which has its roots in an eclectic fusion of Robert Owen's cooperative ideas, the cultural vision of William Morris, Methodist conscience, Chartist democracy and revisionist Marxism: libertarian, egalitarian and above all ethical, placing more stress on personal exemplifications of socialist values than on public ownership or class legislation. And there is always the anarchist and communitarian criticism of and example to these mainstream socialisms. Other categories abound.

Is there a common core of meaning amid all these revolving and colliding concepts of socialism? I dare to think so. Put in the simplest and most basic terms, socialism has both an empirical theory and a moral doctrine. The theory is that the rise and fall and the cohesion of societies is best explained not by the experience and perpetuation of élites (which is conservatism), nor by the initiative and invention of competitive individuals (which is liberalism), but by the relationship of the primary producers of wealth (in an industrial society, the skilled manual worker) to the ownership and control of the means of production. The doctrine asserts the primacy and mutual dependence of the values of 'liberty, equality and fraternity'; and it draws on the theory to believe that greater equality will lead to more cooperation than competition, that this will in turn enhance fraternity and hence liberate from inhibition, restriction and exploitation both individual personality and the full productive potential of society.

The theory is not fully comprehensive: in its strictly empirical and characteristically economic form it is dangerously close at times to being purely a doctrine for the skilled industrial worker. If it speaks to the poor and the dispossessed, it assumes the kind of grounds for believing in human rights or depicting the quality of a good life that one finds in the Christian tradition and in the writings of Jean-Jacques Rousseau and Immanuel Kant. Attempts to explain the meaning of these doctrines in terms of the economic theory seem far fetched or fatuous. Socialist theory has no more made an entirely original contribution to ethics than it has to aesthetics or to science. Socialist theory and doctrine complement each other in practice, but neither logically entails the other, not even together are they fully comprehensive. To think that any political theory and/or doctrine must be fully comprehensive is precisely what I have argued is a totalitarian rather than a political style of thought. Marxists may write about aesthetics and ethics if they will. It is interesting and sometimes useful to see how the popularity, for instance, of cultural or moral ideas can be explained in terms of class interest and social stratification. But their origin, truth and value is never reducible simply to the economic concepts of the general theory. Russian and Chinese Communism have both gone very far in suggesting that there is a correct *socialist* way to do everything – from agricultural research to sexual conduct and artistic production. But this is nonsense, and its meaning is to be found neither in socialist theory nor in doctrine but in the need for uniformity in would-be totalitarian societies.

What is more surprising is that there is no distinctively socialist theory of political institutions, though the doctrine is rather simply democratic. What kind of political institutions does socialism need? Most of the answers come in conventional republican or democratic terms, except that people will or should participate more, make more use of these electoral or parliamentary or informative devices. Few liberals would quarrel with this; indeed this is liberal doctrine, only the rival theories predict different results. Only the commune and the soviet have emerged historically, and then so briefly, as distinctively socialist institutions. But few think that the spirit of Marx's somewhat inconsistent but passionate championing of the Paris Commune of 1870 as the very model of a classless society, still haunts the Soviet Union, even though the Czechoslovak revisionists in 1968 in the 'Prague Spring' invoked the memory of the Commune as if someone in Moscow still cared or could be shamed. But certainly when socialists talk about 'taking over the State', whether by parliamentary or other means, to use it for socialist policies, usually the cross-current of a somewhat contradictory argument arises – one which stresses small-scale things, local communities and industrial democracy as being both the school and the final resting place of socialist values.

Yet socialists do have a distinctive *attitude* to political and social institutions. They are sceptical that institutions of State or those set up by the State in democratic but non-socialist régimes are always as neutral as they claim to be. This is a healthy scepticism, so long as everyone is aware that they are normally dealing with relative, not absolute, degrees of bias or with well meant but impossible attempts at pure neutrality. But if socialists expect 'fair play', they are foolish. Their opponents sometimes seem to believe that they mean what they say more than they do themselves. But if they try to change the rules, say of the press or broadcasting, to get 'fair play', they should remember the suspicion with which the majority of their fellow countrymen still view them, and will continue to do so precisely because they aim to change the known world. This is a large enterprise and to hurry or to proceed at unrealistic speed can be as fatal as simply accepting the rules or trying only to be as humane as possible to the crew in a leaking ship set on the wrong course. Socialists must convince people that change is possible and desirable, yet not hope to convince them by the refining and reiteration of abstract and sometimes incomprehensible socialist theories, but rather by reawakening traditions and memories of successful popular protest and by argument appealing to existing common beliefs and common interests. Is it fair, for instance, that opportunities for work and rewards for labour within the present system should be so accidental and disproportionate? Yet until some idea of a just reward is firmly established, people in jobs and 'reasonably well off' will simply not accept the principle of equal needs. The rules must be changed by the rules. Theory will guide what policies and priorities to select, but to change the present world we must both understand it, and respect people as they are, not simply as they ought to be and can become.

Socialist theory when applied to history can demonstrate that great changes are possible, but must also comprehend that everything cannot change at once and that social systems are rarely as systematic as either classical Marxist or classical liberal theorists have supposed. Marxist theories of a complete indoctrination or 'socialization' by education or the media can induce a quite unnecessary despair or rage for violent change. But these 'systems' are in fact full of imperfections and inconsistencies that, as conservatives often complain, give too many unexpected opportunities to the politically literate radical. Even in the industrial world, mixed economies are not simply façades: they are indeed remarkably mixed. The mixture can be worked upon and varied. Differential advance in different sectors is possible, despite the preconceptions of systematic theory. And in pre-industrial societies there was often a remarkable lack of congruence in the relations between rulers and ruled, the rulers often being an alien aristocracy, speaking a different language, taxing the peasantry ruthlessly but rarely trying to mobilize them or to change or proselytize them in any way. 'Let sleeping dogs lie' was an autocratic adage; and Alfred, Lord Tennyson alleged that peasants ruminated that 'Kings may come and kings may go, but we go on for ever'. And in non-industrial societies in the modern world (which is virtually to say 'the Third World') the case is much the same: the ruling élites are now at least of the same nation as the mass of the people, but their culture and way of life can be very different.

The ideas of free citizenship and of political activity had their origins in what were, broadly speaking, the aristocratic cultures of Greece and Rome, or among the merchants and bourgeoisie of England, France, Holland, Scotland, Sweden and the German and Italian 'free cities'. Even in those societies it was always difficult to prevent any public example of liberties being exercised among the few from exciting the emulation of at least some of the many. Example or mimesis is a basic social mechanism. The source and enduring myth of republican ideas and institutions was in the slave-holding cultures of Greece and Rome; but this does not taint the seed. In many ways the classical ideal of free citizenship is not so much superseded by Marx in his critique of capitalist society, as assumed by him. If all this was not part of his own cultural preconceptions, it would be hard to make sense of his fragmentary, undeveloped but important accounts of what is this autonomous human personality that can be emancipated from the alienating, competitive conditions of an industrial society where man seems divorced from the fruits of his labour. In his early *Critique of Hegel,* for instance, he wrote that 'the essence of *man* is the *true community* of men' and that 'men, not as abstractions but as real, living, particular individuals are this community. As they are, so it is too.' Marx was much closer to both the classical and humanist traditions and to the French enlightenment than many of his most famous disciples.

Thus it is historically false to identify most of the characteristic political institutions of modern 'liberal democracy' with the rise of the capitalist market. Here the theory is often in error. Capitalism accelerated the spread of such institutions for their instrumental use both to liberate new productive forces and to impose new types of control on the working class. Even so, the political and educational concessions involved in establishing a manipulative façade of free institutions proved more important than either side once thought, ultimately threatening any simple class control of the system. The skilled working man demanded by the new factories and the new technologies was a very different human animal from the peasant typical of the agricultural mode of production in autocracies. He had to be literate, for one thing, and was dangerously concentrated in cities, for another, even in capital cities. It was difficult to stop him from organizing, even in restraint of trade, without denying him the skills that the economy required. He was a constant threat to the State precisely because its power and wealth came more and more to depend upon his power and abilities. Small concessions in the franchise always proved the thin end of a wedge. And many of the new weapons of control proved double-edged. His new masters had to educate him and quite naturally sought to control that education and to limit it; but so many teachers were now needed that they were both hastily trained and hard to control completely. They began to constitute a new intelligentsia or at least a special subsection of the middle class, open to new secular ideas or still full of old evangelical ones; and even the oldest ideas of those who taught them were heavily contaminated, through Latin and Greek, with the classical myth of free citizenship. Several generations of school children in Western Europe must have believed that long before the French and American Revolutions (which their teachers would rarely mention, let alone discuss), there was something rather like these revolutions going on all the time in Greece and Rome. And gradually ideologies of progress began to replace myths of the 'good old days'. When the pupils emerged from the partial dark of such utilitarian school rooms, they often saw rudimentary democratic institutions existing already.

Some leaders of opinion like John Stuart Mill argued that the mass of the people should come into their own and exercise political power, if and when they were fully educated; and that if they were fully educated, they would – which has not happened. Others sought to postpone that fearful democratic dawn by restricting education. But the very demands of capitalist technology for skilled and literate workers, quite apart from radical and socialist agitation, heightened the crisis and the demands, if not for new political institutions, at least for popular access to existing ones.

That socialist theory is distinctive but not comprehensive can be seen even in the narrowest claim that control of the mode of production controls all else. To many Marxists economic determinism is almost a banality. Engels said: 'We make our own history, but in the first place under very definite presuppositions and conditions. Among these the economic are finally decisive.' If we must read the words with Talmudic or hermeneutic closeness, the first phrase and the last are of equal importance. If we see these 'finally decisive' economic conditions as outer limits on human action, then there is still much history we can make for ourselves; but if we see these 'definite presuppositions and conditions' as with us constantly and immediately, permeating all our thoughts and limiting our ability to think otherwise, then we can make little history for ourselves: history is then, indeed, 'the recognition of necessity'. Without socialist doctrines or values, more often assumed rather than asserted by Marx and Engels, there would be a pessimistic not a progressive conclusion.

Marx himself said, 'The mode of production in material life conditions the general character of the social, political and spiritual processes of life.' Since he does say 'general character' and 'conditions', and does not here talk about specific features or causal law and necessity, the claim is unexceptionable. We are conditioned but we are not determined. Within these conditions there must be, indeed, as most contemporary Marxists now admit, a 'relative autonomy' of the political, of the State, even of ideology (it is not always easy to explain the growth, let alone the continuance, of ideologies in purely economic terms). But to believe both that economic determinism is false and (more arguably) that Marx and Engels were either not economic determinists or not consistently so, is not to license any kind of idealist fantasy in politics. Marx did establish a mode of thought that all socialists share: first consider what follows for the organization of a society and for possible changes within it from establishing who owns the means of production and how; then consider all other relevant factors, consider how the mode of production must be modified in the interests of the working class.

Although there is common ground between Marxists and democratic socialists, five things especially have either discredited classical Marxist theory in the eyes of democratic socialists or have made them highly sceptical: (i) its lack of a clear ethical doctrine; (ii) the unwillingness of some Marxists to think in anything but rigid economic categories; (iii) a lingering habit of viewing the texts of Marx and Engels as sacred dogma rather than as often the most fruitful starting point (among others) for speculation; (iv) the inability of many Marxists to take pains to write plainly and to express the theory clearly in common parlance (indeed some seem to imply that they have an esoteric, inaccessible knowledge – the usual justification for autocracy); and (v) the common Marxist confusion between the fertile idea that theory and practice always modify each other, are never wholly distinct, and the false idea that in any given situation only one true policy or party line is backed up by theory.

It is always irritating to be told in argument that a rival or alternative policy is 'necessary', 'scientific' or simply 'objective'; and this belief is corrupting to those who hold it. Marxist theory, like any other theory, has a characteristic view of what policies it thinks are most likely to work; but there are simply too many variables in actual social situations, also too many conflicting perceptions and values involved, to make any one policy taken from the book definitively correct. If socialists are marching towards a new Rome, they should be well aware that all roads do not lead there; but that even given a strong will and a true sense of direction, there are always alternative routes, indeed room for false starts and new attempts, not any single royal road of theory and practice. Policies must emerge from the interplay between ethical doctrines and empirical theories in the hands of people who can develop from experience as well as knowledge good political judgement.

The other socialist traditions have commonly shown better political judgement and have had more to say about actual and possible policies than have most Marxists, even if their theories have been less systematic and more eclectic. Democratic socialist doctrines, however, have had much more to tell us than the Marxist tradition about specifically socialist values and thus the priorities of policy they help to define.

Socialist values

> That Liberty, Equality and Fraternity are still the basic socialist values; that all values modify each other; that many other values are held in common; and that the maximization of these values can only evolve, neither will this come suddenly nor only come after 'fundamental changes in social structure' – such changes themselves need changes in values. Nothing determines, everything conditions.

Values are important. When ordinary people have said that they no longer know what socialism stands for, it is unlikely that they are thinking either of details of policy in manifestos or striving for 'the correct theoretical perspective'. Whether we are followers of Labour Parties, Social Democratic Parties or 'true' socialism (of various kinds), values are always involved. Those who 'unmask' the 'hidden curriculum' in education, can themselves be bitten as they bite, or at least asked to come clean whether they believe their holy selves to be 'value free' or simply to be right. Not all hidden values are oppressive, many are benign. There is no objection to people believing that they hold the right values. Everything depends on *how* values are held and asserted and on *how* they are related to other values.

Any values to be realized in the practical, political world keep company with other values and occasionally contradict them. Some values are asserted as procedures and some as goals: we may be sure *what* we want to do, but equally sure that it should not be done *that* way. Because no single practice or policy follows from theory in any circumstance, it is our values that mainly decide what alternative policies to follow.

Two schools of thought, however, seem unwilling to discuss *what* values we should hold, and often seek to avoid talk of values at all: determinist Marxism and managerial pragmatism. But Marx himself in his early writings, as we have argued, seemed to take for granted both the classical tradition of free republican citizenship and a view of human nature found in Kant. He did not believe either, like many of his disciples, that all present values are simply class values and would be wholly different in a classless society. Even when he produced a formal theory of ideology, which seemed to say the *all* values are products of class or of modes of production, his argument still presupposed that these precapitalist, republican values are continual animating forces. Freedom as action, like scientific knowledge, was plainly a special category, and together they form the presuppositions of the theory of ideology, not something to be explained away by that theory. Nonetheless, the theory of ideology notoriously opened the door to the belief that all values and ideas are systematically related *products* of class and the mode of production, and can thus be manipulated by the State or the Party; only in a post-revolutionary society will values and human nature become autonomous, ends in themselves.

This theory is a relative and sometimes salutary truth: we always need to think of the sociological context of ideas, both to understand their historical meaning and their political possibilities. But as a 'necessary logical framework' or as 'scientific laws', these propositions are misleading and untrue. Because they are untrue much of the contemporary academic literature of the 'sociology of knowledge' (Marxist epistemology) is less threatening or challenging than time-wasting, a jargon-ridden arena of pharasitical sectarian jealousies with little or no relevance to political practice.

The other schools of socialist thought that fight shy of values are the pragmatists or social democrats, those who make a cult of being purely practical and of accepting the present system, if administered with decency and humanity. Consider, for gross example, that former leader of the Labour Party, Harold Wilson, who wrote two big books on his administrations, *The Labour Government, 1964–70* and *Final Term,* and another on *The Governance of Britain,* all without once discussing, even rhetorically, theories, doctrines or values of any kind (let alone socialist). He obviously believed that pure description is valid and held a pietistic belief that everything he did, because he held high office, was interesting or of value. To be purely practical in this sense is simply to accept uncritically the existing values of society – so many of which are, indeed, specifically managerial and capitalist, stressing the virtues of acquisitiveness, competition, self-reliance and efficiency. But pure pragmatism is simply impossible, either a self deceit or a public deceit. Wilson's implicit values seem to be conservative ones: a dedication to the business of simply keeping the ship of state afloat, with little hope or care about direction. Now this is a political achievement of a sort in stormy and troubled times; but it is an unnecessarily modest one for a Labour leader. When he claimed that he was 'blown off course' by uncontrollable international economic events, which events were real enough, few people believed that he was by then on any course at all except running with the wind for survival. Politics is not mere compromise and survival. I have called it 'creative compromise'. People like Wilson give politics its bad name.

Social democrats (in the new sense) profess to be pragmatists, but in a less narrow sense than Wilson's. They may indeed have certain future-looking values, though differing amongst themselves about these. But their predominant values are procedural: about *how* things should be done, not about what should be done. For they either lack imagination about the possibilities of deliberate social change or simply believe that only relatively minor technical adjustments are needed in the mix of a mixed economy. Many people indeed sympathize with these humane and limited viewpoints or are frightened of going beyond them. Yet the decline of the British economy and the growth of mass unemployment owes much to pragmatism: the lack both of any sense of direction and of positive values, such as equality and fraternity. Most social democrats and pragmatists simply assume or claim that 'means' constitute 'ends', that social justice is simply a matter of procedural values – like liberty, tolerance and electoral reform.

Procedural values are important, both for understanding politics and for politicians to be at least sufficiently empathetic to understand the minds of their opponents and what they are really up against. Elsewhere I have tried to characterize basic procedural values and named them as 'respect for reasoning', 'respect for truth', 'toleration', 'fairness' and 'freedom'.[2] But these do not of themselves constitute a particular political doctrine, only the presuppositions of any genuine political education and of *all* doctrines that are political – socialism included.

Liberty, equality and fraternity are the specifically socialist cluster of values – if one treats 'cooperation' and 'community' as closely related to 'fraternity'. Only equality is specifically socialist in itself; liberty and fraternity, however, take on a distinctively socialist form when the three are related to each other. And the three values themselves presume that individuals are both the agents and the objects of values, although individualism, as I will suggest, can take on a specifically socialist form.

Liberty

Liberty deserves almost fanatic support from democratic socialists; a truly socialist movement is so committed to more liberty and to more open government that at times it can seem almost incoherent among the multitude of small, good causes who run across the stage of the movement, whether scripted or not, and find support in the wings. And at times it can seem almost paranoiac in its belief that anything less than totally open government is likely to be concealing oppressive weapons behind every lazily or habitually closed door. Liberty, by itself, is indeed an exuberant and unpredictable thing. The actions of free men are always unpredictable. This is why bureaucrats dislike citizens, and this is the unavoidable tension between the theory of socialism

---

[2]See my 'Procedural Values' in Bernard Crick and Derek Heater, *Essays on Political Education* (Falmer Press 1977).

and its moral beliefs. Some 'libertarians', who call themselves socialist and who join socialist movements, seem to believe that anything goes as long as it is an authentic action of an untrammelled personality. If I bite, I bite freely and splendidly. Such political 'street-theatre' is a cross that any democratic socialist movement in a free society must bear as cheerfully as it can. But true socialists are concerned with judging morally the social consequences of individual actions quite as much as with writing accounts of human action in social terms; even here values must be asserted clearly. Bad social conditions do lead to increased delinquency, for instance, but this does not justify delinquency – it only affects our theories of how to diminish it and our views on sentencing policy. True socialists examine how even the most 'authentic' individual actions, whether of violent protest or colourful self-assertion, can affect the equal rights of others or diminish rather than enhance fraternity.

Liberty is not, we have argued, to be abandoned either as a bourgeois concept or on account of its origins. But it need not remain in the narrow nineteenth-century tradition of 'freedom from', simply of not being interfered with by the State or powerful neighbours. Sir Isaiah Berlin has eloquently argued, in his famous essay 'Two Concepts of Liberty', the danger of thinking of liberty in other than negative terms: if we give any positive content to liberty, ascribe to it any objectives, then we end up, all too often, crying out like Rousseau to 'force people to be free' – as it were, 'here is your Welfare State, damn you (or bless you); now you are free!'. The warning is salutary. Reformers need to be careful. In any possible society, socialist societies included, people may not like what they are given and must be free to challenge by public debate (or by turning their backs on it all) both values and policies. But even our good negative liberties ultimately depend on positive political action. The positive assertion of liberty is needed to open doors, to create an open society; but then we do not just sit admiring so many choices of ways forward or back, we need to choose, by free and open debate, the best doors to go through – perhaps never, indeed, completely shutting any. People who use their liberty to avoid political life are more often done down than left in peace. The price of liberty is even higher than eternal vigilance, as Lincoln said: it demands eternal action. Freedom needs its antique, republican, pre-liberal cutting edge restored in modern conditions: freedom is positive action in a specific manner, that of a citizen acting as if among equals; and not merely to preserve rights (says the socialist) but to extend them.[3]

Socialists must add the egalitarian assumption to liberty that not merely must all men and women be treated as citizens, but they must also be helped to count equally as citizens and, above all, be expected to act as citizens. Liberty in this positive sense does not deny liberty in the more liberal, negative sense: it subsumes, complements and extends it. Citizens in socialist societies must have rights against the State as well as a duty to work for commonly agreed purposes. R. H. Tawney long ago argued the complementary nature of rights and duties in his great essays *The Acquisitive Society* and *Equality.*

Thus talk of socialist liberty as being completely different from bourgeois liberty is melodramatic nonsense. Many left-wingers who are libertarians both at heart and in their personal behaviour get themselves trapped in their writings in that bad piece of Marxist logic, that only in the classless society after the revolution can there be true liberty – until then all we have is capitalist liberty and an 'oppressive tolerance' (a phrase of the late Herbert Marcuse). 'Thank God for small mercies', say men actually living in oppressive régimes. Socialists must always try to extend liberty to more and more people and to more and more activities in whatever circumstances possible. They must at least try to persuade those who think that liberty is being left alone in comfort to watch the television or to cultivate one's garden that governments rarely leave people alone or treat justly those who will not stand up for themselves and combine politically.

Often the most convincing anti-socialist arguments come not from liberals who dogmatically believe that liberty depends on the free working of the market mechanism, but from liberal élitists who think that liberty is all very well for the likes of us but an impossible proposition *en masse,* for the likes of them. They fear not so much an egalitarian political tyranny, whatever their rhetoric, as a debasement of their culture. Perhaps they flatter themselves too much to think that it is their culture that popular politicians wish to universalize and hence debase or vulgarize. Their real defence is that their culture is itself a free activity, irrelevant to political considerations except in totalitarian régimes, unless

---

[3]See the critique of Berlin, 'Freedom as Politics' in my *Political Theory and Practice* (London 1971).

they themselves try to make it so by claiming éither that educated élites should rule by virtue of their culture, or should have their culture specially subsidized by the State. The argument in Britain, for instance, that the existence of private education is the absolute test case of freedom, would be more impressive if the private schools were not so brazen and correct in arguing that their education constitutes a good investment. Property rights and educational rights are, indeed, closely linked in both conservative and liberal doctrine. 'The liberal bourgeois is genuinely liberal,' said Orwell, 'up to the point where his own interests stop.' But he also said, what his fellow socialists did not always welcome, 'liberty is telling people what they do not want to hear'.

'In so far as the opportunity to lead a life worthy of human beings is needlessly confined to a minority,' wrote R. H. Tawney, 'not a few of the conditions applauded as freedom would more properly be denounced as privilege. Action which causes such opportunities to be more widely shared is, therefore, twice blessed. It not only subtracts from inequality but adds to freedom.'[4]

Malinowski also assumed that freedom was something positive. If philosophers defined its meaning negatively, he saw it as part of human action and a basic mechanism of social adaptation.

Those who attempt any definition of freedom in terms of negative categories and in terms of an absolute and unlimited absence of trammels, must be chasing an intellectual will-o'-the-wisp. Real freedom is neither absolute nor omnipresent and it certainly is not negative. It is always an increase in control, in efficiency, and in the power to dominate one's own organism and the environment, as well as artifacts and the supply of natural resources. Hence freedom as a quality of human action, freedom an increase of efficiency and control, means the breaking down of certain obstacles and a compensation for certain deficiencies. . . . The instrumentalities of freedom we find in the political constitution of a community, its laws, its moral norms, the distribution of its wealth, and the access to such benefits as health, recreation, justice, and religious or artistic gifts of culture. To scour the universe for possibilities of freedom other than

---

[4]The last words of the Epilogue to the last edition of R. H. Tawney, *Equality,* 4th edn. (London 1952).

those given by the organization of human groups for the carrying out of specific purposes, and the production of desirable results, is an idle philosophic pastime.[5]

As liberty is maximized it will become more participative and positive, more distinctively socialist. Yet always free participation will bring many voices not one; refusal to hear criticism can be no more a virtue in socialist societies than in conservative; and no multiplication of opinions, however democratically contrived, can guarantee 'truth' or sensible decisions about means or ends. 'Participatory democracy' like 'liberty' is a necessary condition of social justice, but far from a sufficient condition. What is it all for?

Equality

Equality is the value basic to any possible kind of socialism. Without a real desire to achieve an egalitarian society any democratic socialist movement loses its dynamic and lapses back into mere pragmatism. But the concept has notorious difficulties and is often parodied: a literal and exact universal equality, whether of opportunity, treatment or result, is almost as undesirable as it is impossible. Nevertheless an egalitarian society is both conceivable and desirable. Certainly some societies are remarkably less unequal than others; but by an egalitarian society is meant a classless society, one in which every man would see every other man as a brother, of equal worth and potential, a genuinely fraternal society with no conceit or constraint of class to limit fraternity. It would not be a society in which everyone was exactly equal in power, status, wealth and acquired abilities, still less in humane end-products of happiness; but it would be a society in which none of these marginal differences were unacceptable, were regarded as unjust by public opinion – a public opinion which would itself become, as differences in living standards gradually diminished, far more critical and active, far less inert and fatalistic than today. These margins would remain perpetually ambiguous, open, flexible, debatable, irreducible to either economic formula or legislative final solution; but less intense and less

---

[5]Bronislaw Malinowski, *Freedom & Civilization* (London 1947), pp. 59 and 65.

fraught with drastic consequences once poverty and unemployment are as antique as slavery.

No difficulties about the concept are so great as to warrant abandoning it or treating it as pure ritual of the socialist church – unless one wants to abandon it. One difficulty is that socialists want, rhetorically and politically, to make something sound positive which is philosophically best stated in negative terms. There is no 'complete equality' which can 'finally be realized', unless genetic engineering were to come to the aid of economic planning (with about equal accuracy and predictability, one would suspect). But there are so many unjustifiable inequalities. If we believe in the moral equality or the fraternity of all mankind, then *all* inequalities of power, status and wealth need justifying. The boot should be worn on that foot. Inequalities can be justified but only if these inequalities can be shown to be of positive advantage to the less privileged. Some inequalities can be justified, many not – particularly if one adds the vital condition of democratic citizenship: actually to ask the disadvantaged and to depend upon their reply. No precise agreement is ever likely to be reached or, if so, only for a particular time and place. Nor can philosophy supply incontrovertible criteria for what is an unjustifiable inequality. Each case will be equal on its merit and opinions will differ. But the important point is to see that inequalities of reward and power are unjustifiable in principle unless only thus can some clear public benefit follow.

Here I have followed the arguments of John Rawls in his monumental work, *A Theory of Justice* (1972), and of W. G. Runciman in his *Relative Deprivation and Social Justice* (1966). Some socialists have misread the implications of their arguments as merely a radical form of liberalism. But even if that was their intent, if in fact all inequalities were constantly called into question, criticized and forced to justify themselves, then one would be in an egalitarian society. The vast differences in power, status and wealth that are in fact acceptable to most people in a class conscious society, will grow less tolerable as income differences diminish and as an egalitarian spirit grows by argument, agitation and example.

Equality does not mean sameness. Men not robots animate an egalitarian spirit. The idea that even a strict and absolute equality of condition would destroy human individuality and character is not so much a tory nightmare as a science fiction fantasy. The fears of tory and 'market liberal' authors that high taxation and state intervention will destroy individuality, these are literally absurd.[6] Do they really think that man is so artificial and individuality so fragile? Can they really not imagine that everyone could have roughly the same standard of living, equal status and equal access to the processes of political power and yet still retain individuality? Or can they, more understandably, simply not imagine how their fancy selves could adjust to such a society? For some people genuinely believe that individuality, character and culture only exist among the prosperous and well-educated, and that 'the masses' are, as the natives used to be, 'all the same'.[7] Masses can be generalized about but not the educated and the gentry. It is the saddest fate of the poor to have their individuality removed from them in principle as well as threatened in practice. Charles Dickens and George Orwell had a different view of the matter: they actually romanticized poverty as a school of eccentricity and character.

R. H. Tawney in 1931 (long before Rawls) first argued that equality was best seen simply as the negation of socially imposed inequalities:

> So to criticize inequality and to desire equality is not, as is sometimes suggested, to cherish the romantic illusion that men are equal in character and intelligence. It is to hold that, while their natural endowments differ profoundly, it is the mark of a civilized society to aim at eliminating such inequalities as have their source, not in individual differences, but in its own organization, and that individual differences which are a source of social energy, are more likely to ripen and find expression if social inequalities are, as far as practicable, diminished. And the obstacle to the progress of equality is something simpler and more potent than finds expression in the familiar truism that men vary in their mental and moral, as well as in their physical characteristics, important and valuable though that truism is as a reminder that different individuals require different types of provision. It is the habit of mind which thinks it, not regrettable, but natural and desirable, that different sections of a community should be distinguished from each other by sharp differences of economic status, of environment, of education and culture and habit of life.[8]

---

[6]For example, Sir Keith Joseph and Jonathan Sumption, *Equality* (London 1979).
[7]For example, Roger Scruton, *The Politics of Culture and Other Essays* (Manchester 1981).
[8]R. H. Tawney, *Equality,* 4th edn. (London 1952), p. 57.

He argued that a socialist society would have more diversity in it, not less, when he expressed

> . . . straightforward hatred of a system which stunts personality and corrupts human relations by permitting the use of man by man as an instrument of pecuniary gain. The socialist society envisaged . . . is not a herd of tame, well-nourished animals, with wise keepers in command. It is a community of responsible men and women working without fear in comradeship for common ends, all of whom can grow to their full stature, develop to their utmost limit the varying capacities with which nature has endowed them.[9]

Now 'less unjustifiable inequality today!' and 'no unjustifiable inequality tomorrow!' may not be slogans that 'warm the blood like wine', but that may be just as well. For 'Onwards to Equality' is a slogan more likely to warm the hearts of party activists than those whom they need to persuade. No one value, be it liberty, equality, fraternity, love, truth, reason, even life itself, can at all times override all the others or be sure never to contradict them. Equality could certainly be maximized in a totalitarian society; but only at the expense of liberty so that genuine fraternity is destroyed. The political socialist, having a theory of society, looks at values together, in their social setting and in relation to each other. He no more postpones liberty until the classless society than he reserves egalitarian and fraternal behaviour and example until the classless society. If he does, he will not get there; and when he does, classlessness by itself will not have solved all problems and removed all possibilities of oppression.

The political socialist as egalitarian need not get drawn into this parody argument which assumes exact equality of income and wealth: that is somebody else's nightmare not his dream. Literal-minded distributive socialism is very hard to find – since the time of the Gracchi and their heir, Graccus Babeuf, at least. 'Soak the fat boys and spread it thin', may be good populist rhetoric, but most people know how thin it would be unless new productive forces arise. Industrial relations are

---

[9]R. H. Tawney, *The Radical Tradition* (London 1954), p. 101, quoted by Christopher Hampton, *Socialism in a Crippled World* (Harmondsworth 1981), an eloquent protest against the separation of the cultural from the political.

bad, not because the men on the shop floor believe that the cow can be milked without being fed; they are bad because men think that it is unfair or unjust that they should be restrained in their wage demands while their bosses actually write to tell newspapers that people with high incomes have no incentive to work harder unless income tax is cut and their children can freely inherit all their wealth. Workers, oddly, use their eyes and see how much patriotic restraint is practised by those who at least try to look like ruling classes.

Socialists claim that with greater equality there can be greater fraternity, hence greater cooperation, hence greater productivity – since wealth basically comes from the worker. Power and status also count for a lot and so does having a worthwhile job. Real managers like to produce, but the English upper middle class prefer banking to industry.

So much scope for action (and alternative action) remains in the business of moving towards a far greater equality. This is not to be represented as jealous levelling but rather as a constant, aggressive questioning of the reasons for, and the justifications of, both the existing distribution of incomes and wealth, and the present divisions of responsibility between 'workers' and 'management'. Such questioning could prove as popular as it is right. More important for socialism than abstract arguments about formal ownership is progress towards taking all wages and income out of the market and determining them by representative arbitration and open comparison of relativities. Public policy should work towards complete openness of all incomes. Many differences can be justified. But they need to be. We need to develop this as a whole new branch of applied social philosophy rather than of traditional economics. Socialist theory *began* as a critique of the theory of wages in the classical economics of Adam Smith and Ricardo: simply that they are unjustly determined in market economies. Free trade unions need free collective bargaining, indeed, as a great but minimal achievement in a market economy. The result, however, is not social justice in any sense, still less 'equality', precisely because trade unions rarely constitute even a majority of the working population, even before long-term mass unemployment returned to mixed economies. In a socialist and egalitarian economy their collective power will concentrate on reaching agreement about national procedures for arbitrating wage differentials as part of the whole complex of real income, not on a multiplicity of local or industry-wide conflicts with employers. Half-way houses will be many in the evolution of an egalitarian society: wage, welfare and tax structure will all take a long time to come together (many still do not see the need nor perceive the connexion), and different institutions will evolve in different societies. But the essential step forward must be the establishment of a national social wage. Set a level not simply to avoid the pain of poverty but to create equal opportunities for full citizenship and participation in everything that is held to be part of the good life;[10] and limit top incomes to a level that does not create life styles or opportunities for inheritance that frustrate the objectives of egalitarian policies. Neither minimum nor maximum can be decided *a priori*; they are a matter for continuing experiment and open debate.

If economic equality is a relative concept, there is one definition of equality that could and should be absolute: the differential rates of mortality between social classes – inequalities of life and death. The matter is flagrant. Even in a still relatively prosperous country such as Great Britain in a reasonably good year, 1971, the death rate for adult men in social class V (unskilled workers) was, according to official figures, nearly twice that of adult men in social class I (professionals). The 'neonatal death rates' (death in the first month of life) were also twice as high, and for the period from one month to one year, actually five times higher.[11] And national comparisons of infant mortality and death rates in poorer and richer countries tell a far more ghastly tale. By a common definition of 'less developed' societies, the average lifespan of men and women taken together is 42 years, and in developed countries it is 71. Quoting these figures, a philosopher discussing possible justifications of violence says: 'It is not too much to say that what we have before us are different kinds of lifetime.'[12] The 'Brandt Report' on world poverty

---

[10]See Peter Townsend, *Poverty in the United Kingdom: A Survey of Household Resources and Standards of Living* (Harmondsworth 1979).

[11]See the 'Black Report', *Inequalities of Health: Report of a Research* (DHSS London 1980), p. 1.

[12]See Ted Honderich, *Three Essays on Political Violence* (Oxford 1977). He takes the figures from Simon Kuznets, 'The Gap: Concept, Measurement, Trends', Gustav Ranis, ed., *The Gap Between Rich and Poor Nations* (London 1972), p. 34. In his *Violence for Equality* (London 1980), he sternly and easily dismisses most justifications of social violence; but insofar as huge inequalities, always resulting in great differences in life expectancy, are deliberately maintained by any government, then he considers that there is always a residual possibility of justifying violence philosophically. The argument is difficult and esoteric: but Honderich simply points out that governments have a greater opportunity (thus moral duty) to end misery without violence than most revolutionaries have to create justice through violence.

and 'North–South' relations simply and prudentially argued that the disparities were so huge that soon the *peace* of the world will depend on a massive reallocation of resources.

The gaps between the social classes even in a relatively wealthy country like Britain are great not merely in the precise matter of death but in the more general incidence of ill-health. In his Galton lecture in 1975 Sir John Brotherston (a former Civil Servant) remarked: 'For the most part the evidence suggests that the gaps remain as wide apart as a generation ago and in some instances the gaps may be wider.'[13] Thomas Hobbes based his philosophy of political obligation on the alleged necessity of individuals to surrender all power to a State that could effectively minimize the chances of violent death. A modern Hobbes might set his sights higher and see the power of the State at its highest when it can maximize the life expectancy of its inhabitants, and at its most precarious when it fails to do so. Certainly if there was no difference in the death rate between social classes, we would know that we no longer had social classes. This is a fairly obvious definition of a classless society: one in which 'life chances' are equal. Ralph Dahrendorf has recently written a book on *Life Chances* which oddly forgets about death and says little about poverty; but equality of opportunity in Dahrendorf's good liberal senses is not equality enough if it perpetuates, sometimes even increases, such real differences in life span. If free governments will not move towards such equality, small wonder that some would tear them down irrespective of liberty. Life and death are intrusive matters.

So an egalitarian spirit arises out of protest as well as reason. But reason must tell us that true equality is no more but no less than the removal of all unjustifiable inequalities; and that it is a necessary condition, but not a sufficient condition for democratic socialism. 'Equality' needs to be related not merely to liberty but to that most rhetorically potent but philosophically least defined of values, 'fraternity'.

Fraternity

'Fellowship is life,' said William Morris, 'and lack of fellowship is death.' Whereas a huge literature exists on 'liberty' and 'equality', 'fraternity' is

---

[13]Quoted in the Introduction to the 'Black Report', *op. cit.*

the least defined of the values of the Left. Nothing is decided by arbitrary definitions. Rather let us simply ask 'when do we find what we ordinarily call fraternal behaviour?' Surely it is when we are performing some common task, work or even a team game, which we agree needs doing and is done in such a way that each of us has something to contribute? A group of men and women who want to get the job done in time and in the right way, a football team, a group of people organizing a meeting, a good committee, an army with high morale in battle, a nation at war, all these furnish examples of situations in which fraternity is helpful, situations which appear to *generate* fraternity. Note that fraternity does not always involve liberty – it can, better that it does; but fraternity can exist under coercive command as much as by voluntary cooperation.

So it would appear that if fraternity is an attitude of mind, it is one associated with activity. Fraternity is not radiating an abstract love of humanity: it arises from people working together towards common ends. For instance, I am doubtful how much it means for me to say that I feel fraternity towards 'Prods' or 'Tigs', Blacks or Whites, unless I am actually working or mixing with them. We may love Blacks, respect them or simply tolerate them; we can even treat them as equals (insofar as we have occasion to be with them at all); but fraternity must at least involve working on common tasks together or living together (like brothers in a family, with their jealousies and independence as well as bonds of circumstance and affection).

The metaphor of brotherhood needs exploring. Actual brotherhood is commonly an odd relationship of affection and rivalry, even jealousy; so fraternity does not necessarily involve men and women being literally equal, still less treating everyone the same. Perhaps fraternity is closer to friendship than to love. Friendship is not a total identification with another and it is rarely, if ever, consistent with trying to make another into some other image than their own – whether the image of an ideology, the image of God or one's own. Why doesn't she agree with me in everything when I love her so much? Fraternity must surely accept people, even friends, as they are – warts and all. By all means seek to involve them in common tasks, and to influence them; but then seek neither to condemn their inadequacy, nor to be jealous of their superiority, nor to avoid being influenced ourselves. If we are to experience genuine fraternity, we must take each other as we find each other, not in fancy dress. We cannot say that there can be no genuine fraternity until the classless society or until 'we are reborn in Christ' – or in Marx for that matter. Fraternity, like friendship, implies simplicity and lack of ostentation and pomposity, but some restraints nonetheless, for we are dealing with other people. There is a difference between 'making oneself at home' in someone else's house, and acting 'as if it belonged to one'. Similarly, if fraternity is treating people equally, this does not mean that one treats everyone as if they are, in all relevant aspects, equal. W. G. Runciman drew an apt distinction between 'equality of respect', which should be universal, and 'equality of praise', which becomes empty if universalized: men do have different talents and aptitudes which should be recognized. The only limitation on praise and reward is that no talents or aptitudes can justify social hierarchy. To a brother I must be neither servile and acquiescent nor censorious and condescending.

So fraternity must involve, firstly, common tasks and activities, and, secondly, an exultant recognition of diversity of character. Fraternity implies individuality not sameness; but, of course, like the socialist ethic in general, it is also concerned with how individuals can work together and contribute best to the common tasks of a reforming society, living in and creating actual communities. 'From each according to his abilities, to each according to his needs.' But can fraternity cut across class lines? Is fraternity compatible with inequality?

The answer is sometimes. Fraternity can – for a moment – cut across the most rigid class lines in the most inegalitarian societies. This is the fraternity engendered on great occasions, be they wars, battles, long marches, last stands or even Labour Party annual conferences. The fraternity of great occasions, however, of *Sturm und Drang,* of Struggle and Passion, is inherently temporary – unless the pressure is artificially kept up, as when Trotsky advocated 'permanent revolution' to ensure the monopoly of power of the Communist Party (in the right hands) and Chairman Mao advocated, even as Machiavelli and Jefferson had done, that every generation should experience the intense comradeship of revolutionary renewal. Sometimes a kind of fraternity is engendered in new nations between the leader and the masses which is real and elevating for a while, but which if continued indefinitely becomes a deliberate fraud: the illusion of the leader as father or as big brother which disguises dictatorship, lack of liberty and continuing gross inequality.

Such false 'fraternity' can lead in wholly terrible directions. Erich Remarque wrote of the 'false fraternity of the trenches' in *All Quiet on the Western Front.* Yet even release from that compulsive and deadly fraternity left years later (as many other interwar writers also noted), a sense of loss, a deep psychological void. Some sought to fill this void from very different sources, including both the Communist Party and the Fascist movements. The Fascists of the 1920s and 1930s tried, even short of war, to recreate this wartime atmosphere of blood brotherhood or false fraternity. A once-famous book by an apostate Nazi, Von Rauschning, *The Revolution of Nihilism,* argued the paradox that at first people did not march with the Nazis because they agreed with them and shared their values, but they marched because they *wanted* to gain a feeling of brotherhood and wanted to agree with them. Camping, drilling, marching, demonstrating, rioting and beating up Jews or Communists gave them the very experience of fraternity they desired so much. They did it for that reason.

Such fraternity of great occasions is not what democratic socialists want; nor is it one that could not apply to any group of men, irrespective of class, race, nationality, religion or intelligence: we want a fraternity for all seasons and for everyone, self-willed and enduring. Fraternity without liberty is a nightmare, fraternity with liberty is humanity's greatest dream. But if fraternity is hard to find in liberal contexts, small wonder that some people may seek it in violent actions, whether motivated by despair or ideology.

In modern society, fraternity is too often only recognized in emergencies. It would be idle to pretend that those who are ordinarily able to purchase what they want (and constantly to invent new wants) are likely to feel any real sense of brotherhood with those who have to struggle all the time to purchase what they need. Rather than brotherhood, the favoured ones are more apt to perceive threat from the disadvantaged – I could wish with more reason. Any abstract fraternity they might feel is empty of real content while their lives do not touch, while their sons and daughters so rarely intermingle and intermarry, while their ordinary relationships with each other are guided by the social distance arising from exploitation and work, command and obedience. The upper classes (while often 'fraternal' among themselves) call for sacrifice and belt-tightening from ordinary wage-earners, but not from themselves. They admit the working classes to be patriotic insofar as they act 'responsibly', especially in matters of wage restraint and when the unemployed do not kick back. They approach the working classes in times of economic crisis rather as Shakespeare's Henry V spoke to his common soldiers on the eve of battle:

> For he today who sheds his blood with me
> Shall be my brother; be he ne'er so vile
> This day shall gentle his condition.

However, there are strong contrary signs of hope. While sociologists point to a declining sense of fraternity and mutual aid in traditional working classes (which is itself a relative and not irreversible matter, especially as the lesson of hard times begins to sink in), others point to an increased fraternity in the younger generation. Despite the class bias of higher education, for instance, most students for over a generation have begun to act in a more classless manner in their dress, speech, life style generally and patterns of friendship. Many try valiantly, some successfully, to sustain this even in the world of commercial and industrial work. And they see themselves as part of a wider largely working-class youth culture, whose music and dress may not have universal appeal, and may be subject to commercial exploitation, but which is nonetheless egalitarian in spirit. This 'youth culture' has now spread throughout the Western world, and tries hard to make links with the Third World consciousness, however artificial, absurd and tentative these links at times can be; and it even penetrates Eastern Europe and is a cause for worry in the Kremlin itself. All this has happened without any conscious government policy, often in the teeth of ruling classes and educational authorities. Schooling everywhere is less dragooned and more informal – even in the private sector that tries so hard to resist change and maintain a proper sense of hierarchy. It only needs to be given a sense of political purpose.

Contemporary women's movements are especially rich in 'fraternity'. The incongruity of the word in this context should indeed make one pause. I myself do not believe that a sensitive use of a historically male-dominated language is necessarily sexist. Some might argue that the very use of 'fraternity' helps perpetuate assumptions that male dominance is natural. It could. Personally I rejoice in how much fraternity at its best is exemplified in women's groups working together for common purposes as equals. But I grant two things to those who have more than nominal worries: the one is that the Fascist perversion of fraternity, the aggressive brothers' band, is indeed a strongly male image, is in many ways a revealing caricature of psychological stereotypes of manliness, aggression, competitiveness and xenophobia; and the other is that 'sisterhood' in some ways is truly a less ambiguous image of what I am trying to convey by 'fraternity'. Think simply of any group of women spontaneously 'rallying round' to help and support one another in need or trouble. 'Sisterhood' then has all the connotations of support, care, practicality, grace, sensitivity and empathy needed for the best definition of politically minded socialists working together. In principle it would be no more strange for men to say 'liberty, equality, and sisterhood' than for women to say 'liberty, equality and fraternity'. Indeed it might be salutary, for 'sisterhood' makes a clear moral point; the concept would then be liberated, indeed, from its less happy associations with 'a brother's band against the world' rather than with good human groups able to relate as equals to all others. In terms of sheer comprehensibility, however, it still seems to me, on balance, more sensible to try to de-sex, even to feminize, old 'fraternity', rather than to pause to rewrite most languages or to impede them with more neologisms. Thus I repeat (but with this qualification) that amid the anti-fraternal competitiveness of capitalist society, women's groups are especially rich in counter-examples of 'fraternity', truly conceived.

Again those who talk as liberals or social democrats of the need for more worker participation in industry and 'co-ownership' and those who talk as democratic socialists of the need for industrial democracy or cooperative ownership of industry, have in common a sense that there is a vast energy and know-how ready to be released if the men and women who do the hard work could influence or control the work. And in Great Britain the 'old tories' or true conservatives in the Conservative Party have a sense at least of the need to preserve communities and community values, unlike the 'market liberals' in their party who seem willing to see communities disintegrate in favour of a model of a purely individualistic, competitive and careerist society – a capitalist system which, indeed, never fully succeeded in destroying the fraternal institutions of working-class life. The task of good government is to create a sense of common purposes and problems that must be solved together: fundamental economic and social policies which actually need widespread support to work for the overriding purpose of creating greater equality and a genuine, active liberty or common citizenship for all in each country and gradually for all mankind.

If more genuine fraternity or sisterhood existed, worries about literal equality and marginal differentials could be less acute. Literal equality would not guarantee fraternity unless there was also a sense of common purpose; and existing degrees of inequality must make fraternity in everyday life excessively difficult. The duke and the dustman, the dictator and the poor peasant, may indeed feel themselves to be members of one nation, but that nation then will be based on a sense of hierarchy, condescension and deference, not on brotherhood: at best only a poor and dependent cousinhood. In Beethoven's *Fidelio* the King is converted to the principles of French Enlightenment and suddenly proclaims: 'Let all men be my brothers'. Nice of him, but it's no good. The master and servant relationship is mutually corrupting. For while there are dukes, dictators and millionaires, such gifts are a sham and a deceit, something never let go of and always returnable. True fraternity can be encouraged by governments and leaders but it cannot be imposed: it must have roots in popular institutions and struggles. Oppression and common enemies can indeed stimulate fraternity; but the only way to maintain fraternity in such conditions is to continue oppression or war (even if the government is now called Communist rather than Czarist).

Both the Communist Party and the Fascist movements of the 1930s sensed a profound human need when they cultivated their emotions of fraternity simultaneously on a very small and local scale (the primal image of the brother's band, organizing in shop-floor cells or in neighbourhood militias) and also on a vast scale (the Movement itself, even for a while the international movement). We need both. The experience of fraternity is learned in small groups; and learned best in small groups which fulfil a variety of roles – working, governing themselves and providing as many of their own services as they can: the image of the commune and of industrial democracy. But it must be extended to all humanity – certainly beyond the nation, otherwise the world will only see the deadly rivalry of East and West replaced by fear of war between North and South. And yet fraternity must be extended in such a way that the large scale does obliterate the small. We do indeed need both.

Consider one example of a problem of balancing the large with the small, for the matter is not easy when brought down from principle and rhetoric to practice. In Great Britain we are now a multi-racial and multicultural society – whether we like it or not (in fact we always have been, with Scottish, Welsh or Irish compatriots). Few people now seem to favour complete *assimilation* of immigrants: that everyone should be English. Most people now talk, albeit vaguely, of a pluralist society and the *integration* of different communities. We recognize that different cultures can live side by side. But can this be an excuse for gross inequalities between them in standard of living and life-chances? The socialist answer, indeed any humanitarian answer, is obvious. Yet can this good recognition of diversity be an excuse for minority cultures sometimes to restrain their members by force, especially their women and their children, from leaving? This problem is more difficult. Surely no amount of communal fraternity can excuse injustices and restrictions on freedom in the light of general principles of liberty, equality and justice? It is hard to know where to draw the line in practice. Some lines must be drawn in public law, but after much debate, bringing these matters out in the open, neither suppressing nor denying them. We must protect greater cultural differences than we have tolerated or known in the past, but we must also protect freedom, especially the possibility for individuals to move during their lifetime from one culture to another and sometimes back again. Both the old nation and the new sub-cultures have to make political and social adjustments: such adjustments are only unjust if the majority use their power imperceptively and inflexibly – unpolitically. If the majority fail to conciliate the minority they may (in a narrow sense) be acting democratically, but they are storing up the kind of trouble for the future (as has happened in Northern Ireland) that can make democracy unworkable.

Socialists must always remind themselves that economic planning will never by itself create a more fraternal society. Simple arithmetical equality could conceivably create even fiercer competitiveness. We must not oversociologize. Social conditions can help or hinder but they cannot guarantee more fraternity, nor, fortunately, always destroy it – as men on strike in hard times show us. Fraternity is an ethic that can grow if believed in freely and practised. It goes with simplicity, lack of ostentation, friendliness, helpfulness, kindliness, openness, lack of restraint between individuals in everyday life and a willingness to work together in common tasks. It doesn't only go with fierce memories of the trials and struggles of a movement's early days or with the happy unison of party meetings.

Yet fraternity does not mean no leadership: it only means no permanent class of leaders tomorrow and no *noblesse oblige* today – no condescension, no giving favours; but rather, leaders receiving trust on account of peculiar skills of both empathy and action which are being used for common and popularly decided purposes. Fraternity does mean creating by public policy, as well as by individual example, common purposes and cooperation both in working life and in leisure. A fraternal society would be one in which there was far more popular participation in all decision-making. Fraternity is frustrated by gross inequalities of income and by the acquired and encouraged acquisitiveness of capitalism: 'the rage for the accumulation of things', as Orwell once remarked, a rage that is obviously never satisfied and which thinks that it only can be satisfied by the exclusion of others.

Nor is fraternity, like the socialist views of positive freedom, necessarily incompatible with individualism, unless brothers simply push too hard – this needs to be said for it worries so many people. If, of course, one builds into the concept of an 'individual' all that Professor Hayek does in his *Road to Serfdom, Individualism and Economic Order* and many other works, which is, to put it briefly, the whole of *laissez-faire* economic theory, then plainly man as such a programmed predator has very little interest in being fraternal, or very little chance. Hayek's individual will obey the law out of utilitarian self-interest; and that law is not able, though it may rashly try, to change the 'laws of economics'. But less cluttered, more general and more humane concepts of 'the individual' should raise no problems for socialists or others. All we need to say, anthropologically, is that mankind is unique and that one aspect of that uniqueness is that each member of the species is unique; and, philosophically, that every man must be treated as an end in himself never as a means to an end. Having said this, there is no greater reason in principle why human beings should not act with fraternity towards each other rather than with aversion, with cooperativeness rather than with aggression or competition. Both images are induced cultural achievements and owe more to nurture than to nature.

Socialism does, however, have a distinctive modulation of this general view of *homo sapiens.* Socialists, after all, stress sociability. Some, like Kropotkin and the anarchists, benignly 'cheat' by building into their account of human nature a cooperative spirit of 'mutual aid', just as some social biologists will picture natural man as 'red in tooth and claw'. Stressing sociability as a cultural achievement, some socialists go overboard in seeing social classes as more real than individuals; so that, once again, true individualism can only exist after that mythic, almost eschatological event, the Revolution. There is no need to go that far. Some suggest, for instance, that it is better to talk of individual human *identity* rather than conservative 'character', Marxist 'class identity' or Rousseauistic 'personality'. Many people today take for granted that the main object of 'a liberal education' and of personal life is to develop something called 'personality'. 'Personality' implies that I am myself at my best when I am performing spontaneous, unique and 'authentic' acts all over the place. Many libertarian Socialists hold this view, but it is a view hard to reconcile with the socialist stress on sociability and cooperation: 'personalities' are very good when challenging established conventions, they are less helpful in creating new conventions of social justice and in working together.

My 'identity', however, implies something both individual and social. It is individual because it is uniquely mine, but what it actually consists of is a series of mutual recognitions with other people in a social context.[14]

It is no use my believing that I have a true but suppressed personality unless I can show some signs of it recognizable and tolerable to other people. And you cannot expect me to take your personal attributes seriously unless they are presented in terms recognizable and tolerable to me. Individualism must be limited by deliberate sociability. Yet sociability is a wider concept than social class. Class in a class society is inevitably a very important part of my identity but it can never be a sufficient account of my individual identity, just as the theory of social class works quite well with aggregate predictions, but is useless to explain 'the exceptions' of individual behaviour, which are often so crucial. Individuals should by collective action cultivate fraternity with tolerance as they move towards an egalitarian society.

---

[14]I tried, very tentatively, to develop this notion of sociability limiting individualism in my *Crime, Rape and Gin: Reflections on Contemporary Attitudes to Violence, Pornography and Addiction* (London 1974). Here I paraphrase Kathleen Nott in her *The Good Want Power* (London 1977): '. . . two postulates: (i) that "identity" is a discernible fact; (ii) that becoming aware of it and accepting it as a fact either for oneself or for others entails a principle of mutual recognition'. But I do not think she would like my socialist gloss on her, since her sub-title is 'An Essay on the Psychological Possibilities of Liberalism'.

Socialism and time

> That what tempts some socialists into authoritarian attitudes and commonly allows even democratic socialist movements to be misrepresented as authoritarian is the lack of a sense of time-scales and of theories of incremental progress.

Politics is a process fully compatible with what could prove to be, in the end, a revolutionary society. The application of socialist values would indeed be revolutionary in contrast to any form of government that exists at the moment, though some base-camps are better prepared than others. But it should be obvious, from history, sociological knowledge and commonsense, that such a transformation cannot occur overnight. When an evolutionary revolution is attempted in countries with long established representative institutions, many conventions are a brake upon progress: but the price of trying to ignore such brakes, experience suggests, is simply too great. When a revolution (as an event) occurs in countries which have not had such a tradition, it is desperately difficult for those in power to see the need to create genuine representative institutions if they even appear to impede the speed of social advance. But such is life, or rather society. All I argue is that in neither condition is democratic socialism impossible. Perhaps some Marxists in both kinds of circumstance truly believe that liberty fatally obstructs progress and that parliamentary institutions are incompatible with socialism; but the Russian leaders' reaction to Czechoslovakia in 1968 and to Poland in 1981 did not follow from such theoretical considerations: theirs was the sadly normal reaction of autocracy faced by popular challenge. In the Soviet Union it is quite clear that liberty has not been consciously and momentarily sacrificed for equality; on the contrary, and from the very beginning, Communist government suppressed criticism of all kinds. Without liberty the popular demand for equality has withered away into a new kind of social stratification based upon party membership and office-holding, largely determined by competitive examination and interview.

Any consideration of the time-scales involved in industrialization in Western Europe, or of the bad consequences of an imposed, rapid industrialism from the top, whether on the Stalinist model in Russia or on the Meiji model in Japan, must convince socialists and their opponents alike that the enterprise is a long one. Even after violent revolutions, old attitudes survive to an astonishing extent; it is as misleading to underestimate the changes in post-revolutionary Russia as it is to ignore continuities. And from a base-camp established amid representative or parliamentary institutions, the time needed for the establishment of a socialist society may appear desperately long. But the built-in political necessity of socialist governments having to carry with them an enfranchised public opinion, as well as an already organized trade-union movement, guarantees that each move of the camp further and further up the mountain will be on solid ground, less likely to slip backwards or simply to get stuck.

The rhetoric of socialist politicians, particularly when the Left-wing struggles for control of a party and a movement against the Right, invariably promises more than is possible in a brief time: the 'life of the next Labour Government', even wildly absurd claims about bringing in 'fundamental and irreversible socialist legislation' in 'the first session' of a new Parliament. Even if they could, the results would be disastrous: great changes can only come in stages.

Do people believe such rhetoric? Most of it is for internal party consumption. Rhetoric is both the curse and the joy of politics. The press are perhaps ungenerous to take rhetoric too seriously, and to imply so wickedly that politicians will do as they say. Journalists are not philosophers. But serious socialist leaders should not promise more than they can fulfil in the short term. The short term is the period of building a base and support for social change. Short-term legislative measures must respond to immediate problems and be popular or at least widely acceptable in the country at large (especially if they need a response in the behaviour of working people to work at all, as so much economic and social legislation does). But short-term measures should be consistent with middle-term theories about *how* to achieve long-term goals, such as an egalitarian society; or at the very least, amid the often desperate contingencies of politics and economic events, not inconsistent with those goals.

The middle period is the period of trying to change attitudes and values, by persuasion or by the removal of institutions whose main function is to maintain privilege and social stratification, be it private education, private medicine or the investment policies of banks and pension funds. Even the removal of some of these institutions is unlikely to work in a socialist direction unless it is done gradually, or unless enough people who work in them are at least willing to serve the new system unobstructively. In retrospect it does not seem to have been a very bright idea of Great Britain's Labour Government of 1945–50 simply to replace the management of so much industry by Civil Servants, without the generation of socialist managers and engineers that was by then the forgotten part of the great vision of Shaw, Wells and the Webbs, the role they cast for the new Polytechnic institutions. Middle-period planning and transition plainly requires at least a generation simply because of the need for changes in attitude; it is not possible in the life of any one or two Parliaments.

Yet amid short-term legislation, middle-period strategies have to be canvassed. People have to be convinced of and made familiar with the new ideas. Educational change has to be undertaken in the short-term programme to provide the personnel and the skills for the strategy of the middle-term structural changes. But such changes and the strategies themselves have to be debated, speculated about, before they can be established. And all the time the long-term values are to be asserted and refined: what will the social differences of the sexes be or the role of cultural minorities in a classless society? A socialist movement needs moral philosophers as well as economists, or rather needs to popularize both modes of discourse in a speculative not a dogmatic spirit. 'The ethically desirable must be the sociologically possible.' The bounds of present possibilities can be extended, but only over time and by debate, not edict.

For a socialist movement simply to campaign on long-term values would be absurd. For it simply to campaign on immediate reforms of the present system is not socialist at all (simply desperate patchwork on a worn-out garment). It needs always to campaign on three different levels: (i) short-term tactical reforms within the system to build a basis of popular confidence for advance; (ii) middle-term strategies to change the system; and (iii) long-term persuasion to work a new system in a new spirit. Manifestos would look very different if written in this manner (more socialist and less Chartist). But even if it may be a long time before *institutions* will exhibit socialist values, *socialists* can. Part of persuasion is reasoning but part is example.

Government must work through stages, but individuals can simultaneously work amid short-term limitations, plan for middle-term change and speculate on the future, without hypocrisy or self-deceit. Young civil servants or managers are not 'selling out to the system' if they implement policies which they think are mistaken, or work within institutions they think to be regressive, so long as their criticisms are made and are heard within or without the workplace. They *can* help change the climate of expectation and should hope to use their knowledge, and expect to be consulted, in formulating middle-term strategies. Social-workers are not 'shoring up the system' if they help people in trouble: they are helping people in trouble. With socialist policies they may be able to tackle problems in better ways, they may have fewer problems, but they must convince not desert their clients. Teachers are not betraying children by following an existing bad syllabus, so long as they use every opportunity they have in the present system to change it or at least to refuse to moralize it. If socialist policies and greater social equality diminish both the feeling of hopelessness and the class labels of learning, however, there may be greater motivation, more learning and less teaching. Factory workers are not working for capitalism, they are working for a living wage. But with socialist policies wage differentials may count for less and their skills may be used to better effect. It is not romantic in the least to think that 'industrial democracy' could be more efficient than private ownership: it is a serious hypothesis to be tested gradually and assessed in many different ways. Working 'within the system', efficiency has to be proved, but in being proved the assumptions of our existing definitions of 'efficiency' can be challenged: is capital intensive machinery really less costly than labour intensive processes of work? Someone has to pick up the bill or pay the cost of labour-saving that becomes unemployment.

As well as the classes, there are the sexes. A woman is not necessarily selling the pass to prove herself as good as a man in a man's world, not unless she rests content with the individual achievement and fails to use her position to try to change the assumptions of that world. Women today are less and less content to work for men in the home, they too work for wages because they need to, or even when middle-class women do not need to, they then work to prove their independence and equality. Expectations of radical change already exist and need but to be built upon. Pressure groups have modified both public policy and public opinion even within our present society. Some women may not have to wait for the classless society to act like equals and to be treated as equals. But equality of the sexes without social equality will be hampered by class differences of opportunity. Progressive middle-class women should beware of imposing their values on working-class women. They campaign, to take an example important for women, to have their babies 'at home'. Being individualistic, they do not like being bullied and categorized in hospitals; and middle-class women are also, on average, healthy so less at risk outside hospital. But they should not (thinking of time-scales) make a cult of home-birth and imply that other women are unnatural not to do so, until such time as bad housing conditions and poverty no longer make infant mortality so dramatically different between the social classes. But middle-class women should not be ashamed of making differential advances to equality in education and employment, for instance: such example is likely to spread.

Advance must be by 'small steps', certainly; but steps if they really are steps should have high rises as well as broad treads, and need to be placed on top of each other, not scattered surrealistically over the landscape as opportunity knocks or according to who holds what Ministry. Nonetheless in both short-term and middle-period planning differential advance can be made. The idea that societies are systems (whether held in Marx's or Hayek's form) is a highly abstract one and should not be applied too literally to practice. Every plan must be flexible enough to allow unexpected opportunities to be seized on one part of the line, costly attacks abandoned for the moment at another, so long as there is a general move forward.

Socialist movements in the west have commonly lost confidence in their leaders' will or ability to move towards a socialist society. The rank-and-file party activists are often grossly unrealistic, often in too much of a hurry (and anything of this kind made in a hurry is not likely to last); but if they are it is at least in part the fault of leaders who are so pragmatic that they both lose sight of and can never talk with conviction about either middle-term restructuring of institutions or long-term attainment of socialist values.

Perhaps this has all fallen between advocacy and defence. But what I would advocate as a socialist has to be defended both against those socialists who are impatient of political means, and sceptics who think that socialism is inherently anti-political or anti-libertarian and that social hierarchy, poverty and mass unemployment is the price that all must pay for the culture and liberties of some. In the long run people will not accept that citizenship can be fully practised other than among equals.

A Final Footnote to Rally Those who Grudge the Price (1992)

There was an old man who supposed
That the street door was partially closed,
But some very large rats
Ate his coat and his hats
While that futile old gentleman dozed.

EDWARD LEAR

'The charge of elitism never fails to amaze me because
the same people who make it will also criticise you for not
prescribing their brand of revolution to the masses.
A writer wants to ask questions. These damn fellows want
him to give answers. Now tell me, can anything be more
elitist . . .? As a writer I aspire only to widen the scope of
self-examination. I don't want to foreclose it with a catchy,
half-baked orthodoxy . . . Writers don't give prescriptions,'
shouted Ikem. 'They give headaches.'

Uproarious laughter.

'Well, on that note we say thank you to Dr Osodi for a most
entertaining evening.'

CHINUA ACHEBE, Anthills of the Savannah

The price of free politics, indeed of peace, can be high. Thirty years ago I began by saying that I simply wanted to make some old 'platitudes' pregnant: that politics is the conciliation of naturally different interests, whether these interests are seen as material or moral, usually both. The activity is to be honoured as the key to freedom, whatever the behaviour of actual politicians.

The thought is perennial, but circumstances have changed and the strategy of this book might be different today. Two sets of circumstances have changed, both greatly for the better; but not without a price. Firstly, the inefficiency of Communist central command economies has been empirically and dramatically demonstrated (just as eighteenth-century and early nineteenth-century reformers had demonstrated the inefficiency of old autocracy in terms of political and economic theory). Secondly, everywhere autocracies now seem less stable than parliamentary régimes, whereas thirty years ago the right-wing dictatorships of Spain and Portugal seemed, for example while not unshakeable, yet realistically to be accepted as part of the most probable order of things in the foreseeable future. And during this period military government came and went in Greece. These countries that seemed worrying exceptions to the European tradition of civic politics and of parliamentary government, suddenly proved comforting examples of the long-term strength of these traditions and their appropriateness to modern conditions. And now demands for multi-party systems, parliamentary liberties and judicial protection of human rights gain ground throughout South America, even in some African countries. These demands will, of course, meet with varying fortunes: as old Machiavelli argued, more shrewdly than either Marx or modern social scientists (be they free-market economists or sociologists), there is *Fortuna* as well as *Necessità* in all forms of political life. However, these tendencies were afoot even before the astounding and heartwarming events of 1989 in Eastern Europe and the equally astounding but tragic events in China.

These events were, of course, a consequence of the reforms of the Gorbachev era, themselves a product of the failure of the Communist Party's vision of total and transformatory control. But there were no other straws for him to snatch at than moving towards (but always a relative term) a free-market economy and free political institutions. Almost everywhere this now seems the only real alternative to either autocracy or totalitarianism, although the forms and modulations political régimes can take are infinite. Political cultures always have a particular and peculiar cultural setting, and are difficult to attain where there has been no prior experience of either entrepreneurial or civic spirit, only a theoretical appreciation of observed and idealized examples elsewhere. But the events in the USSR were only a necessary condition, not a sufficient one, for the revolutions in Eastern Europe. The Communist one-party régimes in Hungary and Poland had already been visibly undermined, over a period of time and amid complex events and steady pressures. But what was so totally unexpected, heartening, indeed heroic (no sane prophets or pundits emerged to say, 'told you so'), was that crowds in Czechoslovakia, East Germany and Romania took to the streets so suddenly, risking their lives for freedom. Neither in Prague and Brno nor in Berlin and Dresden was it clear at the time that the army and the police would not fire – in Romania they did, and in China with terrible effect; no one could be sure that the servants of the oppression would suddenly perceive enemies of the state as fellow human beings, fellow countrymen, fellow citizens even.

Perhaps few governments, even of free societies, can be entirely happy in an uncomplicated way at the spectacle of the masses suddenly becoming a people and tearing down their government, however iniquitous. Should it not have been a time for public political joy? And even if not joy for the freedom of others, at least joy that the long fear of an annihilatory world war was over? Yet there was failure in the West of moral imagination. There was a lack of immediate response, even by great words (which are important), certainly from President Bush and Prime Minister Thatcher, those two self-perceived leaders of 'the Free World' who seldom lacked for instant rhetoric. Margaret Thatcher was not alone in seeming shamefully obsessed by fears of *what it would all cost the taxpayer,* and by ungenerous antique fears of German unity. Perhaps only private people could rise to the heights of those revolutionary events. The day the Berlin Wall was breached I played Beethoven's Ninth Symphony three times between radio and television bulletins; and when eventually I got through on the phone to Berlin to the German friend for whom I first wrote this book, to try to give grounds for hope in troubled times, I discovered that she had done the same. Whether through poor German or good politics I had always misheard the key word *'Freude'* of the final chorus as *'Freiheit'.* But for that heroic moment, both freedom and joy. Only later the bathos, the price to be paid. Mrs Thatcher was sometimes not entirely wrong.

So in this final Footnote I want to reflect on the high price of freedom, peace and politics. And I want to do this not by discussing in detail the new problems created or revealed by the break-up of the old Soviet Empire and the end of the Cold War, but by speculating more generally on the nature of what can appear to be insoluble political problems. Perhaps the examples I took in the book were too glib, or writing during the Cold War it was too easy to make a rhetorical contrast between political rule and totalitarian rule; for anyone free to choose, the choice was obvious. So I now am my own critic and look at some great and continuing problems and dilemmas, not to solve them but to be realistic about the price worth paying for free politics.

I have argued all too easily that all advanced societies contain a variety of values and interests, and that conflicts between them are best settled politically. Politics, it is still important to labour the old Aristotelian point, is both historically and logically prior to democracy. There are some situations in which any simple application of democratic majority rule can make political resolutions more difficult, even stimulate more violent conflict. In Israel and Palestine, in South Africa and – a smaller example, but in some ways more incorrigible – Northern Ireland, the democratic argument has been part of the problem. 'We have the majority and we'll do what we will with it.' My chapter 'A Defence of Politics Against Democracy' was not an argument against 'democracy', only against seeing it as the answer to everything, a single universal and overriding value (Tocqueville and J. S. Mill had long ago said everything that needs to be said on this). Political rule, I said, existed before democratic government, and some dictatorships have rested on popular support and been the stronger for it.

Normal politics breaks down or is impossible to create when rival groups pursue policies which they say admit of no compromise and which are believed to be totally exclusive and contradictory, at least as formulated by the protagonists. Consider Israel and Palestine, Northern Ireland and South Africa. In each of these areas, and elsewhere too, there are normal people who believe that the very survival of their communities as cultural identities, which is so much part of their own self-identity, is threatened by any political compromises whatever of the kind advocated in this tract. 'The slippery slope', 'the thin end of the wedge', 'give an inch, they'll take a yard', 'our land for ever' or 'no surrender!', they say.

Our response to such challenges is often to take the moral high ground and to raise like a flag the question of justice. Who is in the right? 'Oh, I know the history is complicated, but who *basically* is in the right?'

What is the question?

Is this always the right question? An English country story has an almost Hassidic wisdom about it. 'How do I get to Biddicombe?' 'I wouldn't start from here if I were you.' So I want to start with a mild humanistic protest against the prevalence of restating the arguments of the protagonists as if these are possible solutions. Intellectuals and concerned journalists should not 'join in' and 'take sides', as if they were lawyers in an advocacy system seeking to win a case, rather than arbitrators in a tribunal seeking to establish the facts and considering how to obtain the best possible *settlement,* to settle for a peace or conciliation acceptable to the rival parties – not for an ideal solution, nor possibly even a permanent solution. Much good reporting and commentary is also marred not only by clear partisanship, but by presenting problems only in terms of the day-to-day reporting of recurrent injustices, especially the violent injustices, committed by one side or the other. This creates a danger of responding passionately to symptoms and not thoughtfully to causes; the public in Western democracies outside our three troubled areas must sometimes wonder what the underlying conflicts are really about, why are they doing this? 'The atrocities of the terrorists' and the 'excesses of the security forces' are events which are themselves part of the propaganda battle, and often manufactured or provoked for that purpose. And all factual 'balance sheets' of incidents and atrocities are highly subjective in their assumptions. While it is important to ask activists what they want, and to listen empathetically to nuances in their replies, it is just as important, sometimes more so, to stand back from the struggle and to ask other observers close to the ground (such as old-fashioned reporters, churchmen, teachers and small businessmen) what they think is *possible.* One should try to establish a way of looking at extreme problems that can do justice to the claims of rival groups when they each or all may have a quite plausible and, to the individuals involved, even a fully just case.

Politics is a conciliating activity or process, not a set of substantive rules needing agreement or consensus (as unthinking politicians say when trying to be thoughtful) about 'fundamental values' or even 'the rule of law'. Politics can change laws peacefully and find paths of compromise amid differing values so long as there is a broad consensus about procedures. There is more agreement in societies like the USA and the member states of the European Community about *how* to conduct disputes than about the *ends* of policy. Such a distinction is both sensible and civilized. Writing about political education I invoked the concept of 'procedural values': a minimal respect by political activists for freedom, toleration, respect for truth, as well as empathy and willingness to resolve disputes by discussion.

But what happens when these prior conditions for politics do not exist, when 'procedural values' themselves are hotly contested? The three cases I mention, Northern Ireland, Israel/Palestine and South Africa, are at least intellectually interesting to the political thinker, even if there were not moral and practical reasons for all our interests as compelling as in the ethnic complexities, rivalries and hatreds of Eastern Europe, the Balkans, the Russian confederation and many African states and Indian provinces. Political leaders in these situations can appear either not to perceive the complexity of the interests to be satisfied (as if their perceptions are affected by the intensity of the conflicts), or believe that the very safety of the state or the survival of their people, as the case may be, is threatened by any political articulation from rival interests. They then conceive it as their moral duty not to compromise but to oppress, eradicate or simply stolidly and often bloodily endure. They see their opponents as beyond political persuasion. They see them as threatening not merely their basic interests and beliefs but all that they are, their very being, their precise human, cultural identity: thus as literally beyond reason, like another order of beings. They confuse the old order with all possible types of order, even though its autocratic incompetence may have been a cause of disorder. *All* political opposition becomes seen as inherently subversive. Such terrible fears can arise from religious, ethnic, national or class prejudice: the others are not like us as a people and never can be, and nor have we anything to learn from them. And this is often a reciprocal relationship, a self-fulfilling prophecy. 'Treat people like rats,' said Arthur Koestler, 'and they will learn to bite your fingers off.' Protestant and Catholic, Jew and Arab,

Muslim and Hindu, Tutsi and Hutu, etc., etc., can publicly rejoice in deaths of the other.

When large numbers of people are treated as enemies of the state and its rulers, then they may come to attribute to themselves a complete and artificial unity. To amend Browning, 'Oppression makes [even] the wise man mad.' This unity may be false culturally and hard to sustain politically ('Blacks' and 'Whites', 'Arabs' and 'Jews', 'Irish' and 'Brits'; 'they are and we are all the same'); hard to sustain, that, is, without repression within one's own ranks – 'act like a *true* Black!', or a true White, Serb, Uzbeki, whatever. Nationalism for the time of struggle is so unifying and intoxicating that it often tempts leaders elsewhere to continue 'the struggle' even after victory, or victory enough. And there are cases when some of the disenfranchised and dispossessed are as prejudiced, violent and irreconcilable as the rulers. Orwell once said with great honesty that after becoming anti-imperialist it took him twenty years more to realize that 'the oppressed are not always right'. He did not mean they were wrong in not wanting to be oppressed; but they were not right, or necessarily specially admirable, in everything else. Western friends of the oppressed have often been embarrassing idealizers; I prefer Mark Twain's humanism, 'God damn the Jews; they are as bad as the rest of us.' (As a young man I demonstrated against the British attack on Suez and chanted praises of Colonel Nasser. A distinction could have been made.) Orwell's remark is salutary. However, the commonsense moral view must remain that rulers normally have more opportunity for reform, therefore carry a greater moral responsibility for failure to act effectively against endemic disorder, poverty, injustice and (the most telling monitor of all) widely different death-rates between different classes or ethnic groups. Mortality tables are a good rough indicator of political justice or injustice. More revolutions take place because governments break down through the ineptitude of conservatives than through the prophecies, schemes, courage, guns and luck of revolutionaries.

In other words, what happens when normal politics breaks down or remains minimal and locked in a dominant community which is either not accepted by a clear majority of the inhabitants (as in South Africa) or by minorities who consider themselves rightfully a majority but frustrated by boundaries unjustly and arbitrarily drawn (as in Ireland and Palestine)? One odd feature of the actual régimes in these three cases is that none of them are pure autocracies; each has some kind of working parliamentary system, indeed a vigorous and by no means superficial political life within the dominant community. Nonetheless the existing institutions did not furnish a mutually acceptable framework for the resolution of conflicts; rather the discontented see them as part of the problem. The disenfranchised do not merely want, like most American Blacks, to be treated as ordinary Americans; they want fundamental institutional changes as well as in the balance of powers between the communities. Both sides may then refuse to negotiate at all, or in the absence of acceptable common institutions, can negotiate only slowly and suspiciously about how to negotiate – while events can take their bloody course.

One could call such problems 'insoluble' for two formal reasons: (i) that no internal solution likely to guarantee peace can possibly satisfy the announced principles of the main disputants; and (ii) that any externally imposed solution or enforced adjudication is likely to strengthen the desperation and self-righteousness of the threatened group (I first heard the phrase 'laager mentality' in Ulster, long before I heard it in South Africa; and Israel knows 'settler mentality' and 'uncompromising defence of the settlements' too). No one can win in terms of their expressed objectives, 'victory' would be 'defeat', pyrrhic at least. Indeed almost any gain for one side is immediately pictured as a potentially fatal loss for the other. Therefore there typically emerges an ideology and personal ethic of defiant heroism: 'sacrifice for the cause', 'to die for one's people', 'the blood sacrifice', 'better to die fighting than live in subjection', etc. The style of thinking of Zionist settler and PLO, IRA and UDF, and AWB (*Afrikaner Weerstandsbeweeging*), Inkatha's warriors and the ANC's *Umkhonto we Sizwe,* all these have had real similarities with each other as well as famous differences (indeed each, to some extent, 'inspired' the other). And governing communities in such situations commonly claim a unique religious identity, even destiny, as well as an ethnic peculiarity. They are especially prone to irrational fears and to hunting down 'the enemy within the gates' as well as 'the enemy without'.

Equal justice?

In all three cases one can become deeply impressed, almost obsessed, with the equal justice of the broad case put by both régime and rebels – if one knows something of their history and grants their basic premises of argument. Anyone who cannot see the plausibility of the other side's case in each of these three instances cannot think, let alone act, politically.[1] Empathy is painful but may be a better starting point for any possible conciliation than trying to decide *'who is right?'* whether by historical argument (who got where first); by a balance sheet of rights and wrongs (like a judicial arbitration); or by utilitarian argument (who makes or could make the best use of 'the land' or 'our land'). Empathy can be painful and fraught with misunderstandings because supporters of tough and beleaguered régimes are so unused to empathetic understanding, especially from foreign observers, that they can mistake it for moral support. And their opponents may similarly regard any scepticism about their means or ends as hostility, or signs of support for the enemy. Overseas supporters who have generously adopted them as 'a cause' are often especially virulent: 'So you actually went *there*! [Spain, Greece, Israel, South Africa – at different periods]. You didn't believe in a *total* boycott?'

Albert Camus once raged against his fellow intellectuals in France who thought it their duty to take sides in the Algerian War and to provide justifications for 'the right to slaughter and mutilate', each basing their arguments mostly 'on the other's crime':

> The role of the intellectuals cannot be . . . to excuse from a distance one of the violences and condemn the other. This has the double result of enraging the violent group that is condemned and of encouraging to greater violence the violent group that is exonerated. If they do not join the combatants themselves, their role (less spectacular, to be sure!) must be merely to strive for pacification so that reason can have a chance.

Some may follow my 'obsession' or painful empathy into Israel in-Palestine and Ulster-in-Ireland but find it perverse when applied to South Africa. Certainly there are clear arguments why racial prejudice is morally more unjust than religious bigotry or the conceits and constraints

---

[1] Some would make empathy for other viewpoints a formal criterion for 'political literacy' in guidance for schools. See Bernard Crick and Alex Porter (eds), *Political Education and Political Literacy* (Longman and Hansard Society, 1978), and Crick, *Essays on Citizenship* (Continuum, 2000).

of class; and the numbers excluded from the franchise in South Africa are impressive by any standard, especially in a state that claimed to be parliamentary and democratic even in part. But in each of these cases, South Africa not least, a large part of the basic problem is the desperation of historic communities to preserve their identity (originally Afrikaners against the British, quite as much as both the indigenous and migrant peoples against the oppression of both; and sometimes Black against Black).

To have abolished legal Apartheid and sought to remove institutions that can violate basic individual human rights is a necessary but not a sufficient condition for stability and justice in South Africa. Quite apart from the problem of lives stunted by poverty, many – surely most? – individuals in South Africa find a large part of their human identity in being a member of a specific community. And each of these communities can appear, at least, to threaten the others, hence threatening each individual's basic sense of identity, not simply their economic interests or acquired beliefs in democratic (or other) political institutions. To say, as the ANC for instance have often appeared to say (more often their supporters outside Southern Africa), that 'one person one vote' constitutes a solution, is only to point to part of the problem. And this is the same in Northern Ireland and in Israel where the use that the majority made of their power has been both crucial and partial.

In such situations neither side can gain a victory except at a price too great for normal men and women to contemplate or endure ('Where they make a desert they call it peace', cried Tacitus of Rome's razing of Carthage). And in such situations nor can any established juridical or democratic criteria be applied to reach a mutually acceptable result peaceably. The breakdown of normal politics creates the need for a kind of politics that can find guarantees for continuing communal identities as well as common citizenship. Few politicians, few thinkers even, have yet begun to consider the implications of a truly pluralistic democracy. What constitutes a community within a state with different legal rights, whether religious, ethnic or territorial? And if to some degree or other such communities may enforce their own rules, how far should the state go in not merely monitoring those rules but in insisting that individuals (especially women and adolescents) are not imprisoned in their communities? Legal Apartheid is an abomination but in most countries intermarriage between people of different communities (where community involves a strong ethnic or religious loyalty) is still not easy; and in most countries tensions between community values and individual rights hit women particularly hard.

Suppose leaders talked a language of generally *acceptable* compromises rather than democratically *agreeable* solutions? The price for any such accommodations would be painfully high in each of the three cases, in terms of previously announced 'unnegotiable positions' and what communities and their existing leaders conceive to be their rights, both rights against others and rights to manage their own internal affairs without interference. In each case it would involve talking seriously and respectfully to people who may have done 'unforgivable things'. But paying a high price has to be faced at some stage if the alternative in each case would be (as is so often threatened when trying to bring the unruly to the negotiating table) chaos, anarchy or the breakdown of the social order – as actually occurred in Yugoslavia after 1992; or even more likely, a sad continuation of present levels of instability, violence, poverty, tension and injustice – as has been the fate of Northern Ireland since 1968 (to give only a numerically small and local example).

Any dispassionate study of the basic problems of instability and violence in these three areas would show their complexity and might stress the *differences* within what only their opponents and foreign supporters see as a united and monolithic Catholic, Protestant, Arab, Jewish, Black or White camp. Activists on the ground, when one talks to them, are commonly more frank and realistic than their leaders about divisions in their own camp, and talk more about them, almost to a fault, than about the nature and iniquities of their enemies. Nonetheless, in each case the fate of 'moderates' who have attempted to use these differences within their communities to build a political base for compromise is not encouraging. A community when it fears that its very existence is threatened rallies to leaders who will promise to defend it utterly and by all means, even if those leaders' beliefs and methods (as with the Revd Dr Paisley) are not normally acceptable. Such leaders are in many respects unrepresentative except as militant defenders. But advocates of moderation are so often outflanked on both wings.

A scholarly study also might find few direct comparisons between the circumstances of the three areas and offer no easy answers. Almost certainly, there are none. Each area is historically and sociologically unique. The common factors are found not in the empirical facts but in *how we perceive* these problems and in how we try to resolve them. Perhaps the very complexity of them or perhaps a natural impatience at their bloodiness and violence tempts us into specious comparisons and general 'solutions'. These solutions are usually a list of 'self-evident' abstract principles so presented as to lead deductively to a card castle of detailed institutional proposals, favouring one side. When anyone cries 'I've a solution', one knows one is dealing with a fanatic, an innocent or a crank. 'Patience and time', said Tolstoy's General Kutusov to his young officers eager for an immediate all-or-nothing battle with Napoleon.

Strictly speaking, and there is need to speak strictly, only *puzzles* have clear solutions. *Problems* (especially political problems) can either be said to have many possible solutions, or no solutions, only resolutions, settlements, compromises or even ameliorations; none perfect, but several, perhaps many, ranging from the more-or-less positively agreeable to the more-or-less tolerably acceptable. Real differences of interest may continue but they can, with will, skill, resources and good fortune, sometimes be made or become less intense, more peaceful. When idealists aim to eradicate 'the causes of prejudice', as is often said amid multiethnic tensions, they can put the cart before the horse: it is a far more ambitious and long-term goal than containing the consequences of prejudice by law enforcement, reasonable settlements and good behaviour. Indeed, eradication of prejudice would need a prior settlement before it could be sensibly attempted. If we can understand what our differences really are and even tacitly agree to differ, then we can share the same house without any great affection but with reasonable civility to the other – if only because we may both have nowhere else to go.

Such settlements will neither be perfect nor what anyone deeply involved would have rationally agreed to in advance of events and negotiations. Some would say that this is because of the inherent imperfection of human nature (what Reinhold Niebuhr called 'Christian realism'), but I think it a sufficient explanation to point to the simple logical truth that free actions are unpredictable. So we need a way of thinking about such conflicts that avoids dogmatism and neither offers too much nor too little. Reckless impatience in remedying injustice is the mirror of feckless delay by states in tackling conditions that create and sustain suspicion and hostility among communities who live in the same territory and who each claim it as their own.

The price to be paid

My moral is not 'peace at any price' but the terribly high price of 'victory' if it comes to winner-take-all. The price of any negotiated peace in such situations is high enough and painful enough, in terms of disappointing the aroused expectations of activists, but it must be paid if ever the main actors come to want peace more than the triumph or the glory of the continual sacred struggle. A desire for peace can come through exhaustion and weariness (as in Ireland in 1919 and 1920) or through moral conviction amid a diminished fear of losing communal identity. When these conditions begin to appear then, and only then, outside aid and pressure can be of much help, indeed sometimes crucial; until then, each of the three situations suggests that external interventions can actually increase fears and prove counter-productive. And inevitably the form of such interventions owes far more to the nature of the domestic politics of the 'donors' than to any objective appraisal of the needs of the 'receivers'.

The highest price of peace is to give up hopes of total victory, to realize the limits of power, and to tell one's followers so. Israel must not, indeed cannot, be displaced but equally it cannot for ever govern areas which are predominantly Arab; nor can it deny to Arabs in these areas the right to be governed how they choose and by whom they choose. Northern Ireland cannot be governed peaceably from either Dublin or London alone. The province (and it is a province not a state, nor even a normal part of a state, both in relation to Ireland and to Great Britain) *inherently faces both ways.* Few people in the North act as if their identity was exclusively Irish or exclusively British: but leaders do not come to terms with this in their policies, being trapped in a mind-set of conventional nationalisms. And populist leaders of ethnic or religiously identified communities are necessarily more responsive to their peoples. The Anglo-Irish Agreement of 1985 pointed a broad way forward towards institutions of joint responsibility, dual citizenship and bi-communal equality; but its effectiveness was hampered by the exclusion of one community in its formulation. In South Africa any lasting compromises must be between communities, openly or covertly, in the text or between the lines. The ending of Apartheid and the freeing of labour in a more rational capitalist market are steps forward which both sides support, though expecting different consequences; but the non-Whites are so disadvantaged that deliberate economic and social reforms by the state are needed, even if by careful stages through time.

As argued in the previous 'Footnote to Rally Fellow Socialists', the nature of time in society must be considered. What kind of changes (whether of income, education, health, the structure of the economy or basic attitudes) take what kind of 'investment lead-time'? 'Rome was not built in a day' or, as William Blake said, 'eternity loves the products of time'. A real conviction can grow that 'things must change' or at least 'cannot go on as they are'. But opposition leaders must realize that real changes in attitudes among a ruling class and real changes in skills and educational attainment among the dispossessed are the work of decades, sometimes generations, not of a parliamentary session, a 'night of long knives' or any mythical 'first hundred days'. Lasting revolutions are long processes, not quick events. The distinction between revolution and evolution is not absolute. The reforming politician with a sense of time (like Lincoln) is a statesman indeed; the conservative politician who uses time as an excuse for delay is, indeed, a timeserver. No modern state can now turn back, only attempt to make realistic, the rising tide of expectations among its dispossessed, nor frustrate the free movement of people and the free expression of ideas: for these are externally triggered, not so often by deliberate pressure but simply by communications and involuntary example. Both man and monkey are mimetic. Example is a most potent force in politics.

I have stated two general reasons why at least two of these problems might be insoluble. A third contingent one emerges in looking at the three areas separately: the virtual impossibility of successful armed rebellion against each of the governments concerned. But also not to forget that there can be severe political, moral and international limitations on the force that each government can use against internal subversion: hence the relative ease of spasmodic violence and terrorism. The real hope of many terrorists in Israel and Palestine and in South Africa was not to bring down a régime and to take over the state, but to force a government to the negotiating table. (The IRA has been divided on this issue.) In each case terrorism by itself is unlikely to force negotiation. It can stiffen resolve, heighten fears in the régime and provoke counter-terror. But terror when used tactically in combination with demonstrations, strikes, riots and propaganda, can sometimes succeed – and, seen in that light, can *in principle,* under extreme oppression, have some justification. At least it makes it absurd to demand that the oppressed forswear all violence as a condition of negotiations. In such circumstances, negotiations offered by the government are unlikely to be genuine unless constrained; both parties in any real negotiations must believe that the consequences of them breaking down would be worse violence and instability than ever before.

An important difference emerges between terrorists who have political aims – or more precisely those who however vague, idealistic or impractical are their stated aims, yet are capable of acting politically – and those whose behaviour is stridently antipolitical, those to whom *the Struggle* and heroic defiance have become a way of life, ends in themselves. The PLO, the IRA and the ANC all seem to have had, at various periods, real divisions between politicals and militants, as well as tactical disagreements. The politicals can be seen as extremists having some genuine claim to be representative of, as well leaders of, a mass popular *movement,* but the militants while claiming to represent *their* people, in fact act like a *sect.* A sect is internally motivated. Any sect is difficult enough to deal or bargain with, and many sects, mutual rivals for leadership of a movement, are almost impossible to deal with. (The growth of Islamic fundamentalism proves to be a common problem to Israel, Algeria, Egypt, Syria and the PLO.) The PLO and the ANC were not divided into clearly institutionalized political and military wings: each exhibited shifting and tactical moves back and forth from one to the other.

From a stalemate of subversive terror versus state terror, neither able to win but neither able to escape the other, can sometimes emerge a qualified general ground for hope: out of the very eye of the storm can come war-weariness and the meeting face to face of key or honoured leaders on both sides.

Three maxims

Three general perspectives or maxims of political thought seem relevant to intransigent situations. The first maxim concerns the nature of state power. Despite all the abuses of coercion in so many familiar instances, the *limitations of state power should never be forgotten.* There is the inability of governments, when the modern technology of radio is added to time-honoured rumour, to silence both internal criticism and news from elsewhere; and there is the proven inefficiency of over-regulation and over-centralization. There is a vital difference between power as unchallengeability (no one else can do it, even if I can't) and power as the ability to carry out a premeditated intention (getting things done). Some governments can't be overthrown but they can neither by force prevent unrest nor carry their own people into economic reforms or new ways of working. The state's power to get things done, to reform a decayed economy, depends both on an ability to mobilize and convince the beneficiaries of reform, but also on an ability to delegate or devolve authority to agents or elected bodies far from the centre. This balance of central control and local initiative is difficult to achieve; but not impossible, just difficult. Good political judgement *is* difficult.

'Power' to be powerful needs redefining as legitimate authority. Authority is the respect that we give to someone for their skill in performing a function that we think is needed. To get such authority, it is not foolish or empty to say, governments actually have to act legitimately. Their skills have to last and they have to learn to adapt and never to forget that, in the last analysis (as the saying used to be), both power and authority rest on consent. In uncharted transitional situations it is indeed difficult for governments, even when they have accepted the need to negotiate, to treat yesterday's gunmen as the responsible opposition leaders or even as coalition colleagues next month, and to face the possibility of losing power in free elections next year. But the price of refusing to negotiate – perpetual uncertainty, debilitating insecurity, economic decline and foreign ostracism – can come to seem even higher. The price is so high, however, that régimes often come to the edge but then go back or sit on their hands. This is why the common well-meant demand that in such situations oppositions should totally renounce the tactics of civil disobedience or of violence can be both unrealistic and unwise. For the price the régime has to pay is so unwelcome and begrudged that pressure has to be kept up or else the government may lapse back or simply play for time hopefully or hopelessly, simply putting off harsh compromises and facing the fact that the other side can gain office.

The second maxim is that *there can never be peace in the world while we believe that for every nation there must be a state and that the state or national parliament, even, must be fully sovereign.* The need for entrenched guarantees to communities is at the heart of so many problems, whether such guarantees are protected by courts or international treaties. In both Israel and Palestine and in Ireland and Northern Ireland even repartition with better demographic boundaries would still leave many on the wrong side of the line and in each one a formidable territorial problem: the Catholic areas of Belfast and Arab Jerusalem. Questions of minority rights leap across state boundaries: consider the Armenians and the Kurds. Many areas of the world do not fit expectations based on the European experience since the seventeenth century of national state formation and the almost universal emulation or imposition of it elsewhere: consider South America and Africa. Political power is not indivisible, it can perfectly well be divided and limited. The Treaty of Rome is a clear enough example. Elements of federalism and federal thinking are almost inevitable in any lasting settlements, or frameworks for peaceable evolution by consent in divided areas. But some new federal constitutions may have to be communal as much as territorial. The state needs binding constitutionally against harming its own minorities, and sometimes to prevent it favouring them disproportionately; and individuals need protecting by Bills of Right against both state and community.

'Pluralism' was once a philosophy of the state critical of the theory of sovereignty. Some groups, it was argued, do have a relative autonomy that is beyond the power of the state. 'All power is federal', said the young Harold Laski. That is doubtful. We have to think case by case, and function by function within those cases. But some power to be effective can only be federal. Sovereignty thinking, like simple-majoritarian-democratic thinking, can again be more part of the problem than the dominant necessity in any 'solution' or resolution. The claim of 'sovereignty' often precludes any genuine constitutional restraints, hence makes any negotiation still depend on the goodwill (which may be wholly lacking) of the majority or the powerful minority in government. But two or more nations can inhabit one state and preserve their identities. We in the United Kingdom should sometimes look under our noses, as well as to Canada and Belgium, etc. The United Kingdom is a multi-national state not a single nation state, albeit and arguably with inadequate or inappropriate political institutions. Most Scots and Welsh want a parliament both as positive symbol and as a democratic protector of their nationhood, but not a separate state.[2]

The third maxim is that *the basic philosophical concept of a free action as an unpredictable action* (one not logically entailed or determined by any necessary circumstances) *must be related to the nature of political negotiation.* Only in efficient autocracies are the outcomes of 'negotiations' predictable, and efficient autocracies are getting hard to find. Certainly what the leaders of rival groups in the three particular areas say they each want as their unnegotiable objectives are relatively unlikely to occur. They confuse political negotiation with a negotiated military surrender. So if the real object of the struggle is not 'revolution' or 'victory' but is 'to bring to the table' the reluctant parties, then it is wise, while never going into negotiations without preparation, yet to be open-minded about what will emerge. No one will convert the other but in the nature of the problems and of negotiation, no one will get all they want or even quite what they expect. Precise outcomes in difficult situations are unpredictable. Again, only puzzles have unique solutions; problems can be resolved to tolerable levels, if never wholly removed, in different ways. Safeguards, privileges, rewards, opportunities and legal and social rights can all take many forms, and are all negotiable.

By the mid-1980s, for instance, both British and Irish governments began to perceive Northern Ireland as a common problem, so that to some degree they have tried to act jointly, 'in collusion' even (as the rival irreconcilables and invincibles see it). They were uncertain what framework to advocate, both what might work and what might prove acceptable to their very different constituencies. Neither side brought a draft of the 'Anglo-Irish Agreement 1985' with them to the table. It emerged from negotiation, or some might say (but with hindsight) from the logic of the situation. The Intergovernmental Council that emerged was not an instrument of government but rather a reasonably stable forum for consultation and continuing negotiation. But very probably it points, as some fear and others hope, towards some kind

---

[2]See 'Devolution, Decentralism and the Constitution' in my *Political Thoughts and Polemics* (Edinburgh University Press, 1990), and 'The Sovereignty of Parliament and the Scottish Question' in Norman Lewis (ed.), *Happy and Glorious: The Constitution in Transition* (Open University Press, Milton Keynes: 1990).

of evolving joint authority, joint citizenship and some working doctrine of communal equality.[3] But to some on both sides, any negotiation was selling the pass. So sectarians commonly refuse to negotiate or try to wreck negotiations, until their own followers either grow weary of them and rebel, or too often, alas, drop out of politics entirely leaving the fanatics and the 'incorruptibles' unrestrained and pretending to speak for them.

'Oppression makes a wise man mad', and not all begin by being equally wise. But happily this is not always true: oppression can bring out the best in human beings. I found hope not just in new ideas about constitutional arrangements but in what one found when talking to Black South African political leaders recently released from long years in brutal prisons; one found qualities not always associated with normal politics in comfortable, consumer-driven societies: courage, dignity, irony not anger, tactical skill, empathetic understanding of their oppressors rather than a hunger for revenge, and an ability to state the essence of their case cogently – that is, briefly and with absolute relevance as if genuinely to persuade other reasonable people. But if the other side were not so good at persuading, and often, like elsewhere, seemed trapped in their own history, while it made it more difficult to understand their true case and what are their minimal demands, yet it made it more urgent to do so and to take them fully seriously.

So this penultimate defence of politics is a plea for outsiders and observers not to give unqualified and uncritical support to one side or another in the most difficult political problems – Serbs or Croats, say – nor to offer glib solutions. Some causes are more worthy of qualified support than others, but all conflicts need understanding historically and empathetically and all causes benefit from critical support ('A writer', said Orwell, 'can never be a loyal member of a political party' – he was a member of a party when he wrote that.)

Such difficult problems must, indeed, be tackled not evaded, for moral as well as prudential reasons. Decent people should scorn arguments that our government (and all others) should only be concerned with Croatia and Serbia, say, if our material interests are concerned; or should only have helped President Gorbachev or President Yeltsin for

---

[3] See 'Northern Ireland and the Theory of Consent' in my *Political Thoughts and Polemics,* ibid.

the immediate sake of British trade. Common humanity is sufficient reason for the concern, even involvement, of all thinking people; but the greatest good we can do in extreme situations is to keep a clear head and offer independent, critical intelligence, not to add to the passion of the commitments that kill and maim. There is a danger that outsiders can indulge their own passions, as if the tragedies of the world were a street theatre, with either no effect on the problems or bad ones. There is a need for both influence and critical judgement (in Kant's sense) from outsiders, and for insiders to force themselves mentally to act like dispassionate outsiders. Spectators do see more of the game than the players.[4] Informed spectators can influence, not a particular game perhaps, but the general way in which it is played. Such influence is at best indirect: the observer should neither volunteer for the Front nor make high-brow propaganda for the better cause. He or she should try to suggest the preconditions for negotiations between the actual parties involved and stand ready to help, if asked, in assisting or implementing any transitional arrangements. Because such situations involve real and terrible dilemmas and are not perverse tests or puzzles made for our solving, outcomes can vary and will always disappoint, somewhat; there are no perfect or unique solutions. Concerned persons should be less concerned to predict and support most-favoured outcomes and be more willing to imagine and to accept many possible and often quite unexpected outcomes which will give peace and reduce both violent death and death by neglect of state action.

On second thoughts

These considerations lead to two substantial afterthoughts, perhaps second thoughts. I am unrepentant in my argument about the primacy of political thinking over both economic and legal thinking; but in reacting against the exaggerated claims of Marxist economicism and Conservative legalism, I may have underestimated their relative importance. To be told that to observe 'the rule of law' is the overriding maxim for social justice and peace is a dangerous half-truth: those who say so forget that laws can be iniquitous and judges hostile to liberty

---

[4]See Ronald Beiner, *Political Judgment* (Methuen, London: 1983).

and to reform. Socrates broke the law, to begin the whole tradition of free political speculation; so did Brutus; and citizens in Eastern Europe did so spectacularly in 1989, and on a humble scale (foreign readers must forgive parochial triviality) an unjust tax in Britain, the Poll Tax, was destroyed by public disobedience and protest at about the same time. And certainly uncontrolled free markets can no more create the conditions for social justice than can state control: neither the writings of Adam Smith nor Karl Marx are self-sufficient guides to policy (leaving aside that what they both said is somewhat different from what has been made of them by enthusiastic followers and by enthusiastic enemies).

The new struggles for liberty, however, have involved a far greater revival of constitutional law and speculation than seemed relevant or likely thirty years ago. Abrupt attempts to move overnight from an ideology of state control to an ideology of 'a free market in everything' (as old Hungarian friends now say) may, indeed, be a running from one total and rigid ideology to another, both lacking in historical and sociological insight, and may prove dangerous rejections of political thinking about intermediate positions and transitional means. Yet it is now clear that some form of free market, in some context of public law, is a necessary condition for liberty and the institutions of political rule. (I could have said this more clearly in the section on 'Equality' in the 'Footnote to Rally Fellow Socialists'.) Gorbachev realized that in order to get some *perestroika* (economic reform), some *glasnost* (openness, freedom) had to be tolerated, but *glasnost* was not containable and this produced the need for more *perestroika* than he had bargained and prepared for, and let loose the 'wild capitalism'.

So a word, finally, on each of these reservations. If the main precondition for peace and justice in the post-Cold War modern world is a change from centralist sovereignty thinking to pluralistic thinking, then negotiation in extreme situations must take a more legalistic form than has been common of late in European political thought and practice, scarcely at all in the new nations. Negotiations themselves will be about constitutional devices and the only possible outcome will be a just, or acceptable, and better (not perfect) set of constitutional arrangements. Working through these arrangements, substantive issues of social policy would, in the near or middle future, be settled; but not in the constitution itself. Constitutions cannot settle economic policy, neither prescribe redistribution nor embalm or protect specified and precise property rights for ever. The most that can and should be hoped for from negotiation is to reach a consensus on procedures: agreement on rules by which substantive problems can, within a framework of government, be resolved; and also agreement on more difficult processes by which constitutions themselves can be changed.

Put it this way. Remember that the thirteen colonies in British North America that revolted against the homeland found a common bond in a constitution that they created themselves. Constitutionalism was itself a founding and a bonding belief which long preceded any sense of an American nation. A clear and firm sense of American nationhood emerged only during a long and bloody civil war to defend what even then and now was called, not 'the State', but 'the Union'. The first stages of the French Revolution were constitutional, heavily influenced by the American example and by the writings of the Anglo-American republicans and constitutionalists. Only when foreign invasion occurred and internal violence became endemic did nationalism stir, and was stirred, and 'sovereignty of the people' became a sufficient constitutive principle to the Jacobin leadership who used and abused it in the name of 'the people'. The predominate reformist and emancipatory idea everywhere in Europe and the Americas in the early and mid-nineteenth century was to gain or be given 'a just constitution'. There was the American antimonarchical slogan, 'a government of laws and not of men'; and there was the idea of the German parliaments of 1848 to create a *'Rechtstadt',* a state bound by enforceable laws. The belief in general legal rules rather than paternal particularism, 'each case on its merits', was in part a response to particular difficulties of conflicting community, group and ethnic loyalties within states. Britain was and is the exception (to my mind now, the unfortunate exception).

Throughout the latter part of the nineteenth century and into the decade of colonial emancipation in the middle of this century, nationalism seemed to hold sway nearly everywhere, often at the expense of constitutional beliefs that governments should be restrained in some agreed areas by enforceable laws which can only be changed by special procedures. The nation, on the contrary, should have no restraints put upon it, or rather on its devoted leaders: popular sovereignty should be absolute. But there are many areas of the world where different peoples are inextricably bound together by geography or by economic dependence on each other. The collapse of Soviet power released suppressed nationalist passions for ideas of complete independence or of 'ethnic cleansing', which even if possible, prove economically disastrous and morally intolerable. Leaders of the emancipated East European states, of the Baltic Republics, and of the Ukraine and Georgia, etc., have had to consider the practical compromises of 'sovereignty' that states in Western Europe had already taken for their own betterment.

In these areas some of the reasons why constitutional government first arose may be recreating themselves, with the added complexity that relations between 'sovereign states' themselves (as in the EC) can need binding by litigable and enforceable law. National states are not the only possible form of human government, nor necessarily the best. And the idea that the mere assertion of sovereignty can create power sufficient for economic, political and even cultural independence, is a sadly absurd illusion.

Final thoughts

The revolutionary events of 1989 in Eastern Europe have changed the history of the world. But they arose basically from a simple but profound perception by Gorbachev that the economic problems of his country could only be solved politically, not by central command. Nothing has changed the truth of that perception. Economic reform needs political reform, and in the precise sense of trying to create a political system and civic culture, which is not an easy task (as my discussion of the formal conditions for the stability of political systems would indicate; see pp. 142–45 above). And there were, of course, repercussions far beyond Europe; as in a terse remark by Gorbachev in July 1988 that 'there must be a political solution to the Southern African question'. That meant that there would be no more training of guerrillas or money for arms, whether in Africa, the Middle East, South and Central America, or anywhere else.

All this was so unexpected. No political scientists can claim to have predicted these events. The image of the study of politics as aspiring to science rather than to good judgement (say again, political judgement) took a humbling knock (even though such great events leave many scholars undisturbed, still grazing happily in their own narrow fields).[5]

---

[5]When, for instance, the British Political Studies Association held their annual conference at Easter 1990 they were not willing or able to change their programme to include any discussion of the momentous events in Eastern Europe of the autumn before.

Economists had for long proved in theory the inevitable inefficiency of production and distribution of goods and resources in command economies without a price mechanism, and that price mechanisms depend on a free market. But few of them expected that in practice the greatest of these systems would actually break down. Most observers simply thought that it did not work well and could still work worse. Their theories seemed like the rhetoric of Burke who tried to prove that the French Revolution was impossible in the same breath as he berated the iniquities of its success.

Travelling and lecturing in Czechoslovakia shortly after the November risings of 1989, I was startled to provoke puzzled and angry objections by referring (for once without thinking) to 'the November *revolution*'. That very word, like 'socialism' (even with its Western democratic handle firmly nailed to the new broom), was almost untouchable because of its abuse and over-use by the Communist Party. So before we could establish a normal vocabulary to discuss quite what had happened that November and why, I had to go backwards in time to talk about why it is sensible to call the American War of Independence a revolution (certainly in terms of its international consequences) and I had to distinguish patiently between stages of the French Revolution.

The November events were revolutions in certain obvious senses. They were revolts that aimed at far more than a change of government, rather to create a new régime, to transform many basic social institutions and also basic values; and they arose suddenly and almost spontaneously, triggered (to recycle an old concept) by inherent contradictions in the ideology of the ruling class (an ideology of production that could not produce, an ideology of labour that even alienated the working class). But also, like most previous revolutions, the very drama of the events, the very awfulness of the old oppression, combined to create exaggerated expectations of what freedom could immediately bring. And, of course, the revolution swept away one system of distribution, which worked after a fashion, even if so badly, without there being another ready to put in its place.

In fact, of course, no revolution has ever made or could make a complete break from the past; nor are social systems like machine-tools that can be simply bolted into the floor and substituted for outmoded ones. People have traditions, memories and habits. Rome wasn't built in a day and when we rebuild we have to use a lot of old materials, and on the same old site using most of the same people – people perhaps radically changed, but not transfigured; and among those radical changes, the unreal expectations, certainly unreal in the short term.

Small wonder that new régimes come under threat when they have to call for continued economic hardships, perhaps even more than before, to rebuild from the mistakes of the past. The workers have heard all that before. Disillusionment can come quickly, as happened in the former Soviet Union itself, especially when the greatest price of transition to a free economy is something as fundamental and hitherto unexperienced as unemployment coupled to the rising price of necessities. Apart from the risk of violent death, there are no human circumstances that can so discredit a régime and cause many of its inhabitants to drop out from, despise and turn against civil society, as continued mass unemployment and rabid inflation.

There are great dangers in trying to leap from one extreme to another too precipitously: as if one can move from a total central command economy to an unregulated free market as easily as spinning a coin. If we seek to cross from one side of a mountain torrent to another we look for stepping-stones. The great mistakes of command economies are uneconomic subsidy of so-called basic industries, more often symbolically important (like coal and steel in Communist ideology) than economically effective. But not all subsidies are of that kind. I heard Hungarian friends say that *all* subsidies must be removed, even from public transport, from hospitals and from nursery education. When I said weak British things like, 'isn't that going too far?' or 'isn't that wrong?' or simply 'why?', they recited paragraphs to me from the writings of Professor Hayek. What I most tried hard to say was, 'isn't all this politically imprudent?' 'shouldn't you move cautiously and selectively?' They then read me more passages from Hayek.

There can be a fundamental misunderstanding of the nature of Western capitalism. Its early origins were, in some sense, spontaneous, perhaps arguably even a natural tendency. But its institutional development depended not merely on sweeping away a lot of old mercantilist laws, but on the state bringing in new kinds of regulation, notably Company Acts, commercial law in general, regulation of stock markets, and on a great deal of state subsidy of education and the infrastructure for transport and sanitary cities. Borrowing arguments from Neal Ascherson, I bored my Hungarian friends with an account of how much more regulation of this kind there was in the Federal Republic of Germany, far more than was thought good in Thatcher's Britain. That was a better argument; they listened with puzzled patience to my amateur account of the reasons for the success of the post-war West German economy, whereas they reacted impatiently to a brave woman colleague of theirs who went on and on about Swedish social-democracy proving the possibility of mixed economies.

Such middle ways are possible (as I argued in the Footnote on socialism), but perhaps her audience simply didn't want a middle way. But the theoretical point is that just as there was no such thing as a totally totalitarian régime (the desire for total power was real enough, but attempts to exercise it were ramshackle and destructive), so there has never been such a thing as a totally free economy. All economies are mixed economies, and some are more mixed than others. However, it as well to accept that truism: to make deregulation an end in itself can actually threaten a transitional political order. Real leaders must be prudent, must exercise political judgement, must encourage but not surrender completely to the competitive imperatives of the free market.

These conversations caused me to worry that the old régime, Communism I mean, had discredited not only even the mildest elements of democratic socialism and social democracy; it had discredited any respect for politics itself. My basic argument seemed very important to some of them (more so than here), but puzzled others who were in such a mood of reaction against the immediate past that they wanted to take the politics out of everything, even the politics of a freely elected parliament. They imagined that they would thus create a more efficient market economy more quickly; in fact, I argued, they could end up being governed by bureaucrats, lawyers and accountants. Someone has to regulate markets; the real question is whether they are accountable or not to the governed. Totalitarianism indeed was less a relapse into barbarism, as some have argued, than a false modernism: an attempt to remake humanity scientifically and bureaucratically into something more predictable, mechanical and controllable, quite other than human.

To warn against exaggerated expectations is not to belittle the progress that there was. That there are great problems in Eastern Europe in the 1990s, partly the legacies of the past and partly the inadequacy of foreign aid, is no argument for putting the clock back. If we can regret the separation of the Czechs and the Slovaks, we can count it as a blessing that the break-up was peaceful – unlike the bloodshed and anarchy as Yugoslavia tore itself apart. The past was bad enough elsewhere in Eastern Europe, even if not always in immediate material terms to all sections of society, because there was no hope of peaceful change.

Orwell once remarked, in an essay on Koestler, that the 'essence of being human is that one does not seek perfection':

> Perhaps, however, whether desirable or not, it [the Earthly Paradise] isn't possible. Perhaps some degree of suffering is ineradicable from human life, perhaps the main choice before man is always a choice of evils, perhaps even the aim of Socialism is not to make the world perfect but to make it better. All revolutions are failures, but they are not all the same failure.[6]

Betterment has resulted, and free politics is part of that betterment because it is both means and end. It is right that all mankind should live in free political systems and that free political systems have their own means of adjustment, advance, self-renewal and betterment.

Times of transition always entail a high price. Mankind cannot live for long in anarchy or chronic instability, without hope and reasonably clear expectations; but cannot be human or free either if expectations are fixed and rigid. The price of change has been heavy in the Eastern bloc but is worth paying. How easy to say to others! How shameful and lacking in civic spirit that people in the free countries of the West have been so grudging and stinting, found so many rationalizations, so petty-minded and selective, against helping the liberated to restructure their economies on the scale plainly and urgently needed. Are people really so lacking in humanity and vision, or do all our politicians misread us, have no confidence that they can persuade us to look beyond our noses, and thus fail to lead us?

Have they narrowed politics to questions of marginal rates of taxation at the expense of the greater public values of our whole civilization?

---

[6]Quoted in 'Orwell and English Socialism' in my *Essays on Politics and Literature* (Edinburgh University Press, 1989).

Men and women are citizens as well as consumers. The price of liberty is more than eternal vigilance (especially when the objects of our vigilance now appear comfortably on screen); it is eternal commitment to political activity. What has been most proved in the last decade has been the weakness of autocracy, iron régimes have proved fragile; but, alas, the altruism and public spirit of the free, while strong and noble on occasion, is dangerously spasmodic. We are all too apt to watch rather than to act, are too fearful of losing immediate individual comforts to defend intelligently our own long-term interests by working with and helping others.

Epilogue

So revolutions broke out in city after city, and in places where the revolutions occurred late the knowledge of what had happened previously in other places caused still new extravagances of revolutionary zeal, expressed by an elaboration in the methods of seizing power and by unheard-of atrocities in revenge. To fit in with the change of events, words, too, had to change their usual meanings. What used to be described as a thoughtless act of aggression was now regarded as the courage one would expect to find in a party member; to think of the future and wait was merely another way of saying one was a coward; any idea of moderation was just an attempt to disguise one's unmanly character; ability to understand a question from all sides meant that one was totally unfitted for action. Fanatical enthusiasm was the mark of a real man, and to plot against an enemy behind his back was perfectly legitimate self-defence. Anyone who held violent opinions could always be trusted, and anyone who objected to them became a suspect. To plot successfully was a sign of intelligence, but it was still cleverer to see that a plot was hatching. If one attempted to provide against having to do either, one was disrupting the unity of the party and acting out of fear of the opposition. In short, it was equally praiseworthy to get one's blow in first against someone who was going to do wrong, and to denounce someone who had no intention of doing any wrong at all.

Family relations were a weaker tie than party membership, since party members were more ready to go to any extreme for any reason whatever. . . . These parties were not formed to enjoy the benefits of the established laws.

Revenge was more important than self-preservation. And if pacts of mutual security were made, they were entered into by the two parties only in order to meet some temporary difficulty, and remained in force only so long as there was no other weapon available. When the chance came, the one who first seized it boldly, catching his enemy off his guard, enjoyed a revenge that was all the sweeter from having been taken, not openly, but because of a breach of faith. . . .

Love of power, operating through greed and through personal ambition, was the cause of all these evils. To this must be added the violent fanaticism which came into play once the struggle had broken out. Leaders of parties in the cities had programmes which appeared admirable – on one side political equality for the masses; on the other, the safe and sound government of the aristocracy. But in professing to serve the public interest they were seeking to win the prizes for themselves. In their struggles for ascendancy nothing was barred; terrible indeed were the actions to which they committed themselves, and in taking revenge they went farther still. Here they were deterred neither by the claims of justice nor by the interests of the state; their one standard was the pleasure of their own party at that particular moment, and so, either by means of condemning their enemies on an illegal vote or by violently usurping power over them, they were always ready to satisfy the hatreds of the hour. Thus neither side had any use for conscientious motives; more interest was shown in those who could produce attractive arguments to justify some disgraceful action. As for the citizens who held moderate views, they were destroyed by both the extreme parties, either for not taking part in the struggle or in envy at the possibility that they might survive.

As the result of these revolutions, there was a general deterioration of character throughout the Greek world. The simple way of looking at things, which is so much the mark of a noble nature, was regarded as a ridiculous quality and soon ceased to exist. . . . As a rule those who were least remarkable for intelligence showed the greater powers of survival. Such people recognised their own deficiencies and the superior intelligence of their opponents; fearing that they might lose a debate or find themselves out-manoeuvred in intrigue by their quickwitted enemies, they boldly launched straight into action;

while their opponents, over-confident in the belief that they would see what was happening in advance, and not thinking it necessary to seize by force what they could secure by policy, were the more easily destroyed because they were off their guard.

Certainly it was in Corcyra that there occurred the first examples of the breakdown of law and order. There was the revenge taken in their hour of triumph by those who had in the past been arrogantly oppressed instead of wisely governed. . . . Then, with the ordinary conventions of civilised life thrown into confusion, human nature, always ready to offend even where laws exist, showed itself proudly in its true colours, as something incapable of controlling passion, insubordinate to the idea of justice, the enemy to anything superior to itself; for, if it had not been for the pernicious power of envy, men would not so have exalted vengeance above innocence and profit above justice. Indeed, it is true that in these acts of revenge on others men take it upon themselves to begin the process of repealing those general laws of humanity which are there to give a hope of salvation to all who are in distress, instead of leaving those laws in existence, remembering that there may come a time when they, too, will be in danger and will need their protection.

(Thucydides, *The Peloponnesian War*, Book 3, chapter 5)

Darkness

Thucydides in the fifth century BC painted this picture of horrific violence which is not entirely unfamiliar to our more decent, civilized, modern, advanced age of the concentration camps, the gas ovens, Coventry and Dresden (to speak of little local incidents), Nagasaki and Hiroshima, Vietnam, Cambodia, Tibet, Rwanda, Bosnia, Chechenya, etcetera, etcetera, etcetera. 'The progress of mankind', of which eighteenth- and nineteenth-century publicists spoke so warmly, has proved at least a little uneven in its development; indeed, that great phrase was not much heard after 1914 except, for a while, in 'the socialist sixth of the world' and in the USA before the Great Depression. To the revolutionary violence of Thucydides we have added collective passions as strongly motivated as racism, nationalism and – if less frequent than in the early modern past – religion.

There are times when, as Jean-Jacques Rousseau said at the beginning of 'the age of revolutions' (industrial, medical and social, not only constitutional), 'I weep and howl to think that I am a man'. Indeed, the scale and body-counts of the killing fields of our modern age surpass those of either Thucydides or Rousseau, and not only because there are more of us. They follow from premeditated acts of public policy employing modern technology quite as much as from the uncontrolled passions of ethnic hatred, civil war, death in battle and in hot pursuit, the starving of cities, clan vengeance and the killing or maiming of male prisoners and the rape and enslavement of women. But the terse bitterness and angry sorrow of Thucydides' description of the class war in Corcyra is hard to match in modern authors, except in both novels and monographs about the Holocaust and the camps. This may be because he proudly knew that the Greeks, at their best, had already created a unique form of civilization (for he included the Periclean oration – on which I will end this Epilogue) compared to all other nations, empires and tribes in the known world; one which, for all its obvious faults to us, and to some few of his contemporaries too – notably the institution of slavery, the subjugation of women – was unique and wonderful: the *polis* itself, the citizen republic, government by free citizens in public debate.

Jefferson proudly described the new American republic as 'the world's best hope'. If governing in a political manner and resolving problems politically is everywhere and together 'the world's best hope', some rather obvious problems appear of a scale that makes any easy optimism difficult, even foolishly head-in-the-sand. Some problems make life for many or most of the earth's inhabitants, in Hobbes' phrase, 'nasty, brutish and short', certainly short compared with life-expectancies and infant survival rates in the wealthier parts of the world (thinking firmly of *per capita* income rather than gross national product); some, singly or together, undoubtedly threaten advanced civilization, perhaps the species itself.

Consider the continued tolerance of war, poverty and ill-health, the downside of the global market, the despoliation of the environment, and the decline of political thinking and of respect for politicians even in its homelands. Both short-term electoral politics and short-term consumerism, feeding off each other, make long-term problems hard to grasp, even if their threat cumulates.

The tolerance of war

The annual *Human Development Reports* of the UN estimate that since 1945 more than 25 million people have died in wars and other conflicts: 'Global conflicts seem to be changing – from wars between states to wars within states. Of the 82 conflicts between 1989 and 1992, only three were between states.' More than half the conflicts current in 1993 had been raging for over a decade. During that year 42 countries in the world had 52 major conflicts and another 37 experienced endemic political violence of one kind or another. Of those 79 countries, 59 were in the developing world. The end of the Cold War seemed to remove the will and the need of the great powers to keep their former clients and allies in order (in the case of Russia, also the ability). A paper submitted by the US mission to the UN in 1996 estimated that 80 per cent of agricultural land in Angola had been abandoned due to civil war and manufacturing output was only two-thirds of the 1973 level; that in Mozambique only 5 per cent of agricultural land was being cultivated and industry was operating at 20 to 40 per cent of full capacity; and in Bosnia-Hertzegovina at least 20 per cent of the housing stock had been destroyed and much of the public infrastructure. These are but examples.

Rosemary Righter's masterly study of the United Nations Organization states that, while 'ritualized conflict was endemic', enforcement of both General Assembly and Security Council resolutions has been, with few exceptions, weak, often negligent and, when attempted, too often futile.[1] There have been and are some reasonably successful peace-keeping episodes, but peace-making rarely; then only if it suited the national or ideological interests of the Security Council. And, of course, the Charter itself forbids intervention in the internal affairs of the member states, so that interventions to prevent or put down civil wars are resisted by the majority of member states, even if they have international or at least

---

[1] Rosemary Righter, *Utopia Lost: The United Nations and World Order* (Brookings Institution, Washington, DC, 1994).

cross-border repercussions. Changing the Charter to outlaw civil war seems impossible, quite apart from the task of enforcement.

Take the case of Rwanda. The general secretary of the UN, Butros Butros Gali, did warn in advance of trouble coming and asked Western nations to finance and provide the materials and logistics for African states to use their own troops to prevent massacre amid virtual anarchy. The Security Council failed to respond; the result was genocide, with at least a million killed. Righter comments: 'a lack of realism and mere talk had come to play an essential role in the global organizations' (remember that the UN itself is made up of over 100 semi-autonomous organizations: hardly united, scarcely credible).

To preserve or to create free institutions force may be needed. One does not have to read Machiavelli's great *Discourses* to see that.

There was a brief moment of hope at the end of the Gulf War over Iraq's invasion of Kuwait when it looked as if the two great powers, the USA and the USSR, might begin to work together in mutual exasperation at the cost and unpredictable consequences of local wars. The end of the Cold War had made that possible. Butros Gali in December 1992 put before the Security Council a proposal for a volunteer military rapid-reaction force to be controlled and financed by the UN, to be, as it were, the policeman of the world. But this brief hope was only a doomed speculation. The USSR imploded and Russia ceased to have global interests and the USA lost the will, even to pay others to do its fighting. Revulsion at the heavy losses and defeat in Vietnam had been bad enough, but television pictures of dead US troops being dragged through the streets of the Somali capital (a relatively small if bungled incident in itself) finally destroyed any support in Congress for Gali's lonely but rational initiative. Indeed, tactics in the Gulf War, and the failure to follow up victory, were dictated by American aversion to risk casualties even for a demonstrable greater good, as was the reliance on aerial bombardment, and the reluctance to use ground troops, in Bosnia.

Here is power without responsibility indeed. Perhaps the intense localism of the American political and constitutional system is largely to blame, but there has also been an unwillingness of successive presidents to attempt to lead and influence public opinion towards accepting that war and civil war should be outlawed effectively for ever, even at some initial cost and sacrifice. Instead public opinion is accepted as a fixed and given thing. Politics ceases to be effective in face of great problems if it is not believed that elected leaders are able to persuade and change opinion. 'The secret of liberty', Pericles had said, 'is courage.'

The wretched of the earth

Does it need saying that war works against rational and moral attempts to alleviate poverty, malnutrition and chronic deficiency diseases in the developing world? So much money that could be used for aid, too often that is meant for aid, becomes diverted to arms – usually to arm a military régime against its own people. However, what is at issue when looking at measures of poverty and world health is not that overall things are getting worse, for overall in this century life-expectancy has risen dramatically and post-natal mortality fallen in all countries and for all classes – the world has never been healthier or wealthier. What is at issue is acute relative deprivation in wealth, a rapidly growing divergence between rich and poor (reducing some nations and classes to powerlessness compared to others), and differences in mortality statistics, both between social classes in richer countries and between regions of the world – all divergences that are in principle easily remediable if governments had the will and if political mechanisms existed.

Even the growth of world population raises no inevitable spectre of starvation; in principle there is plenty of unused land that could be turned to grain crops which, whether genetically modified or not, have themselves increased dramatically in yield; but again the problem of political will arises and the economics of maldistribution. Many Green prophets of doom, using highly uncertain and contestable statistical projections, as in the global warming controversy, almost certainly overstate their case when it purports to be scientific, empirical and factual (despite their growing anti-science ideology): the far clearer case is moral, as with the need to prevent war and civil war. Such huge divergence of life chances, even when aggregate standards rise, should not be tolerated among fellow human beings. Famine, of course, only occurs in poor countries, because they have nothing to fall back on if the rains fail, or if the paddy fields are hopelessly flooded by inundations, and because international aid is almost always too little and, for many, too late. The UN is inadequately funded, so too is the World Bank; the heart of the matter is that governments of the wealthier nations think themselves, or in fact are, politically constrained from raising enough money through taxation, and also from working together effectively. How worthy are the great voluntary bodies like Oxfam, the Red Cross or Medicins Sans Frontières, but what a sad reflection that they depend so much on the shaking of the collecting-box and the whims and fashions of the private cheque-book.

The despoliation of the planet

We are familiar with what the industrial age is doing to the environment of the planet on which humanity depends. Some ignore the facts. Others hope that they will go away, or that the mysterious guided hand of the free market will blow away the gases, plug the holes in the ozone layer and re-grow cut timber at the speed of a computer. Anyway, for each government and each multi-national (a) it is someone else's responsibility and (b) nothing we can do alone will have any effect.

Let me just set down the main dimensions of the problems, not to discuss them yet again; just naming them reminds us how inadequate and reluctant have been governmental responses. Political compromise can work within countries, but it does not seem to work between countries to control such man-made processes of destruction:

greenhouse-induced climate change
ozone depletion
degradation and loss of agricultural land
depletion and pollution of water resources
depletion of fish stocks

The downside of the global market

Hannah Arendt in *The Human Condition* said that there have only ever been two kinds of comprehensive ideology claiming to hold the key to history: the belief that all is determined by *race* and the belief that all is determined by *economics.* Both racism and economicism are, we should remember, distinctively modern beliefs: before the late eighteenth century the world could get by without such enormous secular claims, and not even religions claimed to *explain* everything. Arendt pointed out that economic ideology took two rival forms, and yet their belief that there must be a *general system* had a common origin and linked them more than their disciples believe: *Marxism* (all is class ownership) and *laissezfaire* (all is market forces). The missionaries and advocates of market ideology in the former Soviet bloc now denounce political interventions in the economy almost as fiercely as did the old totalitarians, although fortunately they are still subject to some political restraints and a few residual cultural inhibitions. In the party politics of Great Britain many of us in the Thatcher and Major times railed against excesses of privatization, the diminishment of public welfare from the state and the attacks of a government on the very concept of a *res publica* or a public interest; and some of us are not entirely sure that those times have gone for ever. Governments can seek to distance themselves from any responsibility for guiding Adam Smith's hidden hand by which the free market becomes the public interest (give or take some emollient oils of private charity and rituals of religious benevolence – thinking of the real Adam Smith). But in a broader perspective, the degree of political restraint upon the children of Hayek – the Reagans and the Thatchers – was also remarkable. They have done to us, for good or ill, much less than they know they ought to have done; and that is, happily, because of 'irrational political factors', as they see it.

Prices cannot be sensibly determined except by market mechanisms; the final breakdown of Soviet planning proved that, however well it may have served for a time of emergency. The new global economy is creating wealth. And capitalism is an international system whose imperatives can be ignored only at a fearful price, as in North Korea and Cuba, or by the luck, while it lasts, of oil in the sand. But it does not follow that price must then determine every human relationship, least of all the civic; nor that there should not be national restraints on world trade that damages fragile native industries or undermines indigenous customs. The effects of the market can be either limited or mitigated by civic action, and some should be: graduated taxation and subsidized institutions for public welfare should be as much subject to local democratic demand as to international tariff and banking rules. *Man is citizen as well as consumer.* Beside the social justice of graduated taxation there is or was public and family morality, strong cultural restraints on the exercise of both economic and political power. New lines of demarcation and mutual influence between the polity and the economy need examining closely and coolly. If people see themselves purely as consumers they will lose all real control of government. Governments will then rule by bread and circuses, even if not by force; and torrents of trivial alternatives will make arbitrary and often meaningless choice pass for effective freedom. For all the absolutist rhetoric, in reality at least a degree of welcome confusion reigns. Only the two extreme positions of All-State or All-Market are untenable; there is a lot of space between. Political and economic factors and principles interact with each, limit each other; but neither can live for long without the other. Amartya Sen has written: 'the real debate associated with globalisation is, ultimately, not about the efficiency of markets, nor about the importance of modern technology. The debate is rather about inequality of power, for which there is much less tolerance now than in the world that emerged at the end of the Second World War.' Less tolerance, perhaps, less willingness to take gross inequalities for granted or to believe fatuously that the wealth of unrestrained capitalism will 'drip down', like tips to underpaid and overworked waiters; but it is still hard to see any real equivalent in international relations to the processes and institutions of free politics within free countries themselves. What there are seem inadequate, deserve minimal defence and little praise.

The decline of political thinking

Even within free countries, there was in the last years of the last century an extraordinary decline in the standard of public debate both among politicians and in the media. Memories are still painful of how, in the American presidential campaign of 1996 and the British general election of 1997 (somewhat mimicking the former), even sustained rhetoric, let alone attempts at reasoned, persuasive discourse, collapsed into sound-bites, and contingent ones at that, reacting to relatively trivial, mainly opportunistic accusations and counter-accusations, a plethora of sound-bites rarely exhibiting either Walter Bagehot's 'stream of tendency', which he thought guided a cabinet, or a coherent 'moral discourse'. All three main parties talked about restoring a sense of morality to politics, but found some difficulty in spelling out what they meant, or even spelling it at all. Even an 'ethical foreign policy' soon became a justification of the arms trade in terms of jobs in key constituencies. Daily in the press and on the radio (which in Britain has supplanted Parliament as the main forum for political debate, or what Bagehot in 1867 called, without irony, 'the political education of mankind'), we hear debate conducted in a Tweedledum and Tweedledee tone of accusation and abuse, difficult questions dodged, trivialities inflated, not reasoned argument on the basis that big problems are complex; rather we hear idiot simplifications and knee-jerk reactions of PR opportunism to immediate events. Simplification of the basic issues of complex problems is a great art, now practised only by a few journalists in the quality, broadsheet, minority press. The paradox is that there was never more political knowledge, with the growth of the social sciences in particular and widespread higher education in general, but never less use made of it in public life, unless psephology is the name of the game.

All this is in great contrast to a hundred years ago and even earlier when 'public' could still be attached to 'political philosophy'. A recent essayist, Mark Garnett, lamented 'the decline of the theoretical polemic' compared to the early nineteenth century, a time when, even if there was no political thought coming out of the ancient universities (although some Benthamism in the new London University), yet there were the *Edinburgh* and the *Westminster* reviews commanding the talent of public intellectuals, publicists, thinkers, call them what you will, and the Mills, Macaulay, Sidney Smith, Brougham, Hazlitt and others were well answered in well-grounded kind by the *Quarterly*'s Tory team of Lockhart, Croker, Southey and Walter Scott *inter alia*. Today one could conjure a list of prominent public intellectuals, perhaps running intellectual chat shows; but they will not be political intellectuals, and anything they have to say in passing about politics will be at best commonplace, more often cynical. The point hardly needs labouring.

The matter is no better in popular discourse. There is now mass literacy compared with the early nineteenth century. But the letters, writings and speeches of early working-class leaders are greatly impressive compared with today. Perhaps it was in part the pride and sense of achievement of the first generation of widespread literacy, and perhaps it was that the first book most commonly possessed and read through was one now seen to be of bewildering complexity and difficult language, the Bible. To its new possessors the new literacy, the product of compulsory education and the free public library, was a wonder and a weapon to be used to the hilt; that is, before the Yellow Press began, slowly but surely, to exploit and debase its possibilities, and long before one could put the newspaper down, or not even pick it up, to relax in front of the TV. If one reads Orwell's *Nineteen Eighty-Four* as savage Swiftian satire, not as prophecy, then one notices that the proles, unlike the inner party, are controlled by *debasement* more than by direct terror: they are given not propaganda but 'newspapers containing almost nothing except sport, crime and astrology, sensational five-cent novelettes, films oozing with sex, and sentimental songs which were composed entirely by mechanical means on a special kind of kaleidoscope known as a versificator'. That was not Communism, it was Orwell's fears for his native England. The culture of competitive capitalism works like God in mysterious ways its wonders of social control to perform. Today one must look for serious political thinking in imaginative literature rather than in the in-grown academy or the sensationalizing, personalizing press.

Contrast, say, the standard of debate on the Irish Question in the 1880s with that of today, or the running debate from the 1870s to the 1930s on the extent and nature of imperialism with that on Britain's relations with the EU today, or the debates on constitutional reform and 'home rule all round' before 1914 with the similar debate now – that is, if one is talking of a discourse beyond the academy. Whether one looks at books, journals, press articles or parliamentary debates, the comparison is not comfortable to ourselves. One must look away from political writing to imaginative literature, philosophy, historical studies and biography to see any sign of what earlier generations would have called 'mental progress'.

The academy, however, has never been better. There is a plethora of books and articles of great learning and thoughtfulness on these constitutional questions. Political thinking and constitutional law are coming together under our eyes, and jurisprudence is being reborn or, rather, reconstituted, not as positivism or textual-literalism but as something moral and political. But there are few signs that this academic thinking reaches even what publishers call 'the intelligent reading public', let alone that it reaches any reading politicians, except occasionally in the ephemeral form of a thousand-word article in the broadsheets. Most MPs now have a university degree, but if they are intellectual at all, they are so in the mode of newsprint, broadcasting and increasingly the Web (or their young assistants scan it for them) but they rarely read a book or tract. There is something paradoxical about Politics as a discipline so rarely relating to politics as an activity. Researchers and thinkers in 'think-tanks' imagine themselves to be mediators between specialized knowledge and the public mind, but if their morale depended on knowing that their messages were heard, rather than on having an agreeable job, it could be very low, and often is. Perhaps the new generation of reforming MPs, having university degrees, many or most in the social sciences of some form or other, think they know it already: outside advice, or even knowledge to be used without the advice, is not needed. The academy is Count Frankenstein and they are our monster children, doing, of course, like our own real children, 'me own thing'. The tradition of political thinking now sustains the Cambridge University Press but rarely even the *Guardian, Independent* and *Observer.*

Political philosophy has become an academic discipline of the highest scholarly standards, both in publications and in intellectual debate. But it has become almost entirely internalized. It has lost any public voice. We talk to ourselves loudly and brilliantly. When celebrated break-outs are made, as if political philosophers might have something to say to politicians and to those who act like citizens (a pity the word 'activist' is tarnished), then even the style, mental vigour and fame of an Isaiah Berlin would not reach beyond a small intellectual community who are far less politically involved and far less 'public-spirited' than in the past. Professionalism now seems to have become an end in itself. Some thinking and writing must always be for the concerns of a profession; but there is something at once tragic and highly comic (in a Swiftian way) in a profession of politics that has so little contact with the activities of politics.

Not that I argue for commitment. That is too easy an answer, and sometimes there has been too much of that. Preaching radical politics in a popularly unintelligible discourse carried few risks within university walls, in Britain as well as in France, Germany and the USA. I argue only for relevance and an independent-minded critical engagement, not uncritical commitment or loyalty to a party. 'A writer', said Orwell, 'cannot be a *loyal* member of a political party.' If what is studied is relevant to civic life, then some pains should be taken to write it up in a form that is accessible to intelligent citizens, or at least aiming to be plagiarized (like *The Political Quarterly*) by the dozen or so columnists and editorial writers who do still read serious books. Outside the walls of academia, economists are held in high regard. Even if their policy recommendations or projections often prove wrong, it is commonly believed that their analytical techniques can narrow the range of alternatives and provide useful comment on the probable consequences of policies. Few people now believe that the analytical methods of academic political philosophers should have any relevance to the political thinking of ordinary citizens. This should not be so.

Some ideas are afoot to revive or create a sense of active citizenship. The schools are under starter's orders to try. We have the luxury of being worried that so many of the younger generation are alienated from political life and public values, whereas some good examples show that this need not be so. In so many other countries of the world people keep their heads down out of habit or prudence as despots, big or small, deliberately deny them political liberties. Myself, I have been much involved in projects to try to instil the aims of citizenship, and the skills needed to fulfil them, into young people; but sometimes one is depressed at the examples in public life, not just sleaze and greed but the low level of debate and the refusal to admit obvious difficulties, as well as the remorseless trivialization and consumerism of the popular media. But there are more hopeful things in our tradition that we can look back to, and then perhaps forward again.

Light

For there was light at the beginning of the tunnel. The United Nations Charter of Human Rights and the Charter of the Rights of the Child are not yet enforced, but every young person in the world should read, mark, learn and inwardly digest the Periclean oration, where Thucydides shows what could be, rather than what too often was, and is.

> Let me say that our system of government does not copy the institutions of our neighbours. It is more the case of our being a model to others than of our imitating anyone else. Our constitution is called a democracy because power is in the hands not of a minority but of the whole people. When it is a question of settling private disputes, everyone is equal before the law; when it is a question of putting one person before another in positions of public responsibility, what counts is not membership of a particular class, but the actual ability which the man possesses. No one, so long as he has it in him to be of service to the state, is kept in political obscurity because of poverty. And, just as our political life is free and open, so is

our day-to-day life in our relations with each other. We do not get into a state with our next-door neighbour if he enjoys himself in his own way, nor do we give him the kind of black looks which, though they do no real harm, still do hurt people's feelings. We are free and tolerant in our private lives; but in public affairs we keep to the law. This is because it commands our deep respect.

We give our obedience to those whom we put in positions of authority, and we obey the laws themselves, especially those which are for the protection of the oppressed, and those unwritten laws which it is an acknowledged shame to break.

And here is another point. When our work is over, we are in a position to enjoy all kinds of recreation for our spirits. There are various kinds of contests and sacrifices regularly throughout the year; in our own homes we find a beauty and a good taste which delight us every day and which drive away our cares. Then the greatness of our city brings it about that all the good things from all over the world flow in to us, so that to us it seems just as natural to enjoy foreign goods as our own local products.

Then there is a great difference between us and our opponents, in our attitude towards military security. Here are some examples: our city is open to the world, and we have no periodical deportations in order to prevent people observing or finding out secrets which might be of military advantage to the enemy. This is because we rely, not on secret weapons, but on our own real courage and loyalty. There is a difference, too, in our educational systems. The Spartans, from their earliest boyhood, are submitted to the most laborious training in courage; we pass our lives without all these restrictions, and yet are just as ready to face the same dangers as they are. . . .

There are certain advantages, I think, in our way of meeting danger voluntarily, with an easy mind, instead of with a laborious training, with natural rather than with state-induced courage. We do not have to spend our time practising to meet sufferings which are still in the future; and when they are actually upon us we show ourselves just as brave as these others who are always in strict training. This is one point in which, I think, our city deserves to be admired. There are also others.

Our love of what is beautiful does not lead to extravagance; our love of the things of the mind does not make us soft. We regard wealth as something to be properly used, rather than as something to boast about. As for poverty, no one need be ashamed to admit it: the real shame is in not taking practical measures to escape from it.

Here each individual is interested not only in his own affairs but in the affairs of the state as well: even those who are mostly occupied with their own business are extremely well-informed on general politics – this is a peculiarity of ours: we do not say that a man who takes no interest in politics is a man who minds his own business; we say that he has no business here at all. We Athenians, in our own persons, take our decisions on policy or submit them to proper discussions: for we do not think that there is an incompatibility between words and deeds; the worst thing is to rush into action before the consequences have been properly debated. . . .

We are capable at the same time of taking risks and of estimating them beforehand. Others are brave out of ignorance; and, when they stop to think, they begin to fear. But the man who can most truly be accounted brave is he who best knows the meaning of what is sweet in life and of what is terrible, and then goes out undeterred to meet what is to come. . . . Taking everything together then, I declare that our city is an education to Greece, and I declare that in my opinion each single one of our citizens, in all the manifold aspects of life, is able to show himself the rightful lord and owner of his own person, and do this, moreover, with exceptional grace and exceptional versatility.

(Thucydides, *The Peloponnesian War*, Book 2, chapter 4)

Classical historians tell us, of course, that Pericles was a demagogue, a kind of would-be democratic dictator. But it is not his behaviour that is here the question; it is what he said when seeking to curry favour and gain support. Could this describe any country now? Could this be said to any audience today? We must work towards it. Only political solutions can meet whole world problems.